THE LEGEND OF

Leggett & Platt®

THE LEGEND OF
Leggett & Platt®

JEFFREY L. RODENGEN

Edited by Stanimira Stefanova
Design and layout by Elijah Meyer

Write Stuff Enterprises, Inc.
1001 South Andrews Avenue
Fort Lauderdale, FL 33316
1-800-900-Book (1-800-900-2665)
(954) 462-6657
www.writestuffbooks.com

The publisher has made every effort to identify and locate the source of the photographs included in this edition of *The Legend of Leggett & Platt*. Grateful acknowledgment is made to those who have kindly granted permission for the use of their materials in this edition. If there are instances where proper credit was not given, the publisher will gladly make any necessary corrections in subsequent printings.

Publisher's Cataloging in Publication
(Prepared by The Donohue Group, Inc.)

Rodengen, Jeffrey L.
    The legend of Leggett & Platt / Jeffrey L. Rodengen ; edited by Stanimira Stefanova ; design and layout by Elijah Meyer ; [foreword by David S. Haffner].

    p. : ill. ; cm.

    Includes bibliographical references and index.
    Issued also as CD-ROM.
    ISBN-13: 978-1-932022-34-6
    ISBN-10: 1-932022-34-1

1. Leggett & Platt (Firm)—History. 2. Bedding industry—United States—History. I. Stefanova, Stanimira. II. Meyer, Elijah. III. Haffner, David S. IV. Title. V. Title: Legend of Leggett and Platt VI. Title: Leggett & Platt VII. Title: Leggett and Platt

HD9969.B434 L44 2008
338.7/68415   2008931649

Completely produced in the
United States of America
10 9 8 7 6 5 4 3 2 1

Also by Jeffrey L. Rodengen

The Legend of Chris-Craft

*IRON FIST:
The Lives of Carl Kiekhaefer*

*Evinrude-Johnson and
The Legend of OMC*

*Serving the Silent Service:
The Legend of Electric Boat*

The Legend of Dr Pepper/Seven-Up

The Legend of Honeywell

The Legend of Briggs & Stratton

The Legend of Ingersoll-Rand

*The Legend of Stanley:
150 Years of The Stanley Works*

The MicroAge Way

The Legend of Halliburton

The Legend of York International

The Legend of Nucor Corporation

*The Legend of Goodyear:
The First 100 Years*

The Legend of AMP

The Legend of Cessna

The Legend of VF Corporation

The Spirit of AMD

The Legend of Rowan

*New Horizons:
The Story of Ashland Inc.*

The History of American Standard

The Legend of Mercury Marine

The Legend of Federal-Mogul

*Against the Odds:
Inter-Tel—The First 30 Years*

The Legend of Pfizer

*State of the Heart: The Practical Guide to
Your Heart and Heart Surgery
with Larry W. Stephenson, M.D.*

The Legend of Worthington Industries

The Legend of IBP

The Legend of Trinity Industries, Inc.

*The Legend of
Cornelius Vanderbilt Whitney*

The Legend of Amdahl

The Legend of Litton Industries

The Legend of Gulfstream

*The Legend of Bertram
with David A. Patten*

The Legend of Ritchie Bros. Auctioneers

*The Legend of ALLTEL
with David A. Patten*

*The Yes, you can of Invacare Corporation
with Anthony L. Wall*

*The Ship in the Balloon:
The Story of Boston Scientific and the
Development of Less-Invasive Medicine*

The Legend of Day & Zimmermann

The Legend of Noble Drilling

Fifty Years of Innovation: Kulicke & Soffa

*Biomet—From Warsaw to the World
with Richard F. Hubbard*

NRA: An American Legend

The Heritage and Values of RPM, Inc.

The Marmon Group: The First Fifty Years

The Legend of Grainger

*The Legend of The Titan Corporation
with Richard F. Hubbard*

*The Legend of Discount Tire Co.
with Richard F. Hubbard*

*The Legend of Polaris
with Richard F. Hubbard*

*The Legend of La-Z-Boy
with Richard F. Hubbard*

*The Legend of McCarthy
with Richard F. Hubbard*

*Intervoice: Twenty Years of Innovation
with Richard F. Hubbard*

*Jefferson-Pilot Financial:
A Century of Excellence
with Richard F. Hubbard*

The Legend of HCA

*The Legend of Werner Enterprises
with Richard F. Hubbard*

*The History of J. F. Shea Co.
with Richard F. Hubbard*

*True to Our Vision
with Richard F. Hubbard*

*The Legend of Albert Trostel & Sons
with Richard F. Hubbard*

*The Legend of Sovereign Bancorp
with Richard F. Hubbard*

*Innovation is the Best Medicine:
The extraordinary story of Datascope
with Richard F. Hubbard*

The Legend of Guardian Industries

*The Legend of
Universal Forest Products*

*Changing the World: Polytechnic
University—The First 150 Years*

*Nothing is Impossible: The Legend
of Joe Hardy and 84 Lumber*

*In it for the Long Haul:
The Story of CRST*

The Story of Parsons Corporation

Cerner: From Vision to Value

*New Horizons:
The Story of Federated Investors*

*Office Depot: Taking Care of Business—
The First 20 Years*

*The Legend of General Parts:
Proudly Serving a World in Motion*

*Bard: Power of the Past,
Force of the Future*

*Innovation & Integrity:
The Story of Hub Group*

*Amica: A Century of Service
1907–2007*

*A Passion for Service:
The Story of ARAMARK*

*The Legend of Con-way:
A History of Service, Reliability,
Innovation, and Growth*

*Past, Present & Futures:
Chicago Mercantile Exchange*

*Commanding the Waterways:
The Story of Sea Ray*

TABLE OF CONTENTS

FOREWORD

BY

DAVID S. HAFFNER
CHIEF EXECUTIVE OFFICER AND PRESIDENT
LEGGETT & PLATT, INCORPORATED

THE INITIATIVE OF THIS BOOK was undertaken for several good reasons, but one was preeminent. Harry M. Cornell, Jr., and Felix E. Wright, the leaders of Leggett & Platt in the second half of the 20th century, were nearing retirement from the company's Board of Directors. Today, these two great friends and very long service partners are blessed with excellent health and sharp memories. The time was right to capture their recollections and observations.

The book is, first and foremost, our gift to Harry and Felix, and an expression of our undying appreciation and affection for them. (Five of the book's eight chapters are, in large measure, about the years during which they exerted a positive and powerful influence on our company.)

The company did not and could not have achieved the success this book recounts without the good work and contributions of literally thousands of Leggett & Platt employee-partners. For every highly placed person mentioned in this book and for every face peering out from its pages, there are countless other contributors unnamed and not pictured. For those who know the company well, many unnamed individuals will come to mind. Because it is impractical to include every important partner, we sincerely hope that the inventors, salespeople, managers, and leaders pictured will be understood to represent all of us.

Finally, we view this book as the Leggett story thus far—only the first 125 years. We've long believed the company is not as good as it is going to be. For many years, our management has embraced a notion expressed by a little sign in Harry's office. It says:

Success is founded on a constant state of discontentment interrupted by brief periods of satisfaction on the completion of a job particularly well done.

This book takes a moment to reflect with satisfaction on a job well done, and it names and thanks some of those responsible for the success. The job of Leggett's success is ongoing. If we are inventive, diligent, hardworking, customer-oriented, and loyal—like our previous leaders—and like Joseph Leggett and C. B. Platt—the best chapters are still unwritten.

I hope you enjoy reading this remarkable story.

Dave

ACKNOWLEDGMENTS

MANY PEOPLE ASSISTED IN THE research, preparation, and publication of *The Legend of Leggett & Platt*. The development of historical time-lines and a large portion of the principal archival research was accomplished by research assistant Regina Roths. Her thorough and careful work made it possible to publish a great deal of interesting information on the origins and evolution of this unique company.

The research, however, not to mention creation of the book itself, would have been impossible without the dedicated assistance of Leggett & Platt executives and employees. Principal among these are John Hale, Bonnie Young, and Dave DeSonier, whose affable guidance, careful editing, and willing coordination of records and individuals greatly assisted our research team. A special thanks goes to David Haffner, CEO and president of Leggett & Platt, for contributing the book's foreword.

The experience of interviewing the many interested and courteous subjects for the book was most gratifying. All the people interviewed—whether current employees or retirees—were generous with their time and insights. Those who shared their memories and thoughts include: Bill Allen; George Beimdiek, Jr.; Howard Boothe; Rich Calhoon; Herbert Casteel; Harry Cornell, Jr.; Jack Crusa; Dave DeSonier; Joe Downes; Ted Enloe; Richard Fisher; Matt Flanigan; Frank Ford; Karl Glassman; Mike Glauber; Dave Haffner; John Hale; Paul Hauser; Dan Hebert; Bob Jefferies; Ernest Jett; Gary Krakauer; Don LaFerla; Sandy Levine; Vincent Lyons; Malcolm Marcus; Eloise Nash; Jack Newman; Dennis Park; Duane Potter; Andy Thomas; Bill Weil; Tom Wells; Wayne Wickstrom; and Felix Wright.

Others who assisted in a variety of ways include: David Ballew and Crystal Hacker (editing); Greg Hall (photography); and various members of Leggett & Platt's Printing Services, Marketing Services, and Legal departments. In addition, Michele Hansford with the Powers Museum and the staff of the Jasper County Records Center, both of Carthage, helped a great deal with supplying and verifying many historical facts.

Finally, a special thanks is extended to the dedicated staff at Write Stuff Enterprises, Inc., who worked on the book. Thanks are due to Stanimira "Sam" Stefanova, executive editor; Elizabeth Fernandez, Anne Forsyth, and Heather Lewin, senior editors; Sandy Cruz, vice president/ creative director; Elijah Meyer and Ryan Milewicz, graphic designers; Roy Adelman, on-press supervisor; Abby Hollister, proofreader; Mary Aaron, transcriptionist; Elliot Linzer, indexer; Amy Major, executive assistant to Jeffrey L. Rodengen; Marianne Roberts, executive vice president, publisher, and chief financial officer; Steven Stahl, director of marketing; and Tania Overby, bookkeeper.

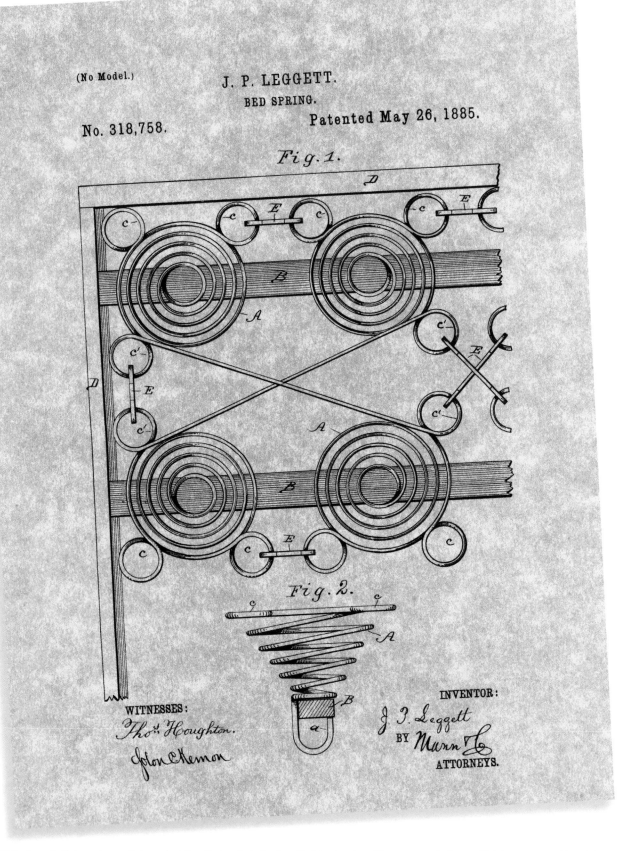

In 1883, Joseph Palmer Leggett invented the first spiral-steel, coiled bedspring. He was granted an official patent on May 26, 1885, as this drawing from the United States Patent and Trademark Office indicates. Though the spring was revolutionary in design, few foresaw the invention growing into a multibillion-dollar industry. *(Drawing courtesy of the United States Patent and Trademark Office.)*

CHAPTER ONE

HUMBLE BEGINNINGS

8,000 B.C. – 1901 A.D.

What a friend is a man's bed! After the toil and care of a long, hard day, or when one's very bones ache from too much play, what luxury it is to feel the gentle softness of a bed! In sickness, nature's own nurse, constant, steadfast, gentle, more healing than any medicine is a bed. And always the vital factor in the bed is the spring it bears.

—Raymond F. Leggett,
son of J. P. Leggett[1]

THE WORLD WAS POISED ON THE EDGE of great change in 1883, bidding silent farewell to the past and entering a period of creativity and innovation. That year, Thomas Edison invented his first electric light, and Louis Waterman devised the fountain pen. Oscar Hammerstein patented a cigar-rolling machine, and the Brooklyn Bridge officially opened to traffic. The Triumph motorcycle made its debut, and the Orient Express made its maiden run between Istanbul and Paris. And in the small town of Carthage, Missouri, inventor Joseph Palmer Leggett shook the hand of blacksmith Cornelius B. Platt, forming a partnership that would eventually evolve into a multinational enterprise. Leggett's idea for a new and improved bedspring would even become the industry standard.

Leggett & Platt would begin with this practical product innovation—a single-cone-coil spring, which proved so successful that diversification into other areas was barely considered until the early 1960s. Over the next half century, however, the company would spread its industrial wings into aspects of production that its founders could never have envisioned.

Today, Leggett & Platt, Incorporated, is a member of both the *FORTUNE*® 500 and S&P 500, and leads the world in the design and manufacture of various components that go into finished mattresses and box springs. The same could be said of Leggett regarding many functions and features embodied in your office chair, your automobile seat, your recliner, your bath mat, several of your appliances, your retail shopping venue, your motorcycle, and even the padding under your carpet.[2] The company also manufactures components found in approximately 80 percent of automobiles manufactured in North America and Europe.[3] If you shop at Wal-Mart, Barnes & Noble, Circuit City, Costco, JCPenney, The Home Depot, RadioShack, Safeway, Target, or hundreds of other stores, you are not only purchasing products whose internal workings are manufactured by Leggett & Platt, but you are also pulling those products from shelves and racks designed and constructed by the company.[4]

Leggett & Platt is the world's leading manufacturer of innerspring and box spring components for residential bedding and a leading supplier of adjustable beds.[5] It is also the world's top producer of recliner mechanisms, sofa sleeper units, and seating systems for the upholstered furniture industry.[6] When it comes to other residential furnishings, the company is the leading supplier in the United States of non-fashion construction fabrics and carpet underlay, as well as a major supplier of geocomponents.[7]

In the field of commercial fixtures and components, Leggett & Platt's customer list boasts more than 1,000 accounts, including most major retailers. It is the world's top manufacturer of retail store fixtures and display products and services.[8]

Many components Leggett & Platt manufactures are integral to the widely recognized brand-name products of its well-known customers. However, none of Leggett & Platt's fine products have a brand name readily recognized by the average consumer. This fact is without a doubt the largest contributing factor to the company's lack of recognition within the general population.

In other industries, Leggett & Platt is a leader in the manufacturing of seating mechanisms and related office furniture components.[9] It further leads the way as North America's No. 1 independent producer of drawn-steel wire.[10] In the industrial sector, Leggett & Platt is a major producer of electric resistance, welded carbon steel mechanical tubing, and other fabricated tubular components.[11] It also manufactures dozens of specialized products,[12] from massage, lumbar, and seat-suspension systems for the automotive industry to quilting, sewing, and wire-processing systems for the bedding, home textile, upholstery, and apparel industries.[13]

Despite Leggett & Platt's size and vast array of sophisticated products, its roots can be traced back to humble beginnings that tell the story of two men, Joseph P. Leggett and Cornelius B. Platt, who built a unique enterprise based upon the old-fashioned ethics of courtesy and honesty common to a small, midwestern town. When J. P. Leggett created the first commercially viable, spiral-steel coiled bedspring in 1883, he revolutionized the idea of a supportive and comfortable sleeping surface. However, the story of his accomplishments—and the company that has kept his name alive—doesn't begin in 1883.

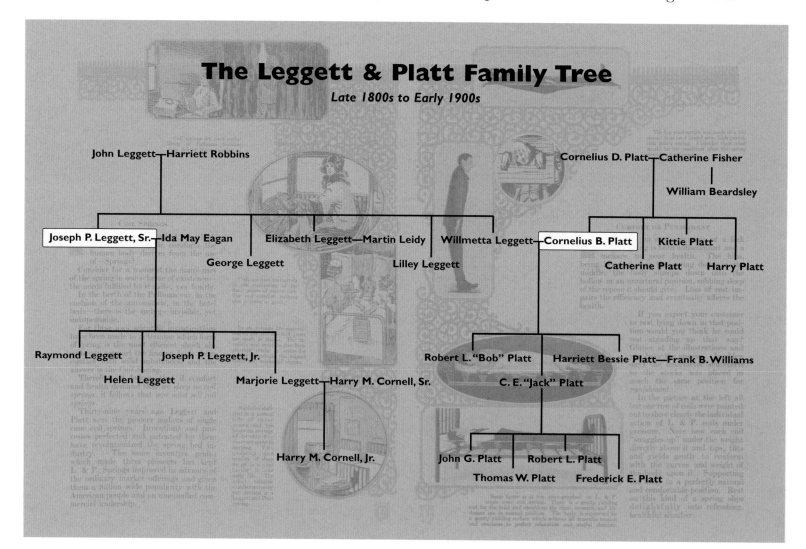

The C. D. Platt Plow Works plant, founded in 1873 by C. B. Platt's father, was located at the corner of Grant and Fifth Streets in Carthage, Missouri. This photo, likely taken between 1883 and 1885, shows a coiled spring bed suspended from the second-story window with a placard reading "Combination Spring Bed."

Rather, it is an important part of an industrial time line that goes back some 10 millennia.

A Brief History of Sleep

A good night's sleep, or at least the comfortable and healthy repose to which we are accustomed, was relatively unknown throughout history. Our ancestors most likely slept in caves on rough ground padded by leaves and grass. Their environment was bereft of comfort, as we know it today.

Roughly 10,000 years ago, however, man first began sleeping on primitive "beds." At the neolithic settlement of Skara Brae in Scotland (dating to approximately 3,400 B.C.) a stone bed hacked from a cave wall was discovered adjacent to a stone hearth and stone sideboard.[14] In the same time period, the Egyptian pharaohs also raised their pallets off the hard ground. This luxury, however, was designated only for the elite; King Tutankhamen, for example, slept on a bed constructed of ebony and gold, while commoners continued to sleep on palm boughs heaped in a corner.[15]

It is believed that the Romans invented the first "mattress" by stuffing reeds, hay, wool, or feathers into a casing, a technique that continued until the late 18th century.[16] During the Renaissance, the general public slept on coarse mattresses that were filled with pea shucks, straw, or feathers, while the upper classes enjoyed beds covered with velvets, brocades, and silks. In the 16th and 17th centuries, mattresses were stuffed with straw or down feathers and placed upon a latticework of rope. By the late 18th century, the cast-iron bed and cotton mattress gained popularity because these setups were less attractive to insects and vermin. Until that time, the presence of mice and insects within mattresses was an accepted fact, even in the beds of royalty.[17]

According to the National Sleep Foundation's 2002 *Sleep in America* poll, 58 percent of adults in the United States experience symptoms of insomnia a few nights a week or more.[18] Oddly enough, the malady has been viewed as a genuine health problem only within the last few decades. Today, however, research has allowed us to realize the true importance of sleep. It is estimated that fatigue resulting from sleeplessness contributes to more than 100,000 police-reported highway crashes, causing 71,000 injuries and 1,500 deaths per year in the United States alone.[19]

Although sleep deprivation arises from myriad sources, including health problems, stress, and the diversions of a fast-paced, high-tech society, studies agree that restful, less interrupted sleep is greatly aided by a supportive mattress and foundation.

Joseph P. Leggett Invents the Bedspring

Patent number 318,758 of the United States Patent and Trademark Office is a simple document adorned with the simple title "BED SPRING."[20] Although bedspring patents were being granted since the 1850s, none had proved commercially viable. That honor would go to Joseph Palmer Leggett on May 26, 1885. In part, the description of his revolutionary creation reads as follows:

My invention relates to springs for bed; and it consists in the detailed construction and combination of the same, as hereafter fully described, whereby the spaces between the springs are in great measure filled up, and the tick or mattress is prevented from falling through between the springs which support it. These springs, by having a very wide spread bearing against the tick or mattress, are prevented from turning over when the weight upon the mattress does not come directly over the center of the springs. ... The manner in which the separate springs are coupled together and combined distributes the weight of any person resting on the mattress over the adjacent springs in addition to those directly underneath and keeps the various parts of the mattress at the same level.[21]

J. P. Leggett was born in Millville, Pennsylvania, on March 6, 1856, to John and Harriett (Robbins) Leggett, who had emigrated from Hall, England, in 1836. A large landowner, John Leggett was a prominent citizen in the Millville community and had secured his son's education at the Millville Seminary. Although historical records are lost, young Leggett probably arrived in St. Louis, Missouri, in the 1870s and worked at various firms in a mechanical capacity while perfecting various inventions.

Although Leggett's first patent, the coiled bedspring, would become his most famous innovation, his accomplishments were not restricted to the world of invention. Leggett was also well respected for his contributions to his community in Carthage, Missouri, where he was elected mayor for three consecutive terms from 1906 to 1912. He also served as president of the Bank of Carthage and a member of both the Benevolent and Protective Order of Elks and the Knights of Pythias.[22]

In 1888, Leggett married Ida May Eagan of Carroll County, Missouri, with whom he had four children: Raymond, Helen, Marjorie, and Joseph Palmer Leggett, Jr.[23] Marjorie would later marry Harry Cornell, Sr., whose role would prove integral

As a result of a business partnership between the inventive mind of J. P. Leggett (below left) and the practical, manufacturing mind of his brother-in-law C. B. Platt (below right), a new industry was born in 1883 with the production of the first commercially viable, spiral-steel coiled bedsprings.

After outgrowing the C. D. Platt Plow Works plant, the first Leggett & Platt bedspring factory was opened in 1890 at the corner of Second and Maple Streets in Carthage. This photo, taken in 1892, shows the company's staff. Although the first and fourth individuals pictured from left to right are unidentified, the rest include Kansas farmer Sam Smith, George D. Leggett, Carthage plumber Karl Speece, J. P. Leggett, and C. B. Platt (far right).

to the success and survival of Leggett & Platt, Incorporated. In turn, one of their children, Harry Cornell, Jr., would eventually take the helm of the company and lead it toward its current position as a multibillion-dollar corporation and global leader.

In 1883, with his idea for a new and improved bedspring firmly in mind, J. P. Leggett attempted to secure a manufacturing facility as well as a partner who possessed both mechanical expertise and the desire to invest in the enterprise. As chance would have it, 20-year-old Cornelius B. Platt, who would become his brother-in-law in 1885, had all the qualities Leggett sought in a partner.

One of five children, C. B. Platt was born on March 6, 1863, in Illinois, to Cornelius D. Platt, a blacksmith, and his wife Catherine Fisher, granddaughter of the famous artist Jonathan Fisher. His parents, both from New York, had married in Allensville, Indiana, in 1846, and lived in Polk County, Iowa, for several years before the family traveled in covered wagons to Carthage in 1873, where

they established themselves as "pioneer citizens, well-to-do and prominent."[24]

On August 12, 1885, 22-year-old C. B. Platt married J. P. Leggett's sister, Willmetta, and they had three children, Jack, Bessie, and Robert. He also co-owned a facility located at 508–514 Grant Street in Carthage called the C. D. Platt Plow Works, which his father had founded in 1873.[25] Within a decade, the enterprise had established a name for quality and was assembling as many as 200 plows per day.[26]

As a family member, good friend, and black-smith—self-taught in metallurgy and engineering—the young C. B. Platt possessed an excellent combination of skills to complement the inventive J. P. Leggett in a partnership to produce Leggett's new and improved spring bed. So, Platt put together several hundred dollars as his contribution to the fledgling venture. His experience with early industrial production would help move the business partnership forward.

After several months of preparation and hard work, the first coiled bedsprings were manufactured with belt-driven machinery at Platt Plow Works in 1883, with the product garnering Leggett a patent in May 1885. Until Leggett had developed the bedspring, bedding in the United States had generally consisted of cotton, feather, or horse-hair mattresses, with no added cushion. Leggett's bedsprings were designed to provide a foundation for these mattresses, with the coils fabricated separately. So, for the next 12 years, bedsprings were produced alongside farm equipment at the facility and then sold to retail merchants. Although the Platt Plow Works sign remained on the building, production focused almost entirely on the manufacturing of bedsprings by the late 1800s.[27]

CARTHAGE, MISSOURI: THE MAPLE LEAF CITY

FOUNDED IN 1841, CARTHAGE, MISSOURI, HAS never been a slow-paced community. While area residents are friendly and laid-back, Carthage is a town where success and prosperity have almost always arrived in a rush.

A historic town located on Route 66 in Jasper County, Carthage was named after a city in North Africa. By 1854, the town was assigned the Jasper County seat, and a new brick and stone courthouse graced the public square. In 1856, John Shirley, father of the notorious would-be outlaw "Bandit Queen," Belle Starr, acquired most of the square's north-side property, where he built an inn, tavern, livery stable, and blacksmith shop, introducing some of the first businesses to the city.[1] He also became a respected member of the county government.

By 1861, the 1,200 citizens of Carthage clashed over the issue of slavery, leading to several historic confrontations. On July 5, 1861, the Battle of Carthage, also known as the Battle of Dry Fork, marked one of the earliest, official engagements of the American Civil War, as 1,100 Missouri State Guard troops led by the experienced Col. Franz Sigel fought 6,000 Confederates under the command of pro-Southern Missouri Governor Clairborne F. Jackson.[2] The one-day battle was a major victory for the Missouri State Guard and played a huge part in determining Missouri's course during the war. The Battle of Carthage also marked the only time a sitting U.S. state governor led troops in the field. The "Second Battle of Carthage" took place in October 1863, but the worst clash occurred in September 1864, when Confederate guerrillas burned down most of the city.[3]

In the late 1800s and beyond, nearby lead mines and limestone quarries contributed significant wealth to Carthage. Burlington limestone, also known as Carthage marble, was a valuable local stone used to build the majestic Carthage courthouse, as well as parts of the Missouri State Capitol, U.S. Capitol, and even the White House.[4] The gray marble was also used in the construction of many large and ornate Victorian homes that still grace Carthage's Grand Avenue. Carthage marble is also present on the exterior of Chicago's Field Museum and at Macy's in New York City.

By 1900, in an architectural survey prepared for the Missouri Department of

Leggett and Platt knew that Carthage was a thriving town. Although the city had been devastated by the Civil War and almost destroyed by Confederate guerrillas in September 1864, within the ensuing decade, the Maple Leaf City had proved its resilience.[28] Boasting a population of nearly 6,000 residents and a number of thriving businesses, Carthage included a grocery and dry goods emporium, several three-story brick buildings, a clothing store, several churches and schools, a large woolen mill, a flour mill, a brickyard, and even an opera house. Both Leggett and Platt realized, however, that the town's market was limited. Thus, the duo took to the road.

The entrepreneurs loaded a horse-drawn carriage with their product, and with the assistance of George Leggett (J. P. Leggett's brother) and Jack Platt (C. B. Platt's youngest son), they visited retailers in nearby towns, such as Joplin, Lamar, Galena, and Lockwood. To conserve space in their wagon, both the springs and the slats onto which they attached were loaded separately and then constructed on the sidewalk in front of the store after an order was received.[29] This attracted curious townspeople, who observed the four gentlemen as they assembled their invention, providing the entrepreneurs with an opportunity to attract even more prospective buyers.

Natural Resources, Carthage was judged as the richest town per capita in the United States.[5] Today, this town of 12,688 is one of the most visually appealing stops in the Missouri Ozarks. The town's beauty is especially apparent in early October, when the Maple Leaf City holds its annual Maple Leaf Festival.[6]

Artist Andy Thomas created this authentic 1895 painting of downtown Carthage after months of painstaking research. Thomas utilized historical photographs, maps of the city from 1893 to 1897, and a bird's-eye panoramic view of the town to help him create an accurate, yet artistic, impression of the area. *(Painting printed by permission, courtesy of Andy Thomas.)*

Foundations for the Future

By 1885, Leggett had already secured what would one day become an extraordinarily valuable patent on his bedspring. Around that time, however, it is believed that Martin Leidy, another brother-in-law of J. P. Leggett, acquired some shares of the company from C. B. Platt, who was temporarily away on an unexplained absence.[30]

Although records are sparse, an old receipt indicates that the partnership was initially known as Leggett & Leidy and later as the Combination Spring Bed Company. However, the weathered receipt also shows "Leidy" crossed out and the name "Platt" written beneath it.[31] Whatever the case, Leidy's involvement was short-lived. Platt returned in 1886 and repurchased Leidy's shares, giving rise to the trade name Leggett & Platt.

From this humble beginning, the business grew on the merit and popularity of its product.[32] As the business began to expand, it required greater production space. In 1890, the partners relocated from the C. D. Platt Plow Works to a 20-by-50-foot building on the corner of Second and Maple Streets in Carthage. The factory was eventually extended from Lyon Street to Maple Street, creating an L-shaped building, with the business office and part of the mechanical department located on Second Street, near Maple.[33]

During this period, Leggett continued to perfect, enhance, and improve his original bedspring product. On January 21, 1896, he was granted a patent for a "Spring Bed Bottom," which better secured the bedsprings in place, while permitting them to yield under pressure.[34] On September 20, 1898, he received a patent for the "Manufacture of Spring Bottoms," which related to the nesting of springs that would form the bottoms of beds, chairs, and other types of furniture.[35] That same day, Leggett received yet another patent—for a "Machine for Attaching Bed Springs to Cross Wire Braces."[36] This latest invention consisted of a machine that would quickly and efficiently connect the bedsprings with the cross wire braces of the frame. On January 27, 1900, he was approved for another patent—his latest improvement for a "Sectional Bed Bottom."[37] The improvements involved pairs of metal drop-hangers, cross-ties connecting the hangers, and longitudinal ties extending lengthwise from the hangers. These ties then supported the bedsprings themselves.

Left: The letterhead of this 1892 receipt bears the Leggett & Leidy Combination Spring Bed Company name. Apparently, Leggett and Platt were conscious of the costs of waste, as a close look reveals that "Leidy" was crossed out and "Platt" written underneath. An ample supply of old letterhead must have been available, since the partnership between J. P. Leggett and C. B. Platt was established in 1885 and Martin Leidy had left the company years earlier.

Opposite: By the turn of the 20th century, Leggett & Platt utilized certain brand names to appeal to retailers that purchased its revolutionary spring beds. "Lure-Sleep"—featured here in a company manual outlining a newspaper advertising campaign—was one of many such names.

The illustrations on this page are reproductions from the new series of electrotyped newspaper ads—read them over and order a set for your local paper—actual sizes are one and two columns in width.

Yes it does

make the cheeks rosy and the eyes bright, sleeping on Leggett and Platt's

LURE & SLEEP

Double Deck Spring

You spend one-third of your life in bed. Make your sleep sweet and restful with a Leggett and Platt Spring. Guaranteed for your lifetime.

Because beauty is *health* and restful sleep is more essential to health than even food or exercise. Come in and let us show you how easily you may own and enjoy this most desirable slumber accessory.

(DEALER'S NAME HERE)

It's Nice

to get up in the morning but it's nicer to lie in bed sleeping on Leggett and Platt's

LURE & SLEEP

Double Deck Spring

Supports the body in a natural, healthful position conducive to perfect relaxation and restful slumber. Come in and let us show you how easily you may enjoy the luxury and soothing comfort of a Leggett and Platt Spring.

(DEALER'S NAME HERE)

NEWSPAPER ADVERTISING

HERE is a quality peculiar to Leggett & Platt Springs and that is the *"ultimate in comfort."* That note has been put into all the various forms of Leggett & Platt advertising.

Newspaper and other forms of local advertising over your own signature form the connecting links in the chain of the modern sales plan. The manufacturer's advertising goes broadcast in magazines and other media of national circulation, acquainting the public with the excellence and desirableness of the article, creating desire for the goods. Obviously, this publicity cannot carry dealers names. The local newspaper goes into the home carrying a similar advertisement, over the name and address of a definite dealer.

Use Leggett & Platt electrotyped ads in your local paper over your own name and address to tell the people of your city where to go for Leggett & Platt Springs. By using these ads in your paper you will transfer to your store all of the sales advantage of the prestige and good will that has been built up thru Leggett & Platt advertising in the past.

It does make a difference

in the way you feel of a morning sleeping on Leggett and Platt's

LURE & SLEEP

Double Deck Spring

Sleep well and you keep well. Your physical and mental condition during waking hours depends on the restfulness of your slumber. Why not enjoy the luxury and comfort of a Leggett and Platt Spring when it may be had for so little?

Each little coil snuggles up under the weight directly over it and supports the body in a comfortable, healthful position conducive to perfect relaxation and restful slumber. Fatigue slips away from the body when perfectly relaxed and mother nature rebuilds you over new every night. Come in and see the Lure Sleep.

(DEALER'S NAME HERE)

"He sleeps well who is not conscious that he sleeps ill."—*Bacon.*

"A Victor Spring will help some." —*Hubbard.*

The patents served as giant steps forward, covering the spectrum from manufacturing beds on a wire base (instead of wood) to what would be known as the Leggett Hinge-Top Spring Bed, originally derived from the "Spring Bed Bottom" patent of 1896 and improved upon in successive years thanks to Leggett's eye for efficiency and function. Perhaps most important, the 1898 patent applied to the concept of interlocking coils, a development far ahead of its time.

The buying public was becoming accustomed to the superior comfort and durability of the Leggett & Platt Spring Bed, and consumer demand made expansion inevitable. In 1895, Harry Platt, brother of C. B. Platt, was offered a franchise to use the Leggett & Platt patents. So he opened a factory in Louisville, Kentucky, and operated the facility until 1903, when the McElroy–Shannon Bedspring Company of

Leggett & Platt's first business office at the factory on Second and Maple Streets reflected the company's humble beginnings. Pictured (from left to right) are J. P. Leggett, Walter W. Hubbard, Col. W. K. Caffee, and C. E. "Jack" Platt.

Carthage purchased it.[38] Charles F. McElroy, who had moved to Carthage from Hannibal, Missouri, in 1881, was a wealthy individual involved in mining and real estate.[39] He was also a shareholder in the Missouri Electric Railway and the founding shareholder of the Carthage Land and Mining Company.[40] Although little is known about his partner, Woodford Shannon, it is known that McElroy took on various partners over the years in his extensive endeavors.

The McElroy–Shannon Bedspring Company was partially controlled by J. P. Leggett. The 1900

Carthage city directory lists the company as located at 211 South Grant Street, with McElroy as president, Shannon as secretary, and J. P. Leggett as vice president.[41] Leggett's name may have been absent from the public lexicon in this enterprise, but in effect, the Louisville plant was still partially owned by Leggett & Platt. The McElroy–Shannon Bedspring Company would later open a bedspring plant in Philadelphia and move the Louisville operation to Waukegan, Illinois, and then back to Louisville. It would continue to remain affiliated with Leggett & Platt until 1922, when it was fully acquired.[42]

By 1901, Leggett had applied for a dozen patents, including a Canadian patent taken out that year as a contingency for selling rights in Canada for the manufacturing of bedsprings. It had become evident that the Leggett & Platt Spring Bed was a popular product with consumers. As the company continued to experience growth and expand across the nation, J. P. Leggett and C. B. Platt decided it was time to implement a formal business structure. That year, they incorporated their enterprise under the name Leggett & Platt Spring Bed & Manufacturing Company in Missouri, and J. P. Leggett was named its president.[43] The other original stockholders included George D. Leggett, William McMillan, W. K. Caffee, J. P. Newell, Kate M. Johns, R. E. Lister, W. W. Bailey, Robert Ornduff, W. E. Hall, B. A. Mevey, M. B. Parke, E. O'Keefe, Dr. M. J. McClurg, and William E. Brinkerhoff.[44]

In less than 20 years, the inventor and the blacksmith had worked to create and market a product that would completely alter the design, construction, and sales of the traditional bed. The days of the hard pallet and horsehair mattress were quickly coming to a close, with the name Leggett & Platt rising to the forefront of sleep technology.

Blast Furnace

Premier Wire is drawn from Open Hearth steel. The oxygen of the air blast blown over and around the molten metal unites with and burns out the silicon, manganese and other elements, leaving the unadulterated iron, which is later combined with the correct proportion of carbon and manganese to produce steel of the proper analysis.

Rod Mill

Metal of the required analysis is drawn from the furnace into a huge ladle and poured into ingot molds. Ingots weigh about 5,000 lbs. each. To keep the quality of steel uniform throughout, the ingot is "soaked" under terrific heat until the entire mass has reached a condition of white hot softness, *even thruout*. It is then quickly passed to the rolling mill.

Washing Rods

Premier Wire used in Leggett & Platt Springs is hot rolled from the original ingots into rods. Scale formed in the rolling process is removed by treating with diluted sulphuric acid and washing in warm water. They are then run slowly under successive sprays of water which, in combination with the slight traces of acid still upon the rod, and the exposure to the atmosphere forms the "sull coat" which is absolutely necessary in the cold drawing process.

Making Premier Wire For Leggett & Platt Springs

WIRE, the most highly finished, skillful and costly product of the steel-maker's art, is brought to its nearest perfection in Premier spring steel wire made for Leggett & Platt Springs.

Made of high carbon, open hearth steel, great care is exercised in its manufacture, from the selection of ores thru the sundry processes of converting, rolling, drawing and tempering.

Long experience has demonstrated the exact point of carbon and chemical and mechanical treatment necessary to obtain the particular structure combining the requisite toughness and strength to endure.

The fact that Leggett & Platt coils after many years of use still retain their resilient properties, that our sales have steadily increased each month of each year, that complaints are almost unknown, indicates that Leggett & Platt Springs are pleasing the public better than any other.

Baking Oven

The rods are next dipped in milk of lime and baked for several hours at a temperature of about 400 degrees. The cooling from this process is carefully regulated to impart the requisite ductility to permit of cold drawing.

Wire Drawing

The annealed rods are cold drawn to the desired size thru steel dies. Repeated drawings harden and compact the crystals of the steel and necessitate the repeated return of the wire to the annealing oven, where the carefully regulated temperatures restore the crystals of steel to uniform and normal condition with respect to each other, and remove all local tension and strain from previous working.

In promotional materials aimed at retailers, Leggett & Platt openly described its manufacturing processes in an effort to demonstrate why iron and steel alloy was a better type of metal for the manufacturing of spring coils.

A BUSINESS SPRINGS TO LIFE

1901–1930

The quantity and quality of sleep we get is a vital factor in our daily life. The most valuable slumber accessory yet devised is a Leggett and Platt Spring.

—"The Beds of Kings"
company brochure, 1923[1]

DEALERS NAME HERE

THOUGH THE WANING YEARS OF THE century had marked a rush of activity for Leggett & Platt Spring Bed & Manufacturing Company with the construction of two factories in five years, the business seemed determined to fulfill one need with one steadily improving product for several decades starting in 1901. Leggett & Platt's bedsprings had proved so durable and well designed that, by the early 1920s, company promotional brochures claimed "thousands of Leggett & Platt springs made 35 years ago are still in everyday use and we believe will last twice as long."[2]

With product sales directed at such retailers as furniture enterprises and general stores, prospective retail customers were provided with sophisticated sales booklets that detailed products and the healthful benefits garnered from sleeping on Leggett & Platt Spring Beds. For instance, one such brochure, subtitled "The Beds of Kings," opened with the following approach to retailers:

When your customer is made to realize that he will spend one-third of his life in bed, that his bed is what the spring makes it, that his physical condition and mental alertness during the day are dependent upon the restfulness of his slumber at night, he will then realize that his bed spring is one of the most important factors in his life, and you will have no difficulty in persuading him to select your best L & P number.[3]

Popular bed models of the time included "Victor," "Crown," and the "Lure-Sleep" series, which, depending on options, were further identified as Number 1, Number 6, Number 11, and so forth.[4] The Leggett & Platt product line even catered to the obese, with "The Dixie Sleeper" billed as "The Double-Deckless for Heavyweights."[5]

Patented features, trumpeted as the epitome of cutting-edge sleep technology, were listed as standard on all beds sold in the early 20th century and considered revolutionary for their time. These features, as lauded in one promotional booklet, made the Leggett & Platt product "the most perfect spring bed in the world today." It included such mechanics as a well-secured bottom fastener, a surface design that allowed every coil to move independently and conform to the body's movements, open construction for easy cleaning, and high-carbon steel used in the wire manufacturing process that helped alleviate noise.[6]

For retailers and consumers who were used to sleeping on hard board pallets covered with a horsehair mattress, these were breakthroughs of unimaginable luxury. Moreover, Leggett & Platt

---

One way Leggett & Platt helped retailers promote its products was through slides shown at movie theatres, such as the one above from a series issued after World War I.

Leggett & Platt employees punch out angle iron for bed frames in the basement of the Carthage plant in the 1920s.

had no compunction about making such claims, as every single one was true. In its brochure, "The Beds of Kings," the company even went so far as to liken sleeping on woven wire or link fabric spring bedding to punishment, while alluding that sleeping on coil springs was an extravagance befitting royalty and world leaders.[7]

Honesty As Policy

Leggett & Platt also made no secret of its manufacturing techniques by including detailed photographs and drawings of its metal molding and wire-making process in promotional pieces aimed at buyers. In one, the company even included a set of images showing in microscopic detail how the iron and steel alloy used in Leggett & Platt manufacturing was stronger, and far superior, to other wire materials used in bed making.[8]

This dedication to openness and honesty is one facet of a company culture that was forged by its founders and, uniquely, has proved a keystone in

the Leggett & Platt story throughout its history. More than just a way of conducting business, it was a philosophy of dealing with clients that stemmed from the personalities of J. P. Leggett and C. B. Platt. Theirs was a winning formula from day one: Establish the standards of extreme loyalty and service to customers and provide a product that is both unique and of high quality.

Expansion and Retraction

It is of little surprise that others wished to become involved in what seemed to be an inevitable expansion for Leggett & Platt. The McElroy–Shannon Bedspring Company was already operating a plant in Louisville, Kentucky, that was franchised to use the Leggett & Platt patents. It had also opened a plant in

Right: Managers at the Leggett & Platt factories ensured that operations ran smoothly at all times. From left to right are W. W. Hubbard, manager of the Louisville plant; C. E. "Jack" Platt, manager of the Windsor, Ontario, factory in Canada; and Robert L. "Bob" Platt, assistant manager at the Windsor facility.

Below: This late 1920s photo shows the paint room located in the original Louisville, Kentucky, factory. Aluminum color was used for most of Leggett & Platt's metal products, including rollaway beds and rails.

Philadelphia and moved the Louisville operation to Waukegan, Illinois, in 1915 to be near the source of raw materials.[9] When the move failed to live up to expectations, the founders moved back to Louisville and carried out operations at 117 North Fifth Street in a rented building.[10]

In 1911, Leggett & Platt opened a branch factory in Windsor, Ontario, Canada, which was managed by Cornelius Eugene Platt (known as "Jack"), the youngest son of C. B. Platt. A few years earlier, rights to the Leggett & Platt patents had been granted to the Pacific Spring Company of Oakland, California, giving Leggett & Platt products an initial introduction on the Pacific Coast. These expansions, while exposing the Leggett & Platt Spring Bed to a larger audience, were relatively short-lived. The Windsor branch soon

merged with Star Manufacturing, which was in turn acquired by L. A. Young Industries, Inc., of Detroit, Michigan.[11] (This company would later become the L. A. Young Spring and Wire Corporation and would figure extensively in the history of Leggett & Platt.) Jack Platt remained as manager of the facility. L. A. Young Industries also purchased Pacific Springs' Oakland factory, originally operated by Curtis Wright, Jr., of Carthage, Missouri, who had contracted for use of the Leggett & Platt patents on the Pacific coast.[12] Robert L. "Bob" Platt, another of C. B. Platt's sons, took over as manager of this Oakland factory.[13]

Loss of a Founder

After many years of continuous prosperity at Leggett & Platt, tragedy struck on May 18, 1921, when J. P. Leggett died at the age of 65. His passing left a void at his company and within the community of Carthage. An articulate, and surprisingly frank, hand-typed copy of his original obituary reflected the following text:

> He found his chief recreation in hunting and fishing. His was a gentle, lovable character. He was quick-tempered, but ever ready to forgive and forget. Indeed, all the gentler qualities of manhood were most happily blended in the character of Joseph Palmer Leggett—not put on like costly apparel for gala occasions, but his every day habit. Everybody therefore liked him because he was attentive, obliging, kind, and generous to all. Though a marked man in many respects, it was in his domestic and social relations that Mr. Leggett was most distinguished and most beloved.[14]

The residents of Carthage mourned the loss of one of their favorite sons, as did the employees of the company he had founded. Time would not stand still for the growing company, however, as upon the death of J. P. Leggett, C. B. Platt took over as president.

THE INVENTIVE MIND
OF J. P. LEGGETT

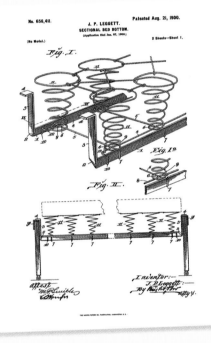

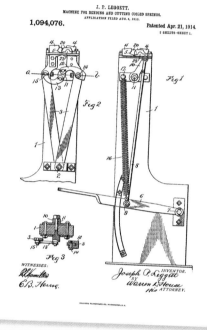

J. P. LEGGETT WAS FIRST AND FOREMOST AN INVENtor, a man in the vein of Edison or Ford, whose mind constantly whirled with ideas. He formulated new concepts, designed and built prototypes, and searched for ways to improve existing products.

    The approval of Leggett's 1885 bedspring design by the United States Patent and Trademark Office was one of many spring-related creations that aided Leggett & Platt in becoming America's premier supplier of bedsprings, innersprings, and related products.[1] He received patents for several inventions, including the "Manufacture of Spring Bottoms,"[2] a "Machine for Attaching Bed Springs to Cross Wire Braces,"[3] and a "Sectional Bed Bottom."[4] On January 21, 1896, he was granted a patent for the original "Spring Bed Bottom"[5] and then received clearance from the patent office on March 3, 1914, for an improved version of the

Besides his original bedspring design, Leggett patented several other spring-related creations, such as a "Sectional Bed Bottom" (above left) and a "Machine for Bending and Cutting Coiled Springs" (above right). *(Drawings courtesy of the United States Patent and Trademark Office.)*

product.[6] Then, only a month later, his "Machine for Bending and Cutting Coiled Springs" was granted official status.[7] Leggett created yet another "Spring Bed Bottom and Manufacture of the Same," which was authorized on August 26, 1919.[8]

    While he excelled in his knowledge of bedsprings, Leggett's inventive mind was not confined to this topic. His "Target Trap," the first such commercially viable device ever created for throwing clay pigeons for the sport of skeet shooting, was given patent approval on November 7,

1905.[9] Known as the "Leggett Trap," the Remington Company purchased this device and advertised it for many years in its sales catalogs.[10] Two years after patenting the trap, Leggett followed it up with an improved "Carrier for Target Traps," which allowed the fast feeding of clay pigeons into the machine, while preventing breakage.[11]

Several of Leggett's other patents were perfectly timed for their era. The 1895 "Lid for Tea Kettles" was a true novelty of the period, whose description in the original patent reads as follows:

The object of my invention is to make a lid through which liquid can be readily poured without removing the lid from the vessel, and which will be self-closing, and which will not open under the steam pressure generated in the vessel.[12]

Yet another Leggett creation was the "Endless Necktie" of 1904, a piece of apparel intended to aid those who might have spilled a bit of soup on their bow tie.[13] The patent description stated:

My invention ... has for its object to provide a necktie consisting of an endless band that may be readjusted from time to time to expose a fresh surface near the ends of a tie for the formation of a tie-bow whenever such portions become soiled or worn.[14]

In 1913, Leggett turned his mind to transportation, designing improvements for electric streetcars, which were popular at the time. In his "Railway Car" patent of 1913, he sought to maximize efficiency and safety of passengers by altering the car's interior.[15] Instead of using "the usual fixed, permanent seats," he believed that "convertible seats" may be "adjusted to positions that will afford greater standing room for the passengers, and furnish means, which may be grasped by them for support."[16]

The automobile, though a new development, also caught Leggett's attention. In 1914, he patented a "Vehicle Propelling Mechanism"[17] that was intended to "provide a structure in which the weight of the motor, employed to propel the vehicle, is used to assist the driving wheels in climbing over an obstruction or to hold the wheels back when they enter a depression in the road."[18] The "Motor Vehicle Transmission System" was also introduced in February 1914 as "a very inexpensive transmission mechanism for motor vehicles, including differential gearing and axle sections, movable to vary the speed of the axle and ground wheels."[19]

J. P. Leggett's last invention, an "Automobile Propelling Mechanism" that was the predecessor of today's front-wheel drive systems and far ahead of its time, was submitted for patent approval six months after Leggett's death by his beloved wife, Ida.[20] The patent received approval on January 29, 1924.

For J. P. Leggett, life was about more than just bedsprings. It was about ideas and making a difference.

In his lifetime, Leggett patented several other interesting ideas that were not spring-related, including (from left to right) the "Endless Necktie," "Target Trap," "Lid for Tea Kettles," and "Motor Vehicle Transmission System." *(Drawings courtesy of the United States Patent and Trademark Office.)*

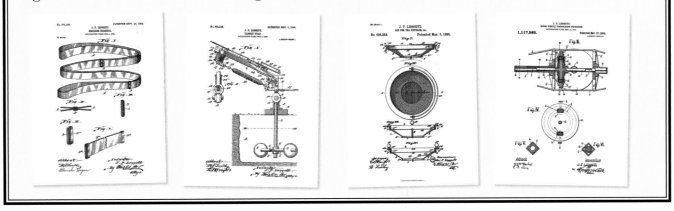

Leadership Changes

As soon as C. B. Platt took over the helm of the company, he immediately implemented several changes. In 1922, patent rights and assets of McElroy–Shannon were repurchased and the Philadelphia plant discontinued.[15] Leggett & Platt, for all practical purposes, also disassociated with the factories in Windsor, Ontario, and Oakland, California. For the time being, production was restricted to the main plant in Carthage and the second facility in Louisville. Raymond F. Leggett, the older son of J. P. Leggett, managed this factory until his death on April 1, 1922. Walter W. Hubbard, who had joined Leggett & Platt in 1906, took over the position and eventually joined the board of directors.

Carthage Growth

Production at Leggett & Platt was concentrated in two distinct locations—Carthage and Louisville. With demand increasing, a new factory was constructed in Carthage in 1925. The plant, located on West Vine Street and adjacent to the Missouri Pacific Railroad sidings (allowing it to place shipments on train cars directly from the factory's loading docks),

AN EMOTIONAL FAREWELL

THE MINUTES OF A CORPORATE BOARD MEETING are typically bereft of emotion. Most are, by design, a record of votes, defined appropriations, approved promotions, and a litany of other matters. Leggett & Platt's record books are no different; from the late 1880s until 1929, written in consistently fastidious handwriting, virtually every page has remained pristine, with no marks, scuffs, or stains.

Such was not the case, however, with the minutes from Leggett & Platt's board meeting on March 27, 1929, which was called for the purpose of electing a president and general manager of the company after Cornelius B. Platt's death six days earlier. Secretary (Dr. M. J.) McClurg, whose penmanship in the board books had been flawless for more than 25 years, appeared shaky and uneven.[1] It was even unreadable in several places. A motion had been put in the form of a resolution, and a copy of the minutes had been sent to Platt's widow.[2] The resolution, highly unusual for the board minutes of a growing corporation, read as follows:

March 27, 1929—It is our sad duty to assemble here today to appoint a successor to our beloved leader and friend, Mr. C. B. Platt. I, W. W. Hubbard, have known C. B. Platt for 30 years. I

knew him in his home, at his work, and at play. I think my long and intimate association with him qualifies me to speak with authority as to the kind of man he was. I never saw him angry. I never saw the time that any employee or associate of his could not go to him, not on the common basis of employee with employer, but as one friend to another, and obtain his counsel and help. When firmness was required, he exerted it, but always tempered with kindness and consideration for the feelings and rights of others. He was ever sympathetic when sympathy was due. I never saw the day so dark he could not see a rift in the clouds with at least a little sunlight shining through. He radiated optimism and cheer and confidence and loyalty. He believed this to be a good and happy world in which to live. And, in so believing, he made it a happy world for himself, and for his family, and for those of us who have been fortunate enough to come beneath the influence of his personality.[3]

The page displaying this letter, which was signed by six directors and Secretary McClurg, was also different in one poignant aspect. It reflected several stains—not coffee stains or tea stains, or the result of aged paper or the ravages of time; they were stains of tears.[4]

was designed for efficiency and with an eye toward future expansions. The initial factory, which would continue to grow over the next several decades, originally covered 49,500 feet of floor space.[16] The building was considered fireproof, constructed largely of reinforced concrete, and considered a model structure for its time. The plant's equipment was considered state-of-the-art, and the building itself measured 80-by-400 feet, with a 30-by-90-foot paint room and a partial basement where bedsprings were designed.[17] This building was so well-constructed and designed that sections of the facility are still maintained as part of the Carthage manufacturing plant.

End of an Era

The new plant in Carthage allowed Leggett & Platt to continue manufacturing bedsprings with greater efficiency, and the product would remain the company's staple offering for the next few years. Unfortunately, however, tragedy struck again on March 22, 1929, when C. B. Platt died at the age of 66. While both of the founding partners had passed away, they had left behind a thriving company that was destined to grow into one of America's most successful enterprises. Citizens and employees heavily mourned Platt, as reflected in the front-page article that dominated that day's edition of the *Carthage Press*. As was also true with his brother-in-law and business partner, J. P. Leggett, Platt had given liberally to community projects and was fast

J. P. Leggett, Jr., was named president and treasurer of Leggett & Platt in 1929 after the death of C. B. Platt.

to support necessary improvements with energy, ideas, and financial donations. He had been a partner with George Porter in a Carthage-based wholesale grocery business, a member of the Carthage Board of Public Works, and a director of the Bank of Carthage.[18]

Second Generation Takes Over

J. P. Leggett, Jr., son of the founding partner, took the helm of the company as president and treasurer. He had joined Leggett & Platt in 1925, overseeing the main offices and functioning as sales manager, while also serving on the board of directors. He had been head of the company for some time, as he had temporarily assumed responsibility for most business affairs during C. B. Platt's long illness before his death.[19] Frank B. Williams was elected as a new director, in conjunction with Leggett, Jr.'s, move to the main office.

Though Leggett & Platt was changing and growing, many aspects remained the same. The company was still largely a family enterprise, as Frank Williams was married to C. B. Platt's daughter, Harriet Bessie Platt. For the first time, the baton had been passed to the next generation, and it was now its duty to uphold the success and traditions established by Leggett & Platt's founding fathers.

The assembly line at the Carthage factory featured a vast array of assembly machines. Leggett & Platt designed, patented, and built virtually all of the equipment.

CHAPTER THREE

SURVIVING DIFFICULT TIMES

1930–1952

All … would do well to purchase Leggett & Platt springs for their beds and thus assure themselves of comfortable sleep.

—Reverend John G. Barden of New York City, advising missionaries bound for Africa[1]

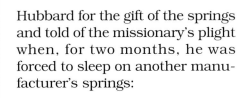

LIKE MANY OTHER SMALL BUT GROWing companies in the United States, Leggett & Platt entered the 1930s with enthusiasm and a product that was gradually gaining acceptance around the world. On December 18, 1929, W. W. Hubbard, vice president and general manager of the Louisville plant, reported to the board and President J. P. Leggett, Jr., that he and the company's eight other salesmen had held a "sales convention" the previous two days and "… brought good results; all were very enthusiastic over it, and it was the intention to make it an annual event."[2]

The quality of Leggett & Platt springs was gaining attention around the world, as evidenced by excerpts from several letters printed in a Louisville publication and sent to the manufacturer. A group of missionaries had written the letters, which told of their trek carrying the springs through many miles of African jungle. The fact that the springs were made in sections and easily reassembled at the final destination had simplified the challenge. According to Hubbard, this unique construction was the only difference between the African-bound mattresses and those in American homes.[3]

One letter, postmarked "Kongolo, Africa" and sent by Reverend Eugene Hendrix Lovell, thanked Hubbard for the gift of the springs and told of the missionary's plight when, for two months, he was forced to sleep on another manufacturer's springs:

We tried the Belgian springs at first, but they were terrible. They use large bolsters under the mattress to hold the head up. So I got busy right away and assembled the spring you gave me, and now— oh, how we sleep. … One has to have sleeping comfort here in Africa if one expects to do good work. How appreciative we are of your gift, and you cannot know how happy we are to use them. They are a thousand times better than other springs.[4]

Another letter from the Reverend John G. Barden of New York City, who had slept on the springs while on a mission to Africa, recommended that " … all who were home on furlough and planned to return to Congo would do well to purchase Leggett & Platt springs for their beds and thus assure themselves of comfortable sleep."[5]

Employees work on individual tables at Leggett & Platt's Bed Spring Assembly Department in the 1930s.

Leadership Changes

While customers around the world praised Leggett & Platt's products, matters on the home front began to take a different and difficult turn. In August 1930, the minutes of the monthly board of directors meeting reflected that turn: "On account of unsettled conditions and decreased earnings causing the present temporary depression, the board thought it best to pass up a dividend at this time. All hopeful of a turn for the better in a short period of time."[6]

By September 1931, matters had not improved, so company directors approved reductions in the salaries of several employees, "cutting expenses wherever possible." In July 1932, the directors unanimously voted to reduce their fees by 40 percent.[7]

In October 1932, J. P. Leggett, Jr., who was suffering from health problems, stepped down as the company's president. In an effort to keep family members as the company's leadership, Frank B. Williams, who was married to C. B. Platt's daughter, Bess, took the helm as interim president. The couple resided

Left: Frank B. Williams, who was married to C. B. Platt's daughter, served as interim president of Leggett & Platt after J. P. Leggett, Jr., stepped down from the position due to illness.

Below: This photo shows a section of the shipping room of the Carthage factory circa 1930. This particular area was devoted to crating innerspring units on the Leggett-designed compressed-air baler. Innerspring units arrived at the crating area from the assemblers via an overhead track and were placed on the crating press (far left) for compression into bundles. The man shown on the right uses a wheelbarrow to deliver crated units to the warehouse.

on Grand Avenue in the Platt home, which was built by the same architect at essentially the same time as the Leggett family home across the street.[8]

The following year, the Carthage plant began to reap some benefits from an expanded product line-up that included innerspring units for mattresses. Until then, the company's manufacturing lineup consisted solely of bedsprings and box springs (foundations for

mattresses).[9] While the Leggett & Platt bedspring had long been a comfortable foundation on which bedding was placed, innerspring units, which were wrapped with bedding materials, were becoming more in demand by mattress makers.

The company's reputation for excellence in manufacturing was also growing in 1933 through its admission into the National Association of Bedding Manufacturers (NABM), which welcomed Leggett & Platt to its membership, hailing the company's success as nothing short of amazing.[10] Founded in 1915, the bedding organization promoted state tagging laws and researched issues that affected consumer health. Its recognition of the company strengthened Leggett & Platt's national reputation.[11]

In 1934, another member of the founding families joined the company's leadership ranks. Harry M. ("Mack") Cornell, Sr., who was married to J. P. Leggett's daughter, Marjorie, was elected to the board of directors. In 1935, he became the company's vice president and sales manager. Although he joined Leggett & Platt with only a high school education, Cornell was known for his outgoing personality and was truly gifted when it came to building relationships. His gregarious spirit and superior sales talent left a permanent impression on the people who knew him and on the company itself.

Outside Leadership

In 1935, Leggett & Platt's leadership would again undergo change. When Walter W. Hubbard passed away following complications from an appen-

Above right: Harry M. Cornell, Sr. (far right) discusses business with engineer Carl Kirchner and another unidentified Leggett & Platt employee. Cornell joined Leggett & Platt's board of directors in 1934 and became vice president and sales manager in 1935.

Right: Edward B. Casey, Jr., managed the Louisville plant before he became a Leggett & Platt vice president in 1938; he was elected to the board of directors in 1943 and was instrumental in establishing the Winchester, Kentucky, factory.

dix operation, Edward B. Casey, Jr., a native Kentuckian and bedding salesman, was hired as manager of the Louisville plant.[12] Casey made an immediate positive impression on the company's leaders. In 1938, he was named a vice president of the company and, in 1943, a member of the board of directors. He served on the board through 1964 and as vice president through 1967. One of the company's most respected and able managers, Casey hired or guided several of Leggett's future managers and leaders.

In early 1935, after the death of an associate in another business forced him to take over matters in that organization, the company's president, F. B. Williams, passed operational responsibilities to George S. Beimdiek, Sr., a board director with the company since 1933. Initially, Beimdiek was named vice president and treasurer of the company and Williams retained the title of president. Beimdiek, however, assumed responsibility for the day-to-day operations of the company.[13]

Beimdiek was born in St. Louis and moved to Carthage after graduating from Benton College of Law in St. Louis in 1905. Rather than practicing law, Beimdiek chose to use his skills first in the quarry business, and later in banking and investing, before becoming a director with Leggett & Platt. While Beimdiek was the first head of Leggett & Platt from outside of the founding families, he was indisputably dedicated to the company's operations

Left: Ink blotters served as popular advertising tools in the 1930s, providing consumers and retailers a low-cost, useful item imprinted with a creative advertisement that caught people's attention. Here, Leggett & Platt compares the Dionne quintuplets to its own "children" named Experience, Promptness, Reliability, Quality, and Satisfaction.

Below: Harry M. Cornell, Sr. (left) and George S. Beimdiek, Sr. (seated center) are photographed with Glenn Joyce (standing) a longtime employee and significant contributor to Leggett & Platt's manufacturing efforts; Ula Payton (facing camera); and another member of the office personnel. In the mid-1930s, Cornell was in charge of the sales staff, while Beimdiek served as president.

and its bottom line. Still, some believed that Beimdiek's lack of lineage might have been a factor contributing to his support of selling the company soon thereafter.[14]

On December 14, 1935, the L. A. Young Spring and Wire Corporation offered to acquire Leggett & Platt for $250,000. L. A. Young Spring and Wire was an automotive and bedding components manufacturer whose leadership included members of the Platt family who had left Leggett & Platt but retained stock in the company. The Platts joined Beimdiek in pushing for the sale.[15]

To vote on whether or not the sale would take place, stockholders called a special meeting at year's end. Prior to the vote, Harry M. Cornell, Sr., who favored keeping the company, borrowed money to purchase additional shares of stock and worked to obtain voting proxies from longtime shareholders. When the vote took place on December 30, 1935, the resolution, which required 3,750 shares to pass, fell short by only 23 votes. For the time being, Leggett & Platt Spring Bed and Manufacturing Company of Carthage, Missouri, would remain intact.[16]

Ebb and Flow

The following year was one of the most profitable periods to date for Leggett & Platt, with net profits exceeding $50,000. In December 1936, the stock-

holders approved an 8-for-1 split of the shares, increasing the number of shares to 40,000.[17]

At the time, Beimdiek informed shareholders that due to concerns over increasing prices and delivery uncertainties in regard to steel, wire, and other products, the board deemed it advisable to keep considerably more raw materials in stock than was customary. Raw materials comprised part of the loss experienced in January and February 1937, when several weeks of steady rainfall led to the flooding of the Ohio River and, in turn, damaged the Louisville plant. While the flood devastated some businesses in the area and forced others to close permanently, Leggett & Platt's operations in Louisville incurred only some $7,000 in recovery costs, largely for the moving, storage, and cleaning of material and finished stock. Luckily, even though more than 11 feet of water had filled the factory's first floor, the machinery remained virtually undamaged.[18]

Nevertheless, the Louisville operations moved from 117 North Fifth Street, which extended through to Bullitt Street, to an adjacent Bullitt Street building the company had already rented for its innerspring production operations.[19] While at first it appeared likely the operations would return to the Fifth Street

Above: Leggett & Platt's office and factory personnel gather for a photo outside the Carthage factory in 1936.

Below left: The Carthage plant was fairly small prior to World War II, before a two-story expansion on the rear of the building more than doubled its size.

Below right: Construction was completed on the original Dallas factory in the 1930s. This early aerial photo shows the facility located on Oak Lawn Avenue in what is today downtown Dallas. Within the next decade, due primarily to city politics and the increasing value of the property, Leggett & Platt would sell the land and move its operations 35 miles south to Ennis, Texas.

location, an explosion at a neighboring plant damaged the Leggett & Platt building and delayed operations for almost three weeks.[20]

With production at the Louisville plant amounting to some 60 percent of the company's total sales at the time, a new location seemed imperative. In 1937, the company moved to a 60,000-square-foot building at 25th and Maple Streets, which it purchased for $30,000.[21] A fire at the new plant in August

GEORGE S. BEIMDIEK, SR.

PRESIDENT, 1938 TO 1953

GEORGE S. BEIMDIEK, SR., was born in St. Louis in 1876, one of 10 children. Raised and educated in the city, he worked for the Fourth National Bank in St. Louis as a young man, while attending night classes at the Benton College of Law. He was admitted to the bar in 1905, the same year he moved to Carthage, Missouri.[1]

In Carthage, Beimdiek helped organize the Superior Limestone Company and played a prominent role in the development of the white limestone business in the city. He was treasurer of Superior and later served as president and general manager of the Carthage Marble and White Limestone Company until 1927, when that business and other Carthage quarries were consolidated to create the Carthage Marble Corporation (a company well-known to longtime Carthage residents).[2]

From 1927 until 1931, Beimdiek was president of the First National Bank of Carthage, which merged with the Central National Bank in 1931.

He was also one of the early directors of the Jasper County Savings and Loan Association, serving on its board from 1931 to 1943.[3]

In 1932, Beimdiek organized the BV Realty & Investment Company with B. L. Van Hoose and remained active in that business until he was named president of Leggett & Platt. He joined Leggett & Platt's board of directors in 1933 and became a vice president and treasurer in 1935, assuming responsibility for the day-to-day operation of the company. In February 1938, he was elected president, treasurer, and general manager.[4]

Beimdiek never actively practiced law, but his legal training and writing skills, as well as his knowledge of real estate, accounting, and banking were of significant value to the then-small Leggett & Platt. In the months before and after he became president, the minutes of the company's board meetings reflected many interesting manifestations of Beimdiek's business and legal experience.

---

caused more than $8,000 in damage, but fortunately nobody was hurt, and operations continued without interruption.[22]

While George S. Beimdiek, Sr., had led the company's operations for nearly three years, he had done so as vice president and treasurer. (In 1937, his title was changed to vice president, treasurer, and general manager.) In February 1938, F. B. Williams relinquished the presidency and was elected chairman of the board; Beimdiek was elected president, treasurer, and general manager of the company.[23]

As operations began to settle down in Louisville, Leggett & Platt opened a factory in Dallas, Texas, in September 1938 in an attempt to capture additional sales originating in the state. James W. Odor, who was hired in 1918 as a salesman, was placed in charge of the Texas plant. Odor knew the growing customer base and its needs very well. In 1939, Odor was named a vice president of the company.[24]

To equip the Texas factory, Leggett & Platt acquired the equipment of the Daltex Company, a small bedspring manufacturer, and shipped addi-

For example, in late 1937, the company evaluated the purchase of the Daltex Company, a Dallas-area spring-making business interested in selling to Leggett & Platt. Beimdiek led a small committee of Leggett executives on a trip to investigate Daltex as well as other Dallas area properties.[5]

The board decided not to purchase the Daltex property, but later acquired its spring-making machinery and moved it to a more attractive location (four acres of land and six buildings) that Leggett & Platt purchased in Dallas.[6] With the board's authorization, Beimdiek guided the real estate and machinery purchases, as reflected in the detailed documents of sale in company records.[7]

Beimdiek's knowledge of law, real estate, and business was also apparent in other Leggett & Platt endeavors. A month before the Dallas land and machinery purchases, Beimdiek and Edward B. Casey, Jr., vice president of Kentucky operations, negotiated the purchase of a new building and two acres of land in Louisville. During the same period, the company completed a complex recapitalization process, and researched and applied for patents on various spring-making machinery (primarily the inventions of Carl Kirchner, the company's mechanical genius). Beimdiek's broad experience and capabilities were well applied in all of these company transactions.[8]

Beimdiek also took pleasure and some pride in writing Leggett's annual reports and letters to shareholders. Beginning in 1936 and continuing through 1952, he authored the "Letter to Shareholders" in 17 annual reports.

In 1910, Beimdiek married Ida Brinkerhoff, whose father was one of the founders of First National Bank of Carthage and served as its president for many years. The couple had one son, George S. Beimdiek, Jr., and a daughter, Martha.[9]

Many years later, following his death in 1963, family members were asked by a grandson to describe George S. Beimdiek, Sr. They remembered him as kind, sincere, active in civic and community affairs, religious, and "great with numbers."[10]

George S. Beimdiek, Jr.

George Beimdiek, Jr., attended the University of Missouri–Columbia, where he earned his bachelor of science degree in business administration. He worked at a St. Louis brokerage before returning to Carthage in 1937 to become president of BV Realty & Investment Company, which his father had cofounded.[11]

In 1959, when ill health caused Beimdiek, Sr., to resign from the board, he recommended his son to be nominated as a director.[12] George S. Beimdiek, Jr., was elected that year and served as a Leggett & Platt director from 1959 to 1985—the same length of time (26 years) his father served on the board (1933 to 1959).

George Beimdiek, Jr., died in 2007 at the age of 94, while this book was being written.

tional equipment to the Dallas operation from the Carthage plant.[25]

With its operations consolidating and becoming particularly strong in Louisville, sales for 1939 would increase by 27 percent, producing a $1.57 dividend for shareholders, more than triple the 1938 dividend of $0.45 per share.[26]

Challenges of War

Leggett & Platt's Texas operations were becoming profitable for the first time when World War II broke out in Europe. By the end of 1940, as raw materials increased 7 percent and labor costs rose 8 percent, the company reported only a 5 percent increase in sales. To battle declining profits and rising competition, Leggett & Platt installed better machinery and focused on improving efficiency.[27]

As the price of raw materials rose to premium levels in 1941, Leggett & Platt turned to defense contracts and diversification to remain afloat. The company began selling its machining, tooling, and engineering capabilities to a range of industries, including aerospace. During this time, Carl Kirchner,

The Leggett & Platt board of directors in the late 1940s included (from left to right) George S. Beimdiek, Sr.; George E. Phelps; C. E. Platt; Edward B. Casey; Harry M. Cornell, Sr.; J. A. McMillan; and J. E. O'Keefe.

an innovative engineer who joined the company in 1923 and greatly helped advance Leggett's engineering capabilities, developed the first semi-automatic, double-sided assembly machine for use in innerspring unit production. The machine enabled the company to reduce its costs and, in time, would help the company rapidly return to pre-war productivity levels.[28]

As a result of the company's progressive and upbeat outlook, Leggett & Platt experienced record sales in 1941. The majority of profits came from defense work, which concerned the board of directors with regard to the company's ability to continue manufacturing products for civilians. The government was rationing raw materials, with priority given to products associated with the war effort. In the 1941 Annual Report, President Beimdiek told shareholders:

Raw materials are becoming increasingly difficult to obtain, both because priorities granted to the bedding industry for civilian manufacture are not suffi-

ciently high to obtain the raw materials, and also because of the increasing demand of direct defense industries on the producers of steel and wire. In addition to the above, certain limitation orders have also become effective and others are in the making, rendering it impossible to determine to what extent your company may expect to continue in the manufacture of goods for civilian use.

Government requirements of our products are comparatively limited, but your company is doing everything possible to obtain a fair share of this business. Competition in this line is extremely keen as most, if not all, manufacturers of bedding products are experiencing extreme difficulty in obtaining raw materials for civilian manufacture.

Your company's machines and equipment can produce little that is required in the war effort other than its regular line of products. For many months, we have diligently pursued a policy of trying to find products required in the defense efforts which might be manufactured with our existing machinery and personnel. We have experienced some small success, but for the most part we are advised that there is little that we can produce which can be used under the present setup. Your company, and with your approval, I am sure, is ready and willing to make a complete conversion to war products, if by so doing we can contribute in any measure to the successful carrying out of our national war effort.[29]

Idleness and Hope

In 1942, with its operations expanding beyond just spring bed coils, Leggett & Platt Spring Bed and

Manufacturing Company shortened its name to Leggett & Platt, Incorporated.[30]

While many Leggett & Platt employees were off to war or redeployed to war-related industries, defense work continued to serve as the company's primary source of income. However, this was not the type of work that would turn a significant profit.[31]

Problems also began to arise in Texas when a group of prominent citizens formed a medical foundation and began plans to establish a premier medical school and clinic. They believed the Leggett & Platt property at Harry Hines Boulevard and Oak Lawn Avenue was the perfect location for their school, as it adjoined the city- and county-owned Parkland Hospital.[32] Through negotiations, Leggett & Platt formed an agreement with the foundation to exchange the Dallas property for land and a building that would be built to Leggett & Platt specifications at an undetermined location. As construction of the new facility would not start until the war ended, Leggett & Platt continued operating at the Dallas site.[33]

With intense restrictions on raw materials throughout 1943, many Leggett & Platt machines

A company truck at the Louisville plant loads up for deliveries. Flex-O-Top is a trademarked Leggett & Platt brand.

were left idle, and the company ended the year with an 18 percent drop in sales. Nevertheless, Leggett & Platt remained optimistic and dedicated. In his letter to shareholders, dated April 5, 1944, Beimdiek wrote:

> ... *officials of the company consider the work beneficial to the war effort and it also assists in the continuing employment of our experienced employees. ...*
>
> *So long as the production of civilian merchandise is limited by the necessities of war and the governmental restrictions and regulations continue, the company's operations will be adversely affected. ... [However,] the cost to reconvert for the resumption of peacetime operations should not present a serious problem. With the easing of restrictions on production of civilian goods, the company anticipates a substantial volume of business in supplying the accumulated demand of the public.*[34]

As the Allies beefed up their forces overseas in 1944, a shortage of manpower at home forced Leggett & Platt to close its Dallas operations in May and continue servicing Texas customers through the Carthage plant's output.[35]

A shortage of workers also forced the company to move assembly operations from the Louisville plant to a rented warehouse 110 miles away in Winchester, Kentucky. At the time, raw material shortages had reduced the company's product lineup from 40 styles of bedsprings to only one, but the company had since expanded into the manufacturing of cushion springs for the furniture industry.[36]

Oscar "Bud" Hougland was sent from the Louisville plant in July 1944 to manage the Winchester operations. Hougland, who started as a factory worker at the Louisville plant in the early 1930s, had been promoted several times—from coiler and assembler, to foreman of the assembly department, to

Oscar "Bud" Hougland joined Leggett & Platt in 1931, working in the bottom wire and top-bending department at the Louisville plant. He was promoted several times through the years and eventually established the new assembly operations in Winchester, Kentucky.

general foreman at Louisville, to superintendent of the Dallas, Texas, plant. In May 1944, Hougland moved back to work at Louisville and was asked shortly thereafter to move again and establish the new assembly operations in Winchester.[37]

By the end of 1944, with the tide of the war changing, Leggett & Platt had fulfilled nearly all of its obligations for the war effort and operated almost entirely for commercial production.[38] Anticipating a return to operations in Dallas, Leggett & Platt continued working toward the exchange of properties and succeeded in locating a suitable new site.[39]

Aftermath

As the war wound down in 1945, Leggett & Platt began to recover slowly. Sales for the year exceeded the three prior years, but had not yet returned to pre-war levels. During the initial post-war years, raw material supplies became more difficult to obtain, a factor complicated by a rash of labor disputes that delayed operations at the nation's steel plants. Operations were further complicated by consumer demand for a better grade of bedsprings and innersprings, which Leggett & Platt supplied as materials became available.[40]

In Dallas, manufacturing resumed on a limited basis. The plant had hired a new crew of inexperienced workers and was making little headway in the production of innersprings. As a result, Carthage was still producing bedsprings for the Texas territory. To add to the frustration, the city of Dallas had now decided to extend its airport operations to encompass the property selected for Leggett & Platt's new site.[41]

A shortage of experienced labor in Louisville also slowed operations there, leaving the facility to produce parts that were then assembled in Winchester, where labor was plentiful. Consequently, the company purchased its Winchester facility in April 1946 and, with the day-to-day guidance and direction of Hougland, began installing machinery and increasing production at that location.[42]

In 1946, Leggett & Platt also solved its Texas dilemma with the purchase and remodeling of a

cotton warehouse in Ennis, Texas, located 32 miles south of Dallas on the Southern Pacific Railroad line and U.S. Highway 75. As before, James Odor would be responsible for the Texas plant. Conducting business in the mid-1940s had proved quite an ordeal, but business was beginning to improve as Leggett & Platt considered expansions to its Carthage and Winchester plants.[43]

An experienced management team was also in place. Harry M. Cornell, Sr., vice president and sales manager, was steadily improving the company's sales force and participating in product development discussions. Fred Bouser and his son-in-law, Bud Hougland, ran the Louisville and Winchester, Kentucky, operations and reported to Edward Casey, Jr., a company vice president. Odor, a longtime employee and company vice president, was in charge of the newly established Ennis, Texas, plant. C. Glenn Joyce, plant superintendent, and Carl Kirchner, a talented mechanical engineer and inventor, continued to improve the machinery capabilities and factory efficiencies at the Carthage plant.[44]

In March 1946, Cornell, Casey, Hougland, and Odor conferred with Glenn Joyce at the Carthage manufacturing plant, comparing production methods and machinery efficiencies in hopes of increasing production and improving the machinery arrangements at all locations.[45]

Growing Demand

By the end of 1947, Leggett & Platt was reporting a year of record growth. Due to increasing demand

---

Above: The original plant in Ennis, Texas, produced innersprings, all-wire bedsprings, and some furniture components. By the end of 1948, Leggett & Platt was already planning the facility's first expansion.

Right: For many years, Carl Kirchner was recognized as Leggett & Platt's machinery and product development expert. He invented and improved many products as well as machinery for the company. Records today still include 11 approved patents filed by Kirchner on behalf of Leggett & Platt.

Left: In the late 1940s, Leggett & Platt products were shipped from plants in Carthage, Missouri; Louisville and Winchester, Kentucky; and Ennis, Texas.

Below: This photo, taken in June 1950, shows 78 of the employees at the Winchester plant in Kentucky.

for box springs to replace open-coil bedsprings, all plants began producing a complete line of box spring constructions for sale to mattress manufacturers in their respective territories.

The Louisville plant was back at capacity and an additional 30,000 square feet of floor space was being built at Winchester. A contract was signed to begin work on another 23,000 square feet of space at Carthage to produce innersprings, rollaway beds, and furniture components. In addition, innersprings, all-wire bedsprings, and some furniture components were being produced at the Ennis plant, although it was not operating at full capacity. The company had also rid itself of the Dallas site, selling it at a profit.[46]

Although obtaining raw materials remained a challenge and cost the company a premium at times, Leggett & Platt's net worth at the end of 1947 was reported as $1.2 million, a fivefold increase over the 1936 figures of $282,000.[47]

Expanding Operations

Expansion continued in 1948, costing the company upward of $400,000 for property and equipment. Savings, however, were gained as Leggett & Platt produced a considerable amount of new equipment through the expertise of fully equipped machine shops at all of its plants. Every plant was also located on a railroad spur for more economical handling of finished product and raw material.[48]

In Carthage, production of innerspring units for mattress makers and cushion springs for upholstered furniture cushions moved to the newly completed addition to the plant, while the original part of the building was retained for manufacturing bedsprings, rollaway beds, and upholstery constructions. In addition, the Carthage business offices moved from 600 West Vine Street on the north side of the building to the central part of the building at 600 West Mound Street, and the former office space was converted to a machine shop.[49]

The Winchester expansion was nearly completed in 1948, bringing the site's total space to 53,000

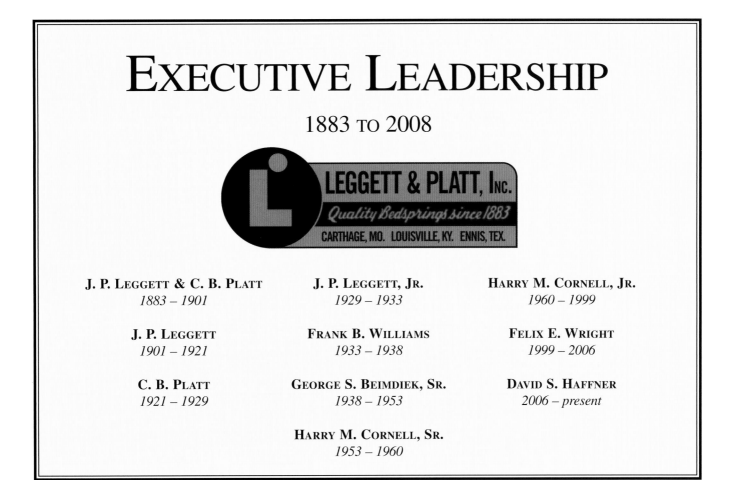

EXECUTIVE LEADERSHIP

1883 TO 2008

J. P. LEGGETT & C. B. PLATT
1883 – 1901

J. P. LEGGETT
1901 – 1921

C. B. PLATT
1921 – 1929

J. P. LEGGETT, JR.
1929 – 1933

FRANK B. WILLIAMS
1933 – 1938

GEORGE S. BEIMDIEK, SR.
1938 – 1953

HARRY M. CORNELL, SR.
1953 – 1960

HARRY M. CORNELL, JR.
1960 – 1999

FELIX E. WRIGHT
1999 – 2006

DAVID S. HAFFNER
2006 – present

square feet. The company also planned to expand the Ennis operations at a cost of $50,000.[50]

New Challenges and Opportunities

As a new decade unfolded, labor strikes continued to plague the steel industry, although they subsided with the onset of the Korean War in June 1950.[51] Leggett & Platt began automating its processes wherever possible, and continued to manufacture much of its own equipment while purchasing other machines designed specifically for the bedding industry.[52] The addition to the Ennis, Texas, factory was completed in 1950, and the company started placing direct-to-customer advertisements in magazines such as *Good Housekeeping* and *Living for Young Homemakers*.[53]

In 1950, another member of the founding families, Harry M. Cornell, Jr., joined Leggett & Platt. Harry, son of Harry "Mack" Cornell, Sr., and grandson of company cofounder J. P. Leggett, had spent a considerable amount of time at the Carthage factory, exploring it when his father worked weekends and working as a laborer and production worker during the summers. Harry had just completed his college education in business administration and marketing at the University of Missouri when he formally joined the company as a sales office assistant in Kentucky.

Unfortunately, at year's end, the company lost a member of one of the founding families with the passing of C. E. "Jack" Platt, son of Cornelius B. Platt. Jack had served on the board of directors since 1947 after retiring from the Windsor, Ontario, operations of the L. A. Young Spring and Wire Company. Upon returning to Carthage, Jack had started the Flex-O-Lator Company, which supplied seating products to the automotive industry.[54] W. E. Carter, president of the Bank of Carthage, was elected to fill Jack's seat on the board.[55]

By the end of 1951, Leggett & Platt's 94 shareholders lived in 17 U.S. states and Canada,[56] with

more than half owning at least 100 shares of stock. The shareholder mix was more female than male, consisting of 34 men and 43 women; the remaining shares were owned by joint, fiduciary, or other shareholders.[57]

This era proved challenging for the company. Unlike the World War II period, when it received many production contracts, Leggett & Platt had been unable to secure any defense contracts since the Korean War began, despite submitting several bids.[58] In addition, conflict at home was cause for concern, as labor unions clashed with the government over wage controls and other developments stemming from the war mobilization process. This culminated in a union boycott of the government agencies put in charge of mobilization efforts, followed by the establishment of the National Advisory Board on Mobilization Policy by President Harry S. Truman. That advisory board subsequently issued a report cautioning against building up the military and recommending only a slight increase in production for mobilization.[59] The report

Company President George S. Beimdiek, Sr. (left) is photographed at the main office at 600 West Mound Street in Carthage in 1952. Beimdiek, Sr., stepped down the following year due to illness and was replaced by Harry M. Cornell, Sr.

also called for controls over wages, pricing, interest rates, and business credit. Company President George S. Beimdiek, Sr., reported that these controls were contributing to a "cloudy" business atmosphere.[60] As a result, he hesitated to predict any expectations for the coming year because of a probable increase in the costs of steel and wire from a pending strike.[61]

The conflict between labor and government reached fever pitch in 1952 when President Truman, threatened with a nationwide steel strike, seized control of the industry.[62] Before his actions could be ruled unconstitutional, the United Steelworkers, Congress of Industrial Organizations (CIO), began a work stoppage that ultimately lasted 53 days.

The strike complicated government regulations allotting steel and forced Leggett & Platt to begin importing the material from Belgium at higher prices.[63] Rather than raise costs to customers, however, the company stayed in line with industry pricing, and subsequently suffered from reduced profits due to higher material costs.[64]

Wire, however, was available, so the company seized its opportunity to diversify. By the end of 1952, bedsprings made up only 20 percent of the company's total sales, with the balance generated by innersprings for mattresses, furniture components, folding cots, box springs, and other products for mattress manufacturers, furniture makers, and dealers.[65] From 1935 to 1952, the company had reinvested nearly $2 million in diversifying its product line, and the results were now becoming evident.[66]

End of a Difficult Chapter

At its meeting on December 16, 1952, the board of directors noted the recent passing of Frank B. Williams, a former president and director of the company. It also heard company President Beimdiek's thoughts about his imminent retirement. According to meeting minutes, "Mr. Beimdiek suggested that the directors be thinking of someone to replace him as president of the company, stating that his age [76] was such that he probably should retire but that he would like to remain on the board."[67]

In April 1953, in a letter to the board, Beimdiek wrote, "In view of the seriousness of my recent illness, I deem it advisable to relieve myself of the obligations incident to the presidency of Leggett & Platt, Incorporated." Beimdiek's resignation was accepted and shortly thereafter the board unanimously elected Harry M. Cornell, Sr., as the company's new president.[68]

The 1935 shareholder proposal to sell Leggett & Platt, led by Beimdiek, Sr., and successfully opposed by Cornell, Sr., was, predictably, a contest neither man forgot. Despite the uneasiness between them, they managed to move Leggett & Platt out of the Great Depression and through a flood, a fire, two wars, and labor and material shortages. Their good work, along with the efforts of many fine managers and employees, made it possible for the company to survive and grow. Under the circumstances, it was a difficult and remarkable feat.

ONE ALONE STANDS OUT . . .

THE STRADIVARIUS VIOLIN
Recognized the world over as the finest violin ever made. A masterpiece of craftsmanship, the Stradivarius was originally made by Antonio Stradivarius in 1737. Some of his more famous instruments are still in existence today.

and among ROLLAWAYS
it's **LEGGETT & PLATT**
FOLD-ER-ROLL

Bedding buyers have acclaimed Leggett & Platt's Fold-Er-Roll as the one rollaway that stands out above all the rest. They know, for instance, that customers appreciate the extra quality that is incorporated into L & P Fold-Er-Rolls.

Dealers enjoy the variety of rollaways that Fold-Er-Roll affords — link or coil springs, Hollywood headboard models, three-position adjustable backrest models — all are offered in Leggett & Platt's complete rollaway line. It provides dealers with a single source for every sale.

The popular "L" Tag means that Fold-Er-Roll is your best rollaway buy. You can depend on year 'round merchandising and advertising of Fold-Er-Rolls with hard-selling ads in leading consumer magazines.

Get complete details soon. Write, wire or phone today for specifications and prices.

Guaranteed by Good Housekeeping

The Symbol of Quality Since 1883

LEGGETT & PLATT
INCORPORATED
MANUFACTURERS OF INNERSPRING UNITS, BOX SPRING CONSTRUCTIONS, SOFA BED CONSTRUCTIONS, COILS

LOUISVILLE, KY.   CARTHAGE, MO.   WINCHESTER, KY.   ENNIS, TEXAS

Leggett & Platt advertisements were commonly placed in publications such as *Good Housekeeping* and *Living for Young Homemakers* in the early 1950s.

CHAPTER FOUR

LEADERSHIP

1953–1969

We had to really get energetic and not be afraid of competition and shaking the markets.

—Harry M. Cornell, Jr.[1]

IN APRIL 1953, THE LEGGETT & PLATT board of directors unanimously elected Harry Mack Cornell, Sr., son-in-law of company cofounder Joseph P. Leggett, as the company's new president. Known simply as "Mack" by his friends, coworkers, and customers, Cornell, Sr., joined the board in 1934 and became an employee and sales manager in 1935. He was an optimistic, courteous, unselfish person, as well as a relationship builder. A longtime director of the company described him as "the most complete people person I have ever known."[2]

In 1930, Leggett & Platt employed only nine salespeople, including one facility manager who also worked as a salesman. Company records do not reveal the number of sales people working when Mack became sales manager in 1935, but by 1951, he and the management team had recruited a capable staff of 31 sales representatives who resided in 20 states and sold in many more.[3]

Mack Cornell's Starting Lineup

Mack's initial challenge as president was not to build a sales team, but to find ways to grow the company profitably in an increasingly complex and competitive market. Predictably, three of his important acts as a new president in 1953 involved the promotion of competent and trustworthy employees.

First, he appointed C. Glenn Joyce, longtime Carthage plant superintendent, as a company vice president and operations manager. Joyce had been recently appointed to the board of directors to complete the unexpired term of veteran director, John O'Keefe, who died the previous year.

Second, with Mack's support, Joyce recommended to the board that Harry Cornell, Jr., be hired to manage the Ennis, Texas, plant. Since James Odor's retirement, the plant's performance had suffered from a lack of consistent management and leadership. The board gave unanimous approval to the appointment. (Despite his age of 24, Harry had already earned the respect and confidence of the board members. Glenn Joyce, for example, had observed Harry's hard work and people skills during his two summers of employment at the Carthage plant, and Edward

Debuting at a Dallas trade show in January 1960, the image of a smiling, black-and-white cat lounging in a Bonnell coil was created by the marketing department in Ennis, Texas. It graced numerous corporate materials, including the Annual Report, for many years. Some claim the logo stems from a real cat that used to enter the plant and curl up in a coil atop a workbench, while others say the image was created to demonstrate the comfort of the coils.

Casey, Jr., had employed Harry as a sales office assistant and trainee at Louisville, recognizing his organizational and leadership talents.)

Third, at the September board meeting, Mack and Joyce asked the directors' opinions about promoting the Missouri territory salesman, Ralph V. Johnson, to assistant sales manager. In this position, Johnson would gradually take on Mack's responsibilities as sales manager. The board approved the promotion, and Johnson began the new job on January 1, 1954. (Johnson eventually became Leggett & Platt's vice president of sales,

serving as a mentor and inspiration for a generation of people in customer service and sales.)[4]

The Leggett & Platt leadership team consisted of four other experienced managers: Frank E. Ford, who had joined the company in 1946 and was elected corporate secretary and treasurer the month before Mack Cornell became president; Edward Casey, Jr., who continued to lead the Kentucky operations; Fred Bouser, who managed the Louisville plant; and Bud Hougland, who managed the Winchester plant.[5]

By the end of 1953, Mack had a team in place to meet the challenge he described in the company's annual Letter to Stockholders:

In the highly competitive market in which we serve it is more vital than ever before to keep costs at the lowest possible level. To this end, an intensive cost reduction and control program is being placed in operation. Every phase of the business has or will be scrutinized for purposes of effectuating economies and obtaining new and additional outlets for the products we are capable of manufacturing.[6]

Above: Glenn Joyce served as a Leggett & Platt vice president and operations manager in the 1950s, providing dependable leadership through many years of company growth.

Below: Frank Ford stands among the Carthage plant's inventory of rollaway beds and bedsprings that were finished in a popular aluminum color. Ford had joined the company's payroll department only a few years before this photo was taken in the early 1950s.

HARRY M. CORNELL, SR.

PRESIDENT, 1953 TO 1959

Harry M. "Mack" Cornell, Sr., was born in Carthage, Missouri, in 1900, and attended the Carthage schools. After graduating from high school, Cornell went to work in the Oklahoma oil fields as a driller. From that position he secured work with the Standard Oil Company drilling wells in Sumatra, Dutch East Indies.[1]

In 1927, between two four-year contracts overseas, Mack came home to Carthage where, on November 5, he married Marjorie Leggett, a former classmate, who was the daughter of J. P. Leggett. Described as charming and intelligent, she was a strong supporter of the company her father had cofounded. Before the year's end, the couple returned to Sumatra, arriving in time to begin Mack's second contract. In October 1928, they had a son, Harry M. Cornell, Jr.[2]

When the oil-drilling contract expired at the end of 1931, the Cornell family returned to Carthage where Mack sold life insurance and served as City Clerk. In 1934, he joined the Leggett & Platt board of directors, and in 1935, he became the company's vice president and sales manager.[3]

Those who knew him remember Mack as outgoing and personable, a kind and considerate man who treated others with respect. He was everyone's friend—employees and customers alike. Many say his personality became ingrained in the company and remains prominent in its culture to this day. As a person with a keen intuition, Mack was a natural sales manager. His investment in relationships paid dividends to the company for years to come.

Mack served as president of the company from 1953 through 1959 and remained its chairman until his death in 1982.[4]

Despite soft fourth-quarter sales in home furnishings and bedding, net sales for 1953 were the best to date—$5.1 million, up 12 percent over 1952. In the first year of Mack's presidency, all of Leggett & Platt's factories realized a sales increase. At Ennis, Texas, where Harry had been assigned, sales rose 128 percent. After-tax income for the company as a whole was up 9.8 percent to $249,900.[7]

Following a slight decline in sales and earnings in 1954, the company enjoyed a healthy rebound in 1955. Net sales were $6.1 million, up 23 percent over 1954, and net earnings were $279,403, up nearly 30 percent from the previous year.[8]

Sales and earnings at the Ennis, Texas, operation continued to improve steadily, and early in 1955, the board of directors unanimously elected Harry

Cornell, Jr., as a vice president of the company. For the next four years, the company's three operating vice presidents—Casey, Joyce, and Cornell, Jr.—provided dependable operational leadership.

Increasing Sales and Adding Capacity

The company's sales team moved Leggett & Platt's net sales to modestly higher, record levels in 1956, 1957, and 1958 ($6.34, $6.38, and $6.71 million, respectively). Although the company was profitable all three years, aggressive competition made it necessary to restrain or lower prices, and profits were held below the level achieved in 1955.[9]

In 1956, Leggett & Platt completed a 17,460-square-foot warehouse expansion at Carthage and

STARTING LINEUP

HARRY MACK CORNELL, SR.
President

RALPH JOHNSON
Sales Manager

FRANK FORD
Secretary–Treasurer

EDWARD CASEY
VP, Kentucky Operations

GLENN JOYCE
VP, Carthage Operations

HARRY CORNELL, JR.
VP, Texas Operations

acquired additional property at Winchester and Ennis. In 1957, a 12,500-square-foot warehouse expansion was completed at Ennis, and in April 1958, the board approved a 15,000-square-foot addition for the Texas location. At the October 1959 board meeting, the directors approved plans for a new 40,000-square-foot facility at Winchester and authorized Harry Cornell, Jr., to begin negotiations for additional industrial property in Ennis.[10]

As noted, in 1958, the company achieved its fourth consecutive year of record net sales ($6.71 million); unfortunately, net earnings ($198,000) were the lowest in more than a decade. The performance of the Ennis, Texas, facility was com-

mendable. Ennis led all others in percentage of net profit to sales and contributed a larger return in actual dollars than either of the larger operations in Missouri or Kentucky.[11]

Unions Selling, Employees Not Buying

Strikes and labor disputes disrupted the U.S. economy in the years after the Korean War. Twice during the 1950s, strikes in the steel industry interrupted raw material shipments to the company, reducing inventories to perilous levels. In this time of union growth and strength, Leggett & Platt employees were frequent targets of union organizers.

In September 1956, in an election supervised by the National Labor Relations Board (NLRB), employees at Louisville narrowly rejected representation by the Firemen and Oilers Union. In October of the following year, Louisville employees again rejected the Firemen and Oilers, but this time by a 4-to-1 margin.[12]

The United Steelworkers Union (USW) attempted to organize employees at Ennis in September 1957. Employees, however, rejected the USW by a substantial margin (64 to 47) in a January 1958 election.[13]

In September 1958, Glenn Joyce reported to the board that the International Association of Machinists (IAM) had petitioned the NLRB for a representation election at Carthage. In November, the Carthage plant employees rejected the IAM by a vote of 72 to 20.[14]

In August 1959, the IAM filed a petition with the NLRB to represent employees at Louisville. In a December election, the Louisville employees also rejected the IAM by a margin of 58 to 41.[15]

During the decade, three different unions petitioned the NLRB for five separate elections at Leggett & Platt facilities. Leggett employees voted five times to remain union-free.

People

Fred Bouser, the longtime superintendent at Louisville, retired on December 31, 1956, and was replaced by Don K. Frederick. (Sadly, the board was informed of Bouser's death the following September.)

In January 1958, the board voted to submit to the stockholders an amendment to the articles of incorporation increasing the number of directors from seven to eight and to add Harry Cornell, Jr.'s, name to the slate of directors submitted to shareholders. Harry was one of eight directors elected by shareholders in February 1958.[16]

In April 1958, George E. Phelps, a director since 1935, died. In his 23 years on the job, Phelps served six years as corporate secretary (from February 1938 to February 1944) and as corporate attorney. Frank Williams, Jr., son of Frank B. Williams, former president and director of the company, was appointed and later elected to fill the vacancy.

In January 1959, George S. Beimdiek, Sr., asked not to be renominated as a director and requested that his son, George S. Beimdiek, Jr., be placed on the ballot. At the shareholder's meeting on February 24, 1959, Beimdiek, Sr., left the board and his son joined it. (Beimdiek, Jr., a successful local businessman and at that time president of BV Realty & Investment Company, would serve as a director until May 1985.)[17]

Harry Cornell, Jr.– Discontent with the Status Quo

When Harry Cornell, Jr., joined the board of directors in 1958, it was a conservative group dominated by far older men. John McMillan was first elected to the board in 1923, five years before Cornell, Jr., was born. George S. Beimdiek, Sr.; Mack Cornell, Sr.; and George Phelps began their service on the board in 1933, 1934, and 1935, respectively.[18]

The board repeatedly found it difficult to agree on a course of action and was slow to act on opportunities. For example, several abridged quotations

Max Baucom, who eventually moved into management at Leggett & Platt, is seen here at the Carthage plant in the early 1950s, tending to one of three pieces of machinery he operated.

from the minutes of six board meetings in the first eight months of 1959 read as follows:

> *... The meeting had been called to consider the purchase of the Ely Walker plant at Verona, Missouri ... we had long considered diversification ... this was a good opportunity. ... After considerable discussion ... it was decided to forgo any action at this particular time.*   —February 7, 1959[19]

> *... The Verona property, which had been discussed at the previous meeting was reported to have been sold.*   —February 24, 1959[20]

> *Mr. Joyce reported on a proposition submitted by a California firm that we produce and market a sleeper construction; however, he had no recommendations to offer at this time.*   —April 29, 1959[21]

> *A lengthy discussion was held concerning possible plant improvements and product diversification after which the meeting was adjourned.*   —May 27, 1959[22]

> *... [Regarding] the proposal of our manufacturing sofa bed hinges and sleeper fixtures ... management had no particular recommendations at this time.*   —June 23, 1959[23]

> *... Developments on the sofa bed hinge and sleeper fixture had not materialized as rapidly as first anticipated, therefore [there was] no recommendation on either matter at this time.*   —August 25, 1959[24]

> *A discussion was held concerning plant expansion in the Louisville–Winchester area, however no decision was reached or action taken.*   —August 25, 1959[25]

All of the previously quoted 1959 board meeting minutes indicated that Harry Cornell, Jr., was in attendance. The aggressive, young vice president said of these meetings: "During those years, the board met monthly. Essentially, the company was being run by the board of directors as a committee. Too often the board was unable to find consensus on matters critical to our future. It was very disappointing ... frustrating."[26]

In contrast to the meeting minutes from early 1959, three abridged quotes from the minutes of the October 28, 1959, board meeting, which reflect Harry's developing influence, read as follows:

> *... Tooling for production of [sofa bed] hinges was in process. ... They would be produced at the Ennis plant [managed by Harry].*
> *... Mr. Beimdiek [Jr.] moved we proceed with plans and specifications for a 40,000-square-foot building at Winchester, Kentucky. This motion was seconded by H. M. Cornell, Jr., and carried unanimously. [The two youngest members of the board made and seconded the motion.]*
> *Mr. Casey moved, seconded by H. M. Cornell, Sr., and unanimously voted that management [Harry] proceed with negotiations for additional land and building area in Ennis.*[27]

The above excerpts clearly illustrate Harry's efforts to reenergize company endeavors to improve and grow.

In 1958, Harry again reported record sales and earnings for the Ennis facility. With a strong desire to create a new, more energetic, and growth-oriented environment for Leggett & Platt, he sought the counsel of business associates and friends.

By the end of that year, Harry had developed a plan to acquire majority ownership of the company. It was a bold plan, but possible. The company had slightly more than 140,000 shares outstanding, and no one person or family owned a near majority of the modestly priced stock. "There were, as you can imagine, a great number of things to think about and work through," Harry recalled. He continued:

> *First, I was very confident Mother and Dad would support the plan, but I didn't want to involve them in the early stages. It would have worried Mother to death, and it would have put Dad in a very awkward situation with the board. I didn't visit with them about the plan until I'd lined up nearly all of the other needed shares.*
> *Second, the preliminary financing for the purchase of the shares was arranged through relationships I'd developed with a Dallas bank. That backing, however, depended on my ability to obtain commitments from several major shareholders to sell their shares.*

I had to be able to demonstrate majority ownership, and the bank wanted various restrictive covenants as part of the deal. [The Bank of Carthage later offered Harry more attractive and less restrictive financing.]

Anyway, I met with a half dozen or so of the major shareholders who had no direct contact with the day-to-day business of the company and obtained agreements to purchase their shares. Trust and confidence were just critical in getting this done.[28]

Harry had another extremely important relationship with Carthage attorney Herbert Casteel, a former fraternity brother at the University of Missouri. In 1952, Harry and Casteel had started a small business, Carthage Wood Products, when Harry was a self-employed, commissioned salesman representing Leggett & Platt and other manufacturers. When Harry was rehired and moved to Texas to manage the Ennis plant in the summer of 1953, Casteel managed the Carthage end of their business, and during the ensuing years, the two men grew that business together.

Casteel was one of the people Harry consulted about the idea of taking control of the company. When it came time to review option purchase letters for Harry to take to shareholders, Casteel assisted. He also borrowed money and purchased Leggett & Platt stock. He recalled:

I didn't know a lot about the company, but I knew a lot about Harry [Jr.]. I was really investing in the man. He was a winner. If he was playing badminton or tennis or golf or anything, he went in to win. And he was willing to make the effort to train himself to win. ... Also, he is, of course, a great people person. He is interested in people, works well with people. I thought he'd build a good management team, work well with management, and I knew he was ethical. I didn't want to invest in a company that was run for the benefit of the executives. I wanted one that was run for the benefit of the stockholders, and I believed he would do that.[29]

Following the adjournment of the directors' meeting in late October 1959, Harry Cornell asked his fellow directors if they would stay a few minutes more, as he wanted to tell them about some important developments.

Harry explained he had purchased the stock of several major shareholders. With shares he owned,

his family's shares, and those of close friends, he could now confidently count on support from shareholders owning a majority of the company's stock. He wanted to lead the company, serve as its next president, and grow the business for the shareholders. "I was nervous and excited, trying my best to be calm and polite, but I also wanted to convey my firm determination to carry the change through," he said.[30]

Harry made it clear that no management housecleaning was necessary; Edward Casey, Jr.; Glenn Joyce; and the other directors were fine people and managers whom he hoped would continue to help grow the company; the board would need to make some adjustments, however.

New Decade, New Leadership

"There's no need to say who was happy or unhappy," Harry Cornell said when asked about the directors' reactions. It appears there were very few unhappy directors. Time had been an ally in Harry's plan.[31]

In 1958 and 1959, the board lost several of its veteran members. Phelps died in early 1958, while Beimdiek, Sr., resigned in early 1959 and his son, George Beimdiek, Jr., joined the board in February 1959. Walter Carter, president of the Bank of Carthage and a Leggett & Platt director since February 1951, died in June 1959.[32]

At the January meeting in 1960, Herb Casteel was appointed to complete Carter's unexpired term. The board voted to reduce its number of members from eight to seven. John McMillan resigned and was thanked warmly for his many years of service. Marjorie (Leggett) Cornell, wife of Harry Cornell, Sr., was nominated to replace one other member of the board. In February 1960, the shareholders voted unanimously for the new slate of directors, and the change in control was complete.[33]

Leggett & Platt became a closely held company for the next few years. "That gave us the ability to plan and carry out our plan," explained Harry. He continued:

Dad was elected chairman of the board. He, Mr. Casey, and Glenn Joyce continued to serve on the board and were very involved in the day-to-day business. Frank Ford, Ralph Johnson, Glenn Joyce, and Mr. Casey were all so supportive of the leadership

change and committed to Leggett's success. We
immediately promoted Glenn to executive vice presi-
dent. George Beimdiek, Jr., stayed on the board, and
he and Herb Casteel were excellent advisors and con-
structive board members for many years.[34]

In 2008, in a letter to Harry, Frank Ford said,
"You provided us with new life when you came to
Carthage and as president. Ralph [Johnson] and I
came up with lots of changes, only to have them
vetoed by the Board of Directors. You provided new
life, and I'll always be thankful."[35]

In 1954, when Harry was managing the Ennis
plant, he hired a high school classmate, Richard P.
"Dick" Fanning, to handle a West Texas sales territory. In 1958, as Harry's responsibilities increased,
Fanning was transferred to the Ennis
office to oversee sales and run the facility. Rising through the ranks to become
the plant manager, he was eventually
elected as a vice president and officer
of Leggett & Platt. When he returned
home to Carthage several years later,
he continued his career as a vice president and later president of the company's bedding group.

The first two years of Harry's
presidency, 1960 and 1961, proved
difficult; sales slowed and competition was fierce. The Bank of Car-
thage and its correspondent bank in Kansas City
stepped up to provide reliable and affordable credit
to the company.

Acquisition Prospects

The pace of growth-related activity at Leggett &
Platt in 1960 was breathtaking. In June, Harry
reported to the board that acquisition discussions
had commenced with the Super Sagless Corporation.
Super Sagless, a manufacturer of sofa sleeper and
recliner chair hardware, had operations in Tupelo,

Richard P. "Dick" Fanning was hired in 1954 as a salesman
in the West Texas territory. Repeatedly promoted through the
years, he was a practical problem solver and decisive
manager who served the company for 45 years.

Mississippi, and Bayonne, New Jersey. In July, the
board held a special meeting to approve an offer
to buy Super Sagless.

In September, Harry reported that the officers of Super Sagless had not accepted the acquisition offer and wanted more cash. Harry did not
recommend sweetening the deal. While the company's young leader was anxious to grow and
diversify the business, he demonstrated patience
and discipline in these negotiations. He also
maintained friendly contacts with members of the
Katz and Bank families, who were the owners.
This kind of relationship building often paid off
later. (In this instance, the payoff came 34 years
later, in July 1994, when Leggett & Platt acquired
Super Sagless from these same owners.)

In September 1960, Harry reported to the board that the company
was investigating the potential purchase of Middletown Manufacturing
Company of Simpsonville, Kentucky
(a competitor of Super Sagless). In
November, he told the board, "... [We
will] not be proceeding further in negotiations with this company."[36] Again,
patience and discipline were shown,
and Leggett & Platt remained in contact with key people at Middletown.
(Eventually, in 1973, Leggett bought
the operation from a subsequent
owner, Lear Siegler.)

In September, the board also heard a report on
the investigation of one other potential acquisition,
Chicago Spring Corporation. The company was not as
diversified as Leggett & Platt, but was considered one
of the foremost producers of high-coil-count units for
mattresses. This acquisition was eventually shelved.[37]

Later that same year (1960), the minutes of a
board meeting reflected: "[The company's] ... interest in producing poly foam ... has been renewed
due to the reasonable cost of polyurethane foam
production equipment."[38]

Board minutes from November 25 reported
that Harry and Glenn Joyce would soon visit several polyurethane foam plants following a National
Association of Bedding Manufacturers (NABM)
convention in Miami. On December 28, they reported
to the board on visits to three of these facilities
in the Southeast.[39]

In February 1961, John Haley, vice president of the polyurethane foam producer Phillips Foscue Corporation, visited Carthage to discuss Leggett & Platt's interest in the urethane foam business. Phillips Foscue had operations in High Point, North Carolina, and Tupelo, Mississippi. However, Leggett did not acquire any urethane foam producers until December 1976, when it finally acquired Phillips Foscue.[40]

One acquisition was completed in 1960. In October, Leggett & Platt purchased all outstanding stock of the C. A. Bissman Manufacturing Company of Springfield, Missouri. The Bissman acquisition provided Leggett & Platt with a new line of products—wood headboards and bunk beds—to complement the company's steel rollaway beds, Hollywood beds, and institutional beds. Bissman would be operated as a wholly owned subsidiary.[41]

Bill Allen, a retired risk manager whose career with Leggett & Platt spanned more than 30 years, remembered that his first day on the job was spent counting Bissman's inventory. Recalling the plan for the acquisition, Allen said:

> We needed a facility where we could manufacture some items—bunk beds, headboards, that sort of thing—that we could sell into the bedding and furniture industry along with our steel products. ... We continued to make some high-end, old-style walnut furniture, just absolutely gorgeous stuff, until we finished all of Bissman's supply of lumber.
>
> ... Then we produced the medium line of case goods, beds, and dressers. ... But, after a few years, we limited our production to bunk beds and headboards.[42]

Although Bissman's product line required revamping, by 1962 the operation contributed to a substantial increase in sales volume. The company's net sales rose to nearly $8.3 million in 1962 from $7.6 million in 1961.[43]

New Products and Expanded Plants

Acquisitions were not the only growth activities at Leggett & Platt in 1960. The company authorized the purchase of machinery to produce two new products:

sinuous-wire and stake-wire bedding units. Sinuous wire was widely used in automotive seats, upholstered furniture, and institutional beds. Stake-wire bedding units were sold to innerspring mattress manufacturers. The sinuous-wire machinery was installed at Ennis. Crimping and closing machines, for the production of stake-wire units, were initially installed in the Kentucky and Texas plants and in a new facility in Phoenix, Arizona.[44]

In June 1960, the board decided to establish a manufacturing facility in Phoenix, which would greatly reduce shipping costs for a growing number of customers in the Southwest and West.[45]

In July, Leggett & Platt leased a building in Phoenix. In August, machinery was being built and ordered for the new plant. In November, Glenn Joyce traveled to Phoenix to supervise installation of the machinery and a tempering oven. Frank Cooper, the Ennis plant superintendent, was relocated to Phoenix.[46]

The Phoenix plant start-up did not go as smoothly as anticipated. By July 1961, Leggett & Platt's senior management was dissatisfied with the plant's uneven production and unprofitability, and considered imposing a "do or die" 60-day trial period.

It was also suggested that a capable young man at the Ennis plant, Felix E. Wright, be sent to Phoenix as a new general manager.[47]

Harry Cornell, Jr., had hired Wright in March 1959 for a position in customer service at Ennis, shortly after Wright's graduation from East Texas State University. The jump from customer service to general manager would be a significant change. Wright, who would become Leggett & Platt's chairman and CEO many years later, recalled he had doubts about his ability to take on the tasks. Those working with him, however, were convinced he was the right man for the job. Wright later said the mentoring he received

A few years after starting his career with Leggett & Platt, Felix E. Wright became general manager at the Phoenix plant and was eventually placed in charge of all sales and marketing west of the Rockies.

from Harry Cornell, Jr., in Phoenix was "one of the best lessons that I ever had in my career."[48]

The first two years of Harry's leadership (1960 and 1961) had been exciting, but challenging. Fierce competition kept profits for both years below earlier levels. In the 1961 Annual Report, Chairman Harry M. Cornell, Sr., described the conditions they faced:

The Year in Review

The year 1961 was marked by extremely competitive conditions in the bedding and furniture industries serviced by Leggett and Platt, Incorporated. This downward trend, which first became evident in mid-1960, became so extreme by mid-1961 that sales and profits were adversely affected … .

The Year Ahead

There is little indication of an immediate improvement in competitive conditions in our markets. To minimize the effect of this situation on earnings, your management is engaged in a vigorous program of cost and expense control. Our policy of product diversification and market development continues. The result of these programs has been gratifying to date.[49]

Fueling Future Growth

Despite the competition, Leggett & Platt's leadership was determined to drive the company forward, while growing and diversifying. By 1963, management had identified and was directing its energy into five steps to fuel future growth. The minutes of the board meetings in early 1963 contain numerous examples of these efforts.

In the first step, with patience and understanding rare among results-oriented business people,

The Phoenix, Arizona, branch was set up in the early 1960s to provide service west of the Rockies.

Leggett & Platt's leaders strived to build long-term relationships with employees, customers, and potential acquisition partners. The board minutes from January 31, 1963, stated: "Under new business … Cornell [Jr.] reviewed his … discussion with the Webster Spring Corporation in connection with the possibility of acquiring Off Set Spring of Memphis."[50]

Leggett & Platt did not purchase Off Set Spring, and a casual reader might overlook the brief entry in the minutes. The mention of discussions with Webster Spring, however, is the important detail. Harry knew the principal owners of Webster, the Levine family, before the acquisition negotiations began, and he maintained a friendly relationship with them afterward. Though they were competitors, they liked and respected one another. Several years later, Harry gave Sandy Levine a tour of Leggett & Platt's wire mill. Levine was impressed and built a similar, smaller mill at his family's company in Oxford, Massachusetts. Many years later, when the Levine family and other Webster shareholders decided to sell their business, they wanted to sell to Leggett & Platt.

The second step to further growth was to extend the company geographically. Board minutes in March 1963 record, for example, that "Felix Wright had been successful in obtaining additional business in Salt Lake City … ." The Phoenix plant, which he managed, reached customers in the Southwest and West more cost-effectively. In the ensuing years, Leggett continued to establish production and distribution facilities in new regions.[51]

The third step was to upgrade and expand the company's existing facilities and machinery. Leggett & Platt's experienced managers and machinists improved plant layouts and designed faster, more efficient machinery. The following excerpts are from January and February 1963 board minutes:

... Mr. Joyce reported that in [Winchester] Kentucky, the new building project was coming along satisfactorily ... .

... [The] increase in production [at Carthage] had been accomplished as planned ... .

... manufacturing costs [at Ennis] were improving ... .

... They [Phoenix] were coming along satisfactorily in all respects ... .[52]

The fourth step was to broaden the company's product lineup. Three new products were mentioned in the January 1963 directors' minutes:

Mr. Cornell [Jr.] reported that the Flotura™ spring construction had now been produced in sufficient quantity and enough tests made that ... this product was now ready for sale to other furniture manufacturers.

A report was made ... concerning the problems encountered with the new Zephyr spring. Construction and sales ... would continue in a limited way ... .

Chittenden & Eastman were buying the walnut bedroom set ... we would begin to develop ... a walnut dining suite.[53]

Leggett's fifth step to achieve growth was to acquire other businesses. As in all company buyouts, while the actual purchasing did not prove overly difficult, negotiating a reasonable price, bringing the acquisition through its transition period, and managing it effectively were complicated processes. Leggett's management team quickly learned the art of successful acquisitions.

In February 1963, Harry told the board, " ... the assets of the Rodman Spring Company and the Harry Keeton Spring Company of Oklahoma City had been acquired ... on a five-year contract, at no interest."[54]

The minutes continued: "Bob Dittberner ... sales manager at Ennis ... transferred to Oklahoma City to serve as district manager there."

Leggett & Platt's acquisition of businesses—the fifth step to further company growth—was dependent on the other four steps. As mentioned, acquisitions often resulted from Leggett's long-term business relationships and extended the company into new geographical regions. They also broadened Leggett's product lineup and improved production and machinery capabilities.

Collectively, the five steps produced the forward momentum for growth. At the same time, Leggett's leaders were beginning to develop and describe a specific, dynamic strategy for growing the company.

The New Strategy

According to Harry Cornell, Jr.:

Our mission during those first years was to bring energy and renewed life to the company, to get the engine firing on all cylinders. We saw opportunities to grow and improve in every direction.

Window and store displays throughout the 1960s touted the durability of Leggett & Platt's innersprings and other products.

HARRY M. CORNELL, JR.

CEO, 1960 TO 1999

BORN IN 1928 IN THE DUTCH EAST INDIES TO MACK and Marjorie Cornell of Carthage, Missouri, Harry M. Cornell, Jr., led Leggett & Platt for nearly 40 years—from a small company to a widely admired, multibillion-dollar, international manufacturing corporation.

In the late 1920s, the Cornell family lived in Talang Akar, Sumatra, Indonesia, where Mack Cornell was working in the oilfields. As a result, when the family returned to the United States in the early 1930s, Harry principally spoke Malay, a native language of western Sumatra.

Harry vividly described the frustrating language barrier he encountered as a 3-year-old boy. "When Mother and Dad hired a baby-sitter, they had to leave a translation list on the kitchen counter, so when I would jabber away, the sitter could understand," he recalled. "It was kind of a struggle. I can still remember my cousins and friends, children my age—I would try and talk and play with them and ended up scaring them to death."[1]

Harry was a Leggett & Platt kid. His grandfather was J. P. Leggett, the company cofounder. His father was a sales manager and later president of the company. For many years, his mother was a member of the board of directors. Even as a grade school boy, he sometimes accompanied his father on customer visits during his summer vacations.

Harry spent two summers working in the Carthage plant during his high school years. His jobs at the plant included unloading rail cars and loading trucks, working at innerspring clipping tables, and operating manual and automatic innerspring assembly machines.

"It was a great experience and big advantage for me later. Most of the machines I learned to run were developed and manufactured by engineers at our in-plant machine shop. I also got to know Leggett's warehouse workers, assemblers, machinists, supervisors, engineers, and managers."[2]

Harry's official career with Leggett & Platt began in 1950 after he graduated with a degree in business administration and marketing from the University of Missouri. From his first position as a sales office assistant and trainee in Louisville, Kentucky, Harry moved into sales, covering the southern Illinois and Ohio territories and successfully established both large and small accounts.

We held regular company meetings with all our general managers, usually a day or two before the board of directors meetings. At management meetings and board meetings, we did a lot of thinking aloud. We talked about what was working, what wasn't, what kinds of products we should produce, and why.

It took a couple of years, but gradually, a coherent growth strategy began to emerge from all our work and all those discussions.[55]

By 1963, Leggett & Platt had developed two product divisions: components and home furnishings. The product offerings of each division were listed on the back page of the 1963 Annual Report. Harry Cornell, Jr., said:

We primarily sold products from the components division to manufacturers of bedding and upholstered furniture. We were regularly adding products to that list and increasing sales successfully.

The products of the home furnishings division were primarily sold to retail stores, and we wanted to maintain a presence and reputation with retailers. But, we also began to see that adding products to that division would be difficult without sometimes competing head-to-head with our customers.

In 1952, Harry left the company for a short time to become a commissioned sales representative in the company's Kansas territory. In the summer of 1953, he was selected to manage Leggett & Platt's struggling Ennis, Texas, plant. He quickly turned the operation around.[3]

In February 1955, Harry was named a company vice president. He was elected to the board of directors in February 1958.

Dissatisfied with Leggett & Platt's lack of growth, Harry formulated a plan to lead the company. He borrowed money and began acquiring stock. By late 1959, along with family members and close friends, he held a majority of the company's stock. In February of 1960, his father was elected chairman of the board, and Harry was elected president and CEO of the company.[4]

During his 39 years of leadership, Harry and his management team led the company from $7 million in annual sales to $3.5 billion, and from four factories to more than 200 worldwide. In May 1999, he smoothly passed the CEO's baton to Felix Wright.

As a leader, Harry was known for his sales acumen, his mentoring, and his team building skills—all traits he attributes to his father's influence. "I really learned the business from watching Dad call on customers and interact with people. He was a tremendous people person; whatever skills I developed, they just came naturally for Dad."[5]

But other longtime employees say those same traits also came naturally to Harry. "Harry has a knack of making people feel like they're on his level," said Howard Boothe, a retired engineer and facility manager. "He was leading this big corporation, but Harry's attitude was, 'I couldn't do it without you.' He made people feel like partners in the business, and consequently, we enjoyed coming to work because we had specific goals to reach. It was a fine company."[6]

Bill Allen, a retired risk manager, agreed. "You knew what Harry wanted you to do, and he gave you the freedom to do it the way you felt it needed to be done. He was one of those people who let you go as far as you could go. If you had a problem or question, he was totally accessible—just a super guy, super boss. He'd chew you out if you did something wrong, but he never did it in public. He always took you aside and told you what the situation was, and that was the end of it. There weren't any more repercussions or anything else. He was really good with people."[7]

We gradually realized that being a components supplier to the bedding and furniture industries was our greatest opportunity for profitable growth.

We continued to produce many home furnishings that didn't pose a threat to our manufacturing company customers. But being a components supplier became our focus and the foundation for our growth for many years to come. A few years later, we even began calling ourselves The Components People®.[56]

More than Words

As previously noted, Leggett & Platt purchased the equipment and inventory of a small spring man-

ufacturer and distributor in Oklahoma City in 1963. To better serve its growing territory, the company also added a new 60,000-square-foot building in Winchester, Kentucky, and new service centers in Denver, Colorado, and High Point, North Carolina.[57]

The following year, the company purchased property adjacent to the Carthage plant for a new machine and product development department. Construction also began on 3,500 square feet of administrative office space, and, by year's end, the company completed construction of 10,000 square feet of manufacturing space and a 30,000-square-foot warehouse. Leggett & Platt also added a data processing system to improve clerical functions.[58]

In "The President's Message" in the 1964 Annual Report, Harry told shareholders and employees:

Growth and expansion are among the words most often discussed around Leggett & Platt. These are meaningful words ... healthy ... strong. That they have been beneficial to the company is evidenced by the aggressiveness of our personnel ... the confidence of our customers ... the expanded plant facilities ... the once-again increasing profits.[59]

Leggett & Platt ended 1964 with a 14 percent increase in consolidated net sales and a 130 percent increase in earnings per share.[60]

In January 1965, the company purchased an innerspring manufacturing facility in DeKalb, Illinois, from the Englander Mattress Company. The DeKalb

---

The Leggett & Platt management team in 1963 included (from left to right) Harry M. Cornell, Sr., chairman; Felix Wright, general manager at Phoenix; Dick Fanning, general manager at Ennis; Harry M. Cornell, Jr., president; Frank Ford, general manager at Carthage; Bud Hougland, general manager of Kentucky operations; and Carl Kirchner, inventor and chief of engineering. Ralph Johnson, sales manager, is not pictured.

plant provided convenient access to many Chicago area customers.

The acquisition of the DeKalb plant was a significant achievement in the company's strategy to become a components supplier. Leggett & Platt would now produce and deliver innerspring units for Englander's mattresses. Englander would finish the mattress, cover it, and sell it. Over the years, many other mattress manufacturers were persuaded to outsource their components manufacturing to Leggett & Platt.

Don Frederick, the former Louisville plant manager, was temporarily assigned to manage the DeKalb facility. In March 1965, Bob Dittberner, the district manager at Oklahoma City, was appointed to manage the plant on a more long-term basis. Herman Meritt was promoted to manage the Oklahoma City plant after Dittberner's transfer.

A Time to Celebrate ... A Time to Mourn

The company's growth in the early 1960s provided abundant advancement opportunities. Felix Wright became the general manager at Phoenix, and was later promoted to vice president and transferred to Kentucky to establish an Eastern division for the company. Dick Fanning became the general manager at Ennis; Bob Dittberner was

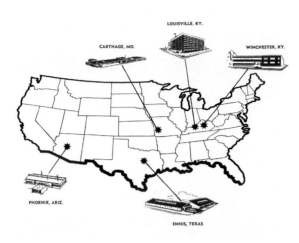

assigned as a district manager at Oklahoma City and later as a plant manager at DeKalb, Illinois. Ralph Johnson became the company's sales manager and later its vice president of sales.

Inevitably, some of the opportunities for promotion were bittersweet. These opportunities arose due to the illnesses and deaths of valued employees.

Due to Edward Casey, Jr.'s, illness in 1960 and 1961, Bud Hougland was promoted to oversee both Kentucky plants. Over time, the Winchester operations were greatly expanded, and the Louisville location was reduced to a warehouse and distribution center.[61]

Glenn Joyce's sudden and unexpected death on March 17, 1963, was an enormous loss. His career with Leggett & Platt had started in 1931 as a Carthage factory worker, and he was promoted several times. He had essentially served as the company's vice president of manufacturing for most of a decade. He was also a member of the board of directors from September 1952 until his death.[62]

Frank Ford was appointed to succeed Joyce on the board, and Ford was named to manage the Carthage plant. The managers of the Oklahoma City and Denver facilities also reported to him.[63]

In February 1963, the board noted and mourned the passing of George S. Beimdiek, Sr., the retired longtime president.[64]

Casey's continued ill-health prevented him from attending board meetings in 1963 and 1964. In December 1964, he expressed a desire to retire from the board. The board appointed James C. McCormick of the Dallas firm Eppler, Guerin & Turner, Inc., in Casey's place, and in 1965, McCormick was elected to the board.[65]

Above: These maps show the company's expansion in the years after Harry M. Cornell, Jr., became president and CEO.

Right: By 1963, Leggett & Platt had developed two product divisions—components and home furnishings. The product offerings of each division were listed on the back page of the 1963 Annual Report.

COMPONENTS DIVISION
Innerspring units
Boxspring units
Sleeper units
Sofa bed constructions
Coil base constructions
Sinuous wire
Sofa bed hinges
Rocker springs
Flotura base constructions
Zeffyr base constructions

ACTION-ARC

DROWSY-BOY

Flex-o-coil

LEGGETT & PLATT, INC.
The nation's leading designer and manufacturer of spring products

ACTION-EEZ

HOME FURNISHINGS DIVISION
Rollaway bed
Bed springs
Bunk beds
Bed frames
Headboards
Bedroom suites
Dining room suites
Dormitory beds
Institutional beds

LURESLEEP

Flex-o-top

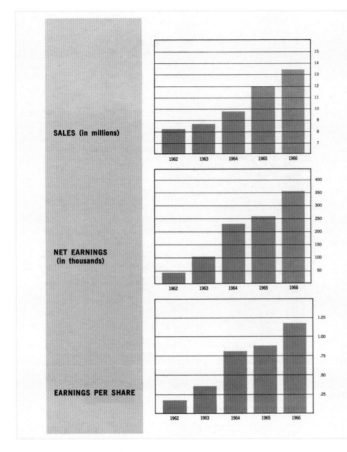

SALES (in millions)

NET EARNINGS
(in thousands)

EARNINGS PER SHARE

In 1967, after 32 years with the company, Edward Casey, Jr., retired from Leggett & Platt's management team. He had served as a vice president for more than 29 years and as a member of the board of directors for more than 14 years. Felix Wright's transfer to Kentucky was timed to coincide with Casey's retirement.[66]

A Remarkable Beginning

It took Leggett & Platt's management and newly energized board most of two years to create the momentum for sustained growth. The Letter to Shareholders in the 1966 Annual Report conveyed the company's remarkable progress from 1962 through 1966.[67]

By 1966, Leggett & Platt's leadership had demonstrated the ability to articulate and consistently execute substantive growth plans. The company's leadership decided the time was right to raise additional capital for growth and extend the opportunity for ownership to a broader public, including a growing number of interested and enthusiastic employees.

Three charts and the opening paragraphs from the letter to shareholders in the 1966 Annual Report stated the company's remarkable progress from 1962 to 1966.

In March 1967, seven years after Harry Cornell, Jr., had established majority ownership and become president, Leggett & Platt went public.[68]

After recapitalization and a stock split in January 1967, the company issued securities consisting of $1 million of 6 percent convertible debentures, due April 1, 1982, and 50,000 new shares of common stock. By the end of 1967, there were roughly 350,000 shares outstanding.[69]

The underwriting syndicate of 19 investment banking firms was managed by the brokerage firm Eppler, Guerin & Turner. Leggett & Platt Director Jim McCormick was a senior vice president of the brokerage firm and provided valuable guidance as the board considered a public offering.[70]

New Acquisitions, New People, More Growth

In 1967, the company expanded its warehouse service centers in Denver, Louisville, Charlotte, and New Orleans. The service centers complemented the company's manufacturing sites and were stocked with a full line of company products, enabling rapid delivery to area customers.

That same year, Jim Bryan was hired as vice president of finance and planning, and, as previously noted, Felix Wright became general manager of the Winchester operations, where he helped form and lead the company's Eastern division.

The following year, Leggett & Platt acquired the Motor City Spring Company of Detroit in March; the Flex-O-Loc Corporation of Lawrence, Massachusetts, in July; and the Kenyon Manufacturing Company of Kenyon, Minnesota, in October. In addition, by that time the expansions of the company's plants in Carthage, Ennis, Oklahoma City, Winchester, Detroit, and Kenyon had been completed or were in process. By the end of 1968, annual net sales were $17.3 million, up nearly $4 million from the two previous years. A little more than half of that increase came from the three acquisitions.[71]

Early in 1969, the company purchased the J. R. Greeno Company of Cincinnati, a manufacturer of "offset" type innersprings, a product not previously offered by Leggett & Platt. The acquisition also included the assets of a Greeno affiliate, Butler Manufacturing Company of Cincinnati, Ohio.[72]

In April 1969, Leggett & Platt acquired the Dalpak Corporation of Dallas, a producer of paper products, including a line of packaging materials used to protect furniture and mattresses in shipment. That year, Leggett hired Michael Glauber as corporate controller to help manage its increasingly complex financial affairs. The company also issued a 5-for-3 stock split.[73]

In only five years, from 1965 through 1969, Leggett & Platt doubled its sales, finishing 1969 with net sales at a new high of more than $25 million (up from $10.6 million in 1964). During those years, the company grew at an average annual compound rate of 18.9 percent in sales and 24.4 percent in earnings.[74]

The Decade Ends

In 1960, a young man named Harry Cornell, Jr., became president and CEO of Leggett & Platt, a small company his grandfather had cofounded in 1883. The closely held company, headquartered in the small town of Carthage, Missouri, had annual sales of roughly $7 million and four manufacturing facilities in three states.

Ten years later, in 1969, the recently turned public Leggett & Platt employed 1,600 people at 13 factories and two warehouse service centers in 12 states. Annual sales exceeded $25 million, and earnings topped $745,000. It was a great new beginning for a grand old firm.[75]

The company's leaders had developed a compelling strategy for growth and an ethical, cohesive team determined to succeed. As the decade ended, several new acquisitions and growth projects were in the works.

Leggett & Platt's most critical raw material was drawn-steel wire. Too often the quality, availability, and price of wire were inconsistent, a serious

This advertisement features the diversity of Leggett & Platt's product lineup in the mid-1960s.

WIRED FOR THE FUTURE

RAWN-STEEL WIRE WAS LEGGETT & PLATT'S most essential raw material. The quality, availability, and price of wire were too often inconsistent—a serious concern. In 1968, Leggett & Platt's leaders decided the best way to eliminate these recurring problems was to operate its own wire-drawing mill.[1]

Leggett & Platt approached four steel companies as potential partners in wire supply—Armco, Laclede, Bethlehem, and U.S. Steel. "They all listened," said Harry Cornell, Jr., "but only Armco and Laclede expressed any real interest."[2]

Laclede was in the middle of reorganizing its management, and Armco seemed a better cultural match for Leggett. After several meetings between senior members of Leggett & Platt and Armco, the CEOs finalized a deal with a handshake in a Kansas cornfield during a hunting trip. "Then, having agreed, we still had to make it happen," said Harry.[3]

The terms of the deal ultimately included building a new plant in Carthage, with each company owning half. An independent board of directors, composed of members from each company, would guide the operation. Armco would supply the steel rod; Leggett & Platt's workforce would draw the wire.

The newly constructed plant began partial production in June 1970. The mill's annual output was entirely consumed by Leggett & Platt in 1971 and 1972. As the mill increased its production, however, surplus wire was sold to outside manufacturers. Having the capability to supply wire to other companies would prove a major competitive advantage for Leggett & Platt. Harry explained the strategy:

The best way to make sure that you're internally competitive when you're vertically integrated is to sell that product to the outside world. So we built into our contract with Armco ... that any excess wire we produced in the Carthage plant, we'd be able to sell to external customers.

The original concept—to be externally competitive in the wire market—always assured us of being internally competitive. It also gave us the opportunity to grow our wire business at a significantly faster clip, particularly during times when Leggett's wire needs were not increasing rapidly.

The mill became successful both internally and externally, and we soon outstripped its capacity. Our spring plants performed much better with the consistent, good-quality wire, and we became a preferred wire supplier for other manufacturers as well.[4]

Fortunately, Armco and Leggett & Platt included a buyout option in their contract; years later, Leggett exercised this option.

The new wire mill in Carthage, which began partial production in 1970, allowed Leggett & Platt to become internally and externally competitive in the wire market.

concern. In 1968, Leggett & Platt and Armco Steel Corporation agreed to build a wire-drawing mill in Carthage, with each company owning half interest in the facility. Armco would supply steel rod from its Kansas City steel and rod mill. Leggett & Platt would supply and manage the people and draw the wire. Even with only half interest, the project was by far Leggett & Platt's largest commitment to fixed assets thus far.[76]

While the wire mill's initial productive capacity would be consumed by Leggett & Platt, the agreement with Armco anticipated excess wire production would be sold to other wire users as well. Leggett & Platt's management was determined to sell to external customers.

The wire supply strategy had two objectives: to provide Leggett & Platt a high-quality, dependable supply of its most critical raw material (an advantage no competitor had), and to create an entirely new growth opportunity for the company through external sales. Management believed that achieving the second objective would ensure that the internally consumed wire was truly price-competitive.

In June 1970, employees were beginning to ramp up production systematically in the newly constructed plant, which had recently installed machinery.

Great growth is often accompanied by great challenges. Leggett & Platt's competitors quickly expressed discomfort over the company's developments, including its acquisitions and wire strategy, and Leggett & Platt became a subject of interest to the Antitrust Division of the U.S. Department of Justice.

Leggett & Platt responded immediately to the Justice Department's inquiries, and CEO Harry M. Cornell, Jr., assured employees and shareholders that Leggett & Platt's dealings were above reproach: "Management is confident that upon completion of the inquiry the Division will conclude that there has been no violation."[77]

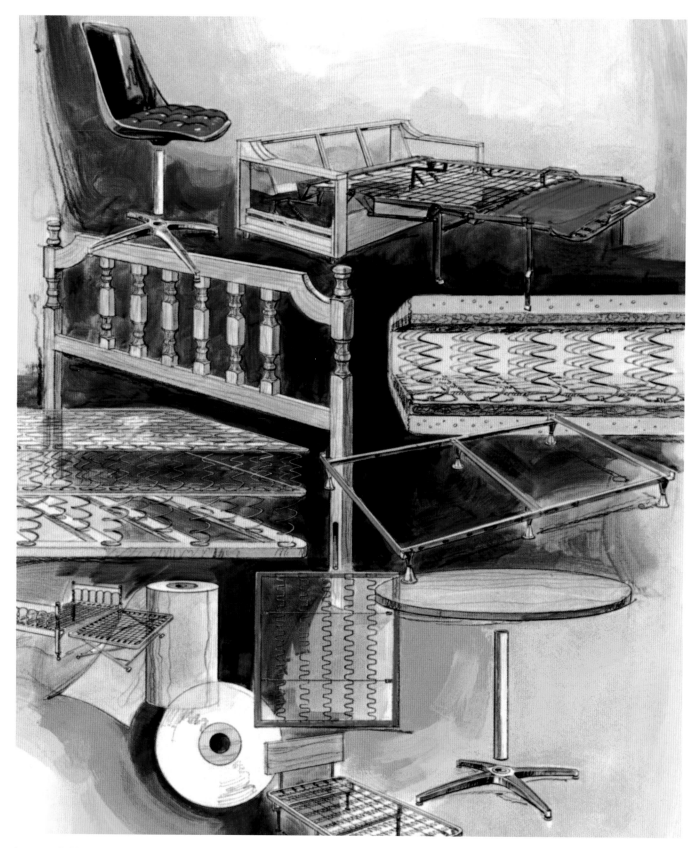

Leggett & Platt's 1972 Annual Report depicted a myriad of products manufactured in the 1970s, including innersprings, box springs, trundle bed frames, sofa sleeper mechanisms, table and chair bases, and many others.

CHAPTER FIVE

A DECADE OF GROWTH, RECESSION, AND LAWSUITS

1970–1979

In those years, Harry and the management team redefined Leggett & Platt and created a better-diversified, growth-oriented company for our employee–partners, management, and shareholders.

—John Hale, senior vice president
of human resources[1]

LEGGETT & PLATT'S 1970 ANNUAL REPORT featured a section titled "A Look at the Future," which reviewed company strategy, the expected growth of the U.S. home furnishings industry, and the predicted demographics that were likely to create unprecedented demand for home furnishings. It also explained the company's evolving role as "a broad line supplier of components to home furnishings manufacturers":

> *This concept ... relieves us of dependence upon the design and marketing of a brand or a few brands of merchandise. Our success is not unduly affected by the success in the retail market of a particular brand name. Instead, as a manufacturer's supplier, we are able to cover a broad front as experts in quality components, many of which are developed and improved by us. Because we are specialists, we usually can produce and sell a quality component more economically than our manufacturer–customers. ...*[2]

Estimating that the home furnishings industry would spend in excess of $800 million on components in 1970, Leggett & Platt conservatively projected that this expenditure could reach $1.2 billion by the end of the decade. With the baby boomers in their early twenties by 1970, it was expected that marriage rates, family formations, and the demand

for home furnishings would boom for several consecutive years.[3]

Leggett & Platt's sales for 1970 were up 17.6 percent over 1969. More than two-thirds of this increase was a result of internal growth. Earnings were also up 28.4 percent.[4]

New Acquisitions

Leggett & Platt's first acquisition of the decade, Signal Manufacturing Company of Los Angeles, in May 1970, provided a West Coast base of operations and a new line of products—sofa sleeper fixtures.[5]

Four acquisitions were completed in 1972. In August, Leggett enhanced its packaging division with the purchase of Kraft Converters, Inc., of High Point, North Carolina. The paper conversion company specialized in the production of packaging for furniture and case goods.[6]

In October, Leggett purchased Metal Bed Rail Company, Inc., of Linwood, North Carolina. In addition to bed rails, its products included bed frames and steel angle components.[7]

In the same month, Leggett acquired Masterack, a division of Southern Cross Industries, Inc., of

---

A member of the Leggett & Platt team hangs an innerspring unit on an overhead conveyer.

Atlanta, Georgia. With this acquisition, Southern Cross became dependent upon Leggett & Platt for various steel and wire components it had previously produced. Masterack also provided Leggett with a new line of products—wire display racks for retail stores.[8]

Roger D. Gladden, vice president of administration and control in the late 1970s, coordinated Leggett & Platt's first inventory at Masterack and helped set up the newly acquired company on Leggett & Platt's

Above: This aerial view shows the company's spring plant and administrative offices in Carthage in 1971.

Right: Roger D. Gladden joined Leggett & Platt in 1972 as an accountant and was repeatedly promoted over the years. He was named vice president of administration and control in 1979 and eventually served as president of the commercial fixture and display group until his retirement in 2002.

accounting systems. When Leggett formed a new fixture and display group several years later, Gladden was initially tapped to lead those operations, which included Masterack.

In December 1972, Leggett & Platt purchased EST Company, Inc., of Grafton, Wisconsin. EST produced cast aluminum, steel, and plastic furniture components used primarily in pedestal-supported chairs and tables. It also cast aluminum components for other manufacturing customers. (Edwin C. Sandham, one of EST's founders, joined Leggett & Platt's board of directors in August 1973.)[9]

Leggett & Platt acquired both Masterack and EST primarily for their furniture and bedding components. While these products proved successful, the sales of both companies' diversified products far surpassed the sales of their furniture and bedding components.

The success of the Masterack wire rack products also led to Leggett's decision to manufacture an extensive line of point-of-purchase retail displays as well as a line of shelving for commercial vehicles. The EST acquisition provided the opportunity for Leggett's initial entry into the aluminum die-casting industry. The company's non-furniture components included lawnmower decks, boat motor propellers, and outdoor light fixtures. Leggett eventually broadened this lineup to include components for barbecue grills, motorcycles, small engines, and diesel truck engines.

New Facilities and Operations

In addition to growing through acquisitions, Leggett & Platt continued to expand by establishing new operations. In 1970, the company constructed a 60,000-square-foot factory in Social Circle, Georgia, to better serve an increasing number of bedding components customers in the Southeastern United States. Warehousing in the facility began late that year, and manufacturing started on March 1, 1971.[10]

Also in 1970, Leggett added a box spring frame operation at Ennis, Texas, and a box spring and frame assembly plant in Houston, both of which received lumber supplies from the company's newly completed sawmill in Naples, Texas. The company's 1970 Annual Report explained the logic behind the expansion of its framing operations:

A growing number of bedding manufacturers prefer to purchase box springs mounted on wood frames rather than perform the mounting operation within their own plants. To meet this demand, Leggett & Platt continues to expand its wood frame manufacturing; and in order to better serve customers, it further disperses the assembly and mounting facilities.[11]

Leggett & Platt's board of directors and officers in 1971 included (left to right, at the table) Ralph V. Johnson; Richard T. Fisher; Don V. Long; Mrs. H. M. (Marjorie) Cornell, Sr.; Harry M. Cornell, Sr.; Harry M. Cornell, Jr.; James F. Bryan; Felix E. Wright; Michael A. Glauber; R. Ted Enloe III; George S. Beimdiek, Jr.; Herbert S. Casteel; James C. McCormick; and Frank E. Ford. In the back corner (from left to right) are Richard (Dick) P. Fanning; W. E. (Bill) Allen; and Guy W. Ewing III. Larry Higgins is not pictured.

ACQUISITION STRATEGY

ACQUISITIONS HAVE BEEN AN IMPORTANT ASPECT of Leggett & Platt's growth. In the early 1960s, when the company began to acquire other businesses more aggressively, Harry Cornell, Jr., the company's new president, encouraged the management team to view the bedding and furniture industries as a single, large market. Leggett determined it would become a broad line supplier of components to those industries.

In the 1960s and 1970s, manufacturers of bedding and furniture typically bought components from small local and regional businesses, which made excellent acquisition candidates for Leggett.

Initially, Leggett & Platt focused on acquiring spring businesses, knowing it could produce spring products more cost effectively than either competitors or vertically integrated mattress manufacturers. Later, the company acquired manufacturers of springs for furniture, and then producers of furniture hardware components—recliner, chair control, and sofa sleeper mechanisms. Eventually, as the company redefined and broadened its growth strategy, businesses producing aluminum castings and store fixtures and displays, among others, were also acquired.[1]

Felix Wright, who was promoted to executive vice president and chief operating officer in 1979, remained actively involved in many of the company's acquisitions. He recalled:

Looking back, it's easy now to see why our acquisition program worked so well. The owners of those small manufacturing companies were often glad to sell to us. These folks had worked hard to build their companies, and selling to us gave them a chance to get paid for all that work. In many cases, the purchase price would pay off all their debts, and they would end up with a nice

In the following years, Leggett & Platt opened several more framing operations near customers' manufacturing plants, supplying them with assembled box springs that simply needed to be covered and finished. This production technique, later widely known and practiced by companies such as Toyota, is called "just-in-time" manufacturing.

In June 1970, the Carthage wire mill also became operational. Although production that year totaled less than 10 percent of the annual capacity, the mill operated at a profitable rate by year's end.[12] By November 1971, it supplied 60 percent of Leggett & Platt's wire; by December 1972, it produced 90 percent of the company's wire supply.[13]

New Products and New Machines

In the early 1970s, Leggett & Platt obtained licenses and designed machinery that enabled the company to manufacture and sell the latest and most innovative components. For example, the company worked to develop machinery to produce Mira-Coil®, a recently patented continuous coil innerspring unit. (It would be several years, however, before the machinery and manufacturing processes for this product were perfected.)

In 1971, Leggett & Platt obtained a license from Boston-based Standard Box to manufacture and sell a newly designed box spring unit eventually named Lectro-LOK®.[14] That same year, Leggett received a license from Spühl AG in Switzerland to produce a new type of molded mattress core, consisting of an innerspring unit encased in cold-cure urethane foam—the precursor of the foam-encased innerspring initially sold to and marketed by Lifetime Foam, a Sears subsidiary.[15]

Besides obtaining production licenses from other companies, Leggett & Platt also worked on developing and patenting its own products. For example, the company's Dalpak subsidiary had a patent pending for an improved type of mattress package.

nest egg of Leggett stock, or they would have stock and cash.

Before we came along, those small business people were trying to finance their own growth and were struggling to keep up with tax law changes and with workplace safety and environmental laws. They were trying to provide employee benefits and a host of other things. We could help them manage all those complicated tasks, and in return, they helped us expand our product offerings and our customer base.

We could take a good product or a manufacturing technique used by that small business, and very quickly, we could sell that product or use that technique on a national basis.

Many of those owners stayed with us, and many were great employee–partners. It was just a good deal for all involved! [2]

When evaluating a potential acquisition, Leggett & Platt considered more than the financial aspects of the deal, according to Robert Jefferies, longtime general counsel for the company. "One of the things they taught me when I came down here was that we initially did not focus on the financial statements. … We asked ourselves, 'How will this business integrate with us? How will it fit?' And we used 'fit' in the broad sense of the term … fit in technology, fit in products, fit in people, fit with our other business units." [3]

Felix Wright agreed with Jefferies' comments. He said:

Fit was certainly important. Over the years, at trade shows and the like, we got to know lots of the business owners and key people in companies we eventually acquired. Those deals often got done because of our relationships. Those ethical, hardworking, customer-oriented, business owners—those were the people we really wanted to bring into Leggett.

Don't get me wrong. We'd buy a business for an innovative product or to get in the door with a good customer, but if the people weren't a good fit, we'd maybe only buy a patent or the physical assets of the business. It's just not a good idea to bring in people you can't trust. They won't be with you long-term, and you can't build a business that way. [4]

Challenges Early in the Decade

In 1971, the U.S. Department of Justice filed an antitrust suit against Leggett & Platt concerning the 1960s acquisitions of Motor City Spring Company and certain assets of the J. R. Greeno Company. With the U.S. Department of Justice seeking the divestiture of these acquisitions, Leggett vigorously contested the suit. President Harry Cornell, Jr., assured shareholders that the company had not violated any laws, but it would be several years before the courts reached a decision. [16]

In 1972, the sawmill in Naples, Texas, struggled with continuing inventory losses, despite

The success of the Masterack division, acquired in 1972, led to its relocation in Atlanta, Georgia, only two years later. The acquisition brought Leggett & Platt the capability to produce a wide variety of point-of-purchase display racks and shelving.

company efforts to improve efficiency to help the mill reach a break-even point by the first quarter of 1973.[17] Also in 1972, Leggett faced a 31-day strike at the Winchester, Kentucky, plant, which affected earnings by 5 cents per share.[18]

Notwithstanding these challenges, the company celebrated a significant milestone in 1971, when net earnings reached more than $1 million. In 1972, earnings rose another 30.6 percent (even without including acquisition income). For 11 consecutive years, Leggett & Platt had increased earnings.[19]

Although the company grew significantly in the early 1970s, it remained a close-knit organization. Donald G. LaFerla, who was hired in January 1973 as Leggett's first data processing manager, witnessed the number of employees climb to 3,700 by the end of his first year—nearly a 50-percent increase from 1,900 employees in 1971.[20] LaFerla recalled how the growing company maintained a cohesive atmosphere:

Left: Donald G. LaFerla was the first head of data processing and an officer of Leggett & Platt for almost 30 years. He coordinated the construction of two major additions to the corporate office complex in Carthage.

Below left: This chart shows the company's products and markets in the early 1970s.

Below right: Spring wire, drawn at the new wire mill in Carthage, sits on a take-up carrier.

One of the things that I remember when I went to work at Mound Street ... about 10 o'clock, over the paging system, you'd hear this voice say, "Coffee is ready." ... Everybody in the whole office used to get up. ... We didn't even have a cafeteria. We had a little area and a couple of Coke machines where we sold nickel Cokes in the little original Coke bottles, and everybody would go down there and sit around ... for 10 or 15 minutes and then go back to our offices.

Three o'clock in the afternoon, same thing. ... It was something that brought all of the people together, so even if you were a new employee who knew virtually no one in the company, within a

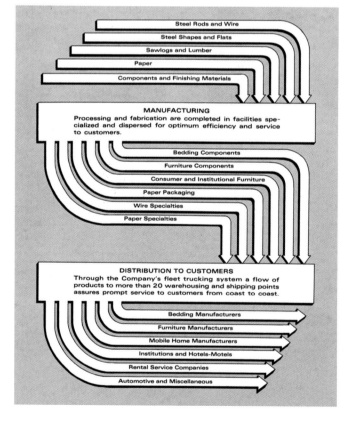

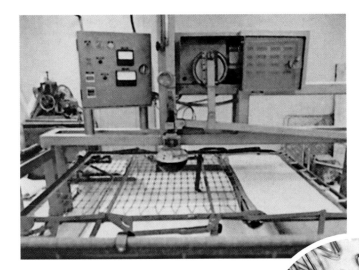

Above left: Using a Cornell Tester developed by Cornell University, Leggett & Platt tested its sofa sleeper mechanism by maintaining pounding pressure on the unit all day long.

Above right: This grid top welder machine was used in the manufacturing of a new box spring design.

Center: A close-up of one of the company's mattress innerspring units.

matter of a week or so, you were certainly going to get exposed to all those people.[21]

Don LaFerla's responsibilities grew along with the company, and he eventually served as vice president of information technology and as a company officer until his retirement in 2001.

Growth and Obstacles

In the first half of 1973, Leggett & Platt acquired two more complementary businesses. In February, it purchased Paramount Paper Products Company of Alma, North Carolina. As a manufacturer of cellulose wadding, padding, and other products for the furniture industry, Paramount was added to Leggett's packaging division.[22]

In April, the company acquired Middletown Manufacturing, Inc., of Simpsonville, Kentucky. Middletown produced mechanical assemblies for

recliners and swivel rockers as well as other metal furniture components. This acquisition gave Leggett an innovative mechanism, later named the "Wall Hugger®," which allowed a recliner to be placed one inch from a wall.[23]

Although the company continued to benefit from acquisitions in 1973, higher interest rates, increased material and operating expenses, and heavy start-up costs stifled earnings. Harry Cornell, Jr., identified three of the difficult start-ups in the 1973 Annual Report: "Compared with the preceding year, 1973 was significantly penalized by losses in start-up situations—principally at Hominy, Oklahoma; Mason, Ohio; and a new sleeper fixture plant at Ennis, Texas," he said.[24]

Expansion costs for manufacturing and warehouse properties totaled $7.3 million and included 60,000 square feet at Linwood, North Carolina; 17,000 square feet at Grafton, Wisconsin; and 32,000 square feet at Phoenix. Fire damage at a nearly complete 50,000-square-foot addition to the Dalpak plant in Dallas delayed occupancy into the next year.[25]

Despite these costs, the slowing economy, and other operational challenges, production was under way on two of the new products licensed in 1971: Spühl AG's molded mattress core and Standard Box's Lectro-LOK® box spring unit.

Machinery design for Lectro-LOK® proved difficult. After experimenting with a few prototypes, Leggett & Platt hired the Frank L. Wells Company to build an efficient machine that allowed Leggett to supply proprietary versions of Lectro-LOK® to select customers.[26]

The production of this unit was vital to the proliferation of the company's box spring frame assembly facilities throughout the country. "The initial Lectro-LOK® box spring ... was the first version of Leggett transferring from the old coil ... into a more automated box spring, which finally got us over to our products that we're currently in today," explained Felix Wright, then vice president of Leggett & Platt and Eastern division manager of the products group. "So that was kind of a middle step."[27]

Thomas J. Wells, Sr., of the Frank L. Wells Company, joined Leggett & Platt as director of manufacturing services in 1974. He said Lectro-LOK® represented a new mindset for the industry as a whole:

It was a huge, huge paradigm shift for [box spring] foundations and allowed Leggett to get a greater market share of the industry ... and it allowed Leggett's customers who were using that innovation to get a higher margin on their finished foundations at retail.

It was a unitized top, just all one piece. Heretofore, those tops had all been hand-laced together with multiple shapes of wire and springs and a lot of labor and a lot of noise and not much firmness and a lot of material content. It was almost like day and night—the two foundations—although they did the same thing. They performed so differently that it led almost everybody in the industry to use it. Competitors were forced to try to design products that went around our patents but provided some of the same advantages.[28]

Left: From his start date in 1974 to his retirement in 2003, Thomas J. Wells, Sr., and the teams he led continually improved Leggett & Platt's machinery, manufacturing processes, and products. He had 72 innovations patented in his name or with his name as a co-inventor or member of the patent applicant group.

Below left: Lectro-LOK® box springs, with their grid top design, became popular worldwide. This photo shows how two extra-long, twin-size box springs appeared when manufactured for a king mattress.

Recession

By 1974, the nation was experiencing an economic recession. For the first time in 12 years, Leggett & Platt did not increase its annual earnings, which dropped 11.9 percent, from $3.7 million in 1973 to $3.3 million in 1974.[29]

Part of this decline resulted from a change in the company's method for valuing its steel rod and wire inventories. On January 1, 1974, Leggett changed from a FIFO (first in, first out) method of accounting, to a LIFO (last in, first out) method.[30]

Earnings were further reduced by a scarcity of raw materials until late in the year, at which point the industry experienced a drastic drop in retail demand. As a result, dealers and manufacturers were caught with excessive inventories and ordered fewer products from Leggett, reducing its sales and earnings.

Lack of sustained profitability led Leggett & Platt to close its sawmill in Naples, Texas. The company suspended operations in April and placed the property for sale in August. In July, the company acquired an internal source of plastic products, Foothills Manufacturing, Inc., of Forest City, North Carolina. This business produced injection-molded plastic components for furniture manufacturers.[31]

Concerning manufacturing and facility expansions, Leggett increased its production of Lectro-LOK® and enlarged its aluminum die-casting operations at EST in Grafton, Wisconsin. In Springfield, Missouri, the company completed an 80,000-square-foot expansion. In Atlanta, Georgia, it acquired land and a 426,000-square-foot building to relocate Masterack across town.[32]

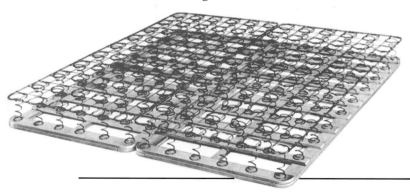

In Carthage, a new technical center, designed to serve both customers and personnel, was nearly completed. It would be staffed by specialists engaged in product testing and in research and development of new products and equipment.

That year, the U.S. Department of Justice filed another civil suit against Leggett & Platt, alleging antitrust violations in the 1972 acquisition of the Metal Bed Rail Company. Like the previous antitrust suit, the government sought divestiture of this acquisition. As for the suit filed in 1971, the U.S. District Court in Cincinnati dismissed the case in August 1974. Unfortunately, the government appealed the decision, causing the case to carry over into another year.[33]

Strengthening Its Position

While the recession lessened Leggett & Platt's profitability well into the second quarter of 1975, net sales rose 4.2 percent to more than $98 million by the end of the year. Earnings, however, dropped 1.5 percent to $3.2 million.[34]

In the nation's bicentennial year of 1976, the company also celebrated historic achievements. Harry Cornell announced:

The year 1976 was fittingly one of considerable accomplishment. ... It marked the end of a decade, our first as a publicly owned company. ... Sales in 1976 increased 19.7 percent to $117.7 mil-

Leggett & Platt often explored potential acquisitions through contacts at its trade shows. The above display is from a trade show in the 1970s.

lion, exceeding the $100 million level for the first time. Net earnings were a record $2.01 per share, up 59.5 percent from the earlier recessionary level of $1.26 per share.[35]

That year, Leggett added a sleeper fixture operation at Middletown Manufacturing and also established eight box spring assembly operations to better serve customers in the Western and Southeastern United States.

Late in 1976, the company acquired 92.3 percent ownership of Phillips Foscue Corporation, a manufacturer of polyurethane foam purchased mainly by the upholstered furniture industry. This acquisition strengthened the company's position as a leading components supplier to the household furniture industry, which was estimated to grow 11 percent in the next year.[36]

In 1977, disruptive winter weather and an eight-day strike at the Simpsonville, Kentucky, plant impeded earnings early in the year. Earnings were also affected by a restructuring of marketing methods in the Atlanta operations, which eliminated manufacturers' representatives, and by the closure of an unprofitable operation in the packaging division.

Sales improved, however, by the end of the first quarter and continued to increase throughout the year.[37]

In 1977, Leggett & Platt expanded beyond the U.S. border by purchasing 50 percent equity in Globe Spring and Cushion Company, Ltd., of Toronto, Ontario. Globe produced springs for mattress and upholstered furniture manufacturers in Canada and gave Leggett a manufacturing source and distribution center there.[38]

In an effort to expand its wire-drawing capabilities, in January 1977, the company acquired a 97 percent ownership in Adcom Metals Company, which had plants in Jacksonville, Florida, and Nicholasville, Kentucky. For the fiscal year that ended in October 1977, Adcom had net operating earnings of $1 million on net sales of $17 million.[39]

With capital expenditures in 1977 totaling $5.7 million, which included five new satellite operations and two major plant additions, Leggett & Platt had enough assets in place to support an annual sales volume of more than $200 million.[40]

Also in 1977, Leggett & Platt began construction on a new 35,690-square-foot corporate headquarters. Set in the countryside four miles west of Carthage, the building's rustic exterior of cedar and locally quarried stone was designed to appear at home amidst the natural surroundings. Anticipating expansions to this facility, management purchased a substantial quantity of additional stone to be used in future additions.[41]

In 1977, Leggett & Platt began construction on a new 35,690-square-foot corporate headquarters built of native stone in a meadow about four miles west of the town of Carthage. Additional quantities of stone were quarried and held for later expansions.

At this time, Leggett was investing more than $1 million annually into research and development, focusing largely on designing new products and improving existing ones through customer feedback. Those products improved through customer input included the Lectro-LOK® box spring and the Wall Hugger® recliner hardware.[42]

Dennis S. Park, senior vice president and head of commercial fixturing and components, joined Leggett & Platt in 1977. Concerning research and development, he said:

> We're constantly challenging ourselves from a development standpoint to make sure that we are bringing that next innovation, that next development opportunity to our customers. Sometimes that will come within an acquisition. Sometimes it will come internally. But we're prepared to take both of those cases as long as we know we're taking to the customer what we think is the highest value component for their business mix.[43]

By the end of 1977, only a year after reaching the $100 million sales mark, the company had increased net sales 33.3 percent to $159.9 million and raised net earnings 22.7 percent to $6.5 million.[44]

Resolution

On January 25, 1978, Leggett & Platt and the U.S. Department of Justice agreed to settle the two pending antitrust lawsuits. In June, when the final settlement was made, the court found no fault on the part of Leggett & Platt, but required the company to sell its J. R. Greeno Company spring assets in Cincinnati and its metal fabrication plant in Hominy, Oklahoma. At the time of the settlement, these facilities provided less than 3 percent of the company's consolidated sales.[45]

Many who were involved in the lawsuits recalled that they came about essentially because Leggett & Platt was a minor player attempting to make major acquisitions at a time when regulators scrutinized almost every acquisition. Harry Cornell, Jr., commented on the lengthy litigation process:

It would have been much easier to ... acquiesce. But you say that the first time, and it's a lot easier to say it the second and third. ... This was when we started getting things going and didn't want to slow it down.

We had three lawsuits going on ... Motor City Spring ... Greeno ... and ... Metal Bed Rail. The Motor City acquisition was finally settled after a lengthy investigation by the Justice Department out of their Chicago office. This process of several years took a heavy toll on me personally. Up until the time that Bob Jefferies joined the company as general counsel in 1977, I was totally involved in dealing directly with our outside counsel in both Dallas and Cincinnati and attended every deposition. I sure got a lesson in antitrust law and trying to deal with the Justice Department.

Ultimately, we came up with the theory of substitution of assets [the exchange of like production and some machinery]. ... We negotiated a deal that was to our liking; we did not have to divest the assets we most wanted to keep. And those were really key operations; we got great customers in good markets geographically dispersed. We were very fortunate that our corporate counsel, Locke–Purnell, gave us good guidance and eventually referred us to additional counsel in Cincinnati. Our outside counsel stimulated us and could think with us.[46]

The resolution ultimately came about in 1978, in part because of wise counsel from Robert A. Jefferies,

Top left: Liquid urethane, poured for the foaming process, was set to a predetermined density and used in the manufacturing of furniture components.

Top right: Drawn wire began as raw bundles of steel rod, which were cleaned in acid and hot water vats and moved through the process with the aid of a gantry crane operator.

Bottom left: Wire inventory at the Carthage wire mill awaits shipment to company plants nationwide. The mill provided Leggett & Platt with an internal source for materials and enhanced its ability to branch into other complementary industries.

Bottom right: Finished wire, in specified sizes, fed onto carriers that were later transferred to wire working areas.

who was hired as general counsel in 1977 and faced the unenviable task of providing Harry, his new boss, with a surprising perspective:

[Harry] was quite frustrated by the lack of progress, and one of my first unfortunate duties was to tell him that one of the biggest reasons for our lack of progress was our CEO. ...

Harry likes to win everything 100 percent, and part of the discussion was that we would not win this 100 percent. This would never end. It would go on and on and on. Harry was the sort of person who couldn't let go. He took a very active role, and part of the reason that he wanted me to come was to find a way to constructively interject myself so that he wasn't constantly dealing with the "Gordian Knot." ... But a big turning point was the realization,

I think, on his part, that we couldn't keep everything that we had bought, that we were going to have to part with some assets, and it was just a question of what was least valuable to us.[47]

The lawsuit settlements, however, imposed two stipulations on the company. For 10 years, Leggett & Platt could not acquire any bedding spring manufacturers, and for five years, it was not allowed to purchase any manufacturers of metal bed frames or specified related products east of the Rockies without obtaining prior consent. These stipulations did not preclude Leggett from acquiring spring plants from vertically integrated mattress manufacturers or innerspring manufacturers that were liquidating, in bankruptcy, or near bankruptcy with no other likely buyers.[48]

MARKETING WITH WIT AND WISDOM

IN 1954, RALPH V. JOHNSON, A MISSOURI TERRItory salesman, was promoted to work for Harry M. Cornell, Sr., as Leggett & Platt's assistant sales manager. Johnson subsequently served as sales manager and, later, vice president of marketing and sales. From the mid-1950s until 1985, he led Leggett's marketing and sales efforts, with a special emphasis on bedding products.[1]

Ralph V. Johnson, pictured above in 1980, was an extraordinary leader in Leggett & Platt's marketing efforts. Coworkers Jay Sanders (immediate left) and Eloise Nash (far left) supported him for many years, helping create a fun, hardworking marketing group.

Fortunately, the company was already well along the path to diversification—a path Harry Cornell, Jr., and the management team had created nearly two decades earlier.

Around the time of the lawsuits' resolution, the company restructured its operations management to match its product lineup, creating a diversified products group, a fabricated steel and wood products group, and two bedding and furniture component groups, divided geographically (East and West). A corporate vice president who reported directly to Felix E. Wright, executive vice president and chief operating officer, led each group.

In the 1978 Annual Report, Wright told shareholders the company's focus on research and development was strengthening its position as a leading supplier of home furnishings components. Successful examples of R&D output included the Snap-LOK™ technology, which joined the Lectro-LOK® box spring lineup, and various types of "action" or "motion" hardware for furniture components, including the three-way Imperial Wall Hugger® mechanism for rockers and the Flotura™ assembly for convertible sofas.[49] Wright also announced:

> *Recently received machinery will enable Leggett to produce the Continuous Coil with enhanced efficiency and commercial feasibility. This revolutionary bedding component has lacked until now the machinery breakthrough justifying a capital investment for mass production.*[50]

As product demand rose, Leggett & Platt increased its wire capabilities by forming a wholly

Coworkers Eloise Nash and Jay Sanders (among others) supported Ralph Johnson for many years. Nash coordinated customer service nationwide for bedding products; as vice president of national internal sales and bedding components, she was one of Leggett's first female officers. A friendly, lively woman, Nash was also known to have a hearty laugh that could be heard many offices away. Sanders, also an interesting story and joke teller, became vice president/director of marketing and sales–bedding components upon Johnson's retirement in 1985. They were hardworking, fun, and successful.[2]

Robert A. Jefferies, Jr., then vice president, general counsel, and secretary of the company, wrote Ralph V. Johnson's Rules of Marketing in 1980. A framed version of the rules was presented to Johnson at a meeting of the company's divisional marketing and sales people in April that year.

The rules were intended to be humorous, but were also full of homespun truths, neatly capturing Johnson's wit and wisdom. The reading of the rules brought laughter and knowing nods from the sales staff, with the event typical of the high-spirited fun this group of Leggett partners enjoyed.[3]

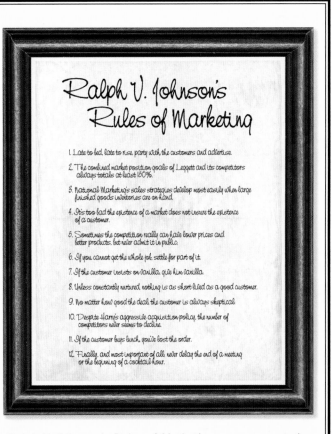

Ralph V. Johnson's Rules of Marketing were presented to divisional marketing executives of Leggett & Platt on April 24, 1980, at the National Technical Center in Carthage, Missouri.

owned subsidiary, Leggett Wire Company, through which it acquired all the outstanding capital stock of Adcom Metals Company, Inc. This acquisition then became half of a partnership with a wholly owned subsidiary of Armco, Inc., forming a new company known as Adcom Wire. Armco agreed to supply steel rod under a long-term contract.[51]

After adjustments for a 3-for-2 stock split in September 1978, Leggett & Platt finished the year with dividend payments 20.5 percent higher than the previous year.[52]

Joining the Big Board

In 1979, the company acquired several operations, including a spring plant in High Point, North Carolina, as well as two facilities in Los Angeles—a fabricated steel plant and certain assets of the De Lamar Bed Spring Corporation.[53] Art Glassman, who later became president of Leggett's Western division, came to the company in the De Lamar acquisition.[54]

The company also purchased a large number of outstanding shares of the Missouri Rolling Mill Corporation (MRM). (Leggett later acquired the remaining outstanding shares as well.) Located in St. Louis, MRM fabricated steel angle products for Leggett and other companies in the Midwest.[55]

Leggett & Platt experienced two unsuccessful acquisitions in 1979. In April, the company pur-

chased 50-percent interest in Futron Plastics of North Carolina. By the fourth quarter, it was apparent that Futron's earnings for the first three quarters were significantly overstated. In November, the investment in and loans to Futron were completely written off.[56]

Leggett also purchased 50-percent ownership in Tiffany Textile Corporation, a small, West Coast distributor of bedding ticking, which was expected to broaden Leggett's product line into mattress and furniture ticking and fabrics and to extend Tiffany's markets through Leggett's national distribution. Unfortunately, the venture did not perform well and was soon liquidated.[57]

In addition, five years after its closing in 1974, the assets of the Naples, Texas, sawmill were sold for a nominal gain in 1979.[58]

The completion of new corporate offices in 1978 allowed Leggett & Platt to relieve the pent-up demand for additional staff in 1979. Six employees from the "Class of 1979" earned senior-level responsibilities. Pictured (from left to right) are John Hale, senior vice president of human resources; Rich Calhoon, vice president of investor relations (retired in April 2002); Ernest Jett, senior vice president and general counsel; Susan Higdon Downes, treasurer (retired in December 1997); Jeff Dymott, staff vice president of operations; and Matt Emmert, assistant corporate controller.

Photographed at the New York Stock Exchange, where Leggett & Platt's stock was listed in June 1979, are (from left to right): Felix E. Wright, executive vice president; Harry M. Cornell, Jr., president; G. Louis Allen, vice president and treasurer; and Robert A. Jefferies, general counsel. *(Photo courtesy of Wagner International Photos, Inc.)*

Perhaps the most significant news of 1979, however, came in June, when Leggett & Platt celebrated its listing on the New York Stock Exchange (NYSE) under the ticker symbol LEG. During the following quarter, the stock's closing price ranged from $12.38 to $15.63; the quarter's volume totaled 237,300 shares traded. At year's end, shareholders of record numbered 2,056, with some 500 employees holding approximately 10 percent of the shares, and roughly 20 percent held by officers and directors.[59]

By the end of the 1970s, Leggett & Platt had become a larger, stronger, and wiser corporation. In December 1979, the company had approximately 5,400 employees, with sales totaling $215 million.[60]

For the 10-year period, 1970–1979, Leggett's sales and earnings increased at compound annual rates of 19.6 percent and 16.2 percent, respectively.[61] With a solid strategy, a sound financial foundation, and a seasoned management team, the company was prepared for further growth.

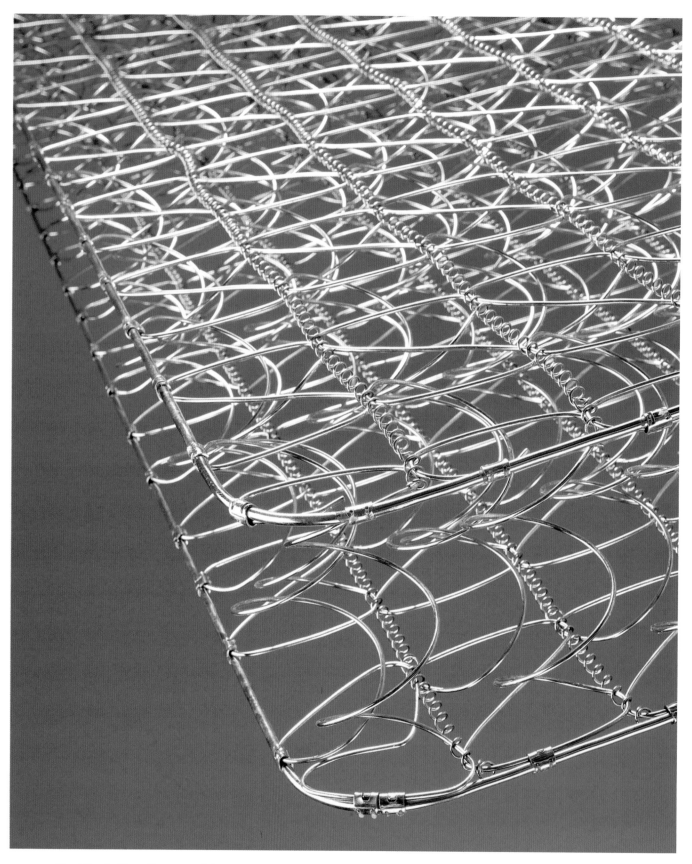

The Mira-Coil® continuous coil innerspring unit grew in popularity in the 1980s and was patented in 23 countries.

CHAPTER SIX

BROADENING ITS BASE

1980–1989

*We firmly believe that service to our industry and to every customer is
Leggett's reason for being and its opportunity.*

—Harry M. Cornell, Jr.[1]

LEGGETT & PLATT'S 1980 SALES GREW to a new record of $229 million, resulting in earnings of $2.06 per share, a 21.2 percent increase over 1979. Issues that dampened the company's 1980 earnings included a first quarter diminished by inflationary costs and an acceleration of the recession, leading to a sharp decrease in demand in the second quarter.[2]

Though Leggett & Platt had become a company of nine-digit sales, it was also proving quite nimble. Over the course of the year, the company maintained its profitability by paying close attention to production schedules, inventory levels, labor costs, and utilization.[3]

The patent infringement lawsuit the company had battled since 1973 was finally resolved in its favor in 1980, allowing Leggett & Platt to proceed with uninhibited production of its Wall Hugger® recliner mechanisms.[4]

Furthermore, the company's research and development efforts were benefiting from output at two major facilities—the original National Technical Center in Carthage and the "Tech Center" showroom in High Point, North Carolina. The latter of these, located in the heart of the furniture industry, served as a display area for the company's full line of components.

At a corporate development and strategic planning meeting at year's end, committee members reviewed the company's objectives. Originally formulated in the 1960s, these objectives were reassessed and discussed over the years and provided broad strategic guidelines aimed at enhancing shareholder return.[5] In 1980, the committee specifically discussed the potential pursuit of acquisitions in broader market segments, including segments not particularly complementary to bedding, furniture components, or other current holdings. Although, at that time, the committee decided not to pursue such acquisitions, the members agreed that acquisitions needed to be "larger in size [and] involve more profitable companies, with good management in place."[6] Such periodic strategy discussions helped set, and sometimes modify, the vision and strategy that drove Leggett & Platt's activities.

On the bedding products side, the company had begun limited production of its long-awaited Mira-Coil® continuous coil innerspring. In 1981, the company reported that the Mira-Coil® product and the machinery for its production were patented in 23 countries.[7]

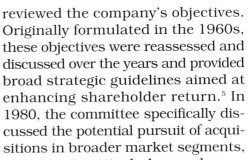

Products manufactured at the EST division for a major customer included a variety of propellers that were cast, polished, and painted.

That same year, Leggett & Platt also formed an international division, which pursued opportunities for licensing agreements and sales of machinery with international finished product manufacturers and components suppliers. The division's president, Larry Higgins, met with bedding manufacturers worldwide, spreading word of Leggett & Platt's expertise in spring-making machinery, technology, and manufacturing

Above: The "Super Excalibur" display units, manufactured by the Masterack division and introduced in 1980, enlarged retail store beverage sections by 25 percent.

Right: Larry Higgins was named president of Leggett & Platt's international division in 1983. He traveled worldwide selling and leasing Leggett & Platt's innerspring production machinery.

processes. This international scope of operations complemented the company's goal to become nationally recognized as The Components People® in the household furniture industry.[8] In the 1981 Annual Report, Felix E. Wright, then executive vice president and chief operating officer, explained how the company was prepared to meet this goal:

Leggett & Platt's operating style reflects the effective combination of two fundamental ingredients: first, an aggressive marketing policy complemented by various supporting services; and second, a willingness of management to commit capital as needed to gain market position and operating efficiencies, thereby improving profitability.

Our management organization has been developed in anticipation of and responsive to the needs of growth. Strong emphasis is placed on decentralized management of operations in coordination with central policies. Operating management responsibilities generally emphasize geographic rather than product-line distinction. Corporate officers and staff administer centralized functions and provide various supporting services to group, division, and plant management.

Internal management development is encouraged and compensation programs include the concept of profit incentives at all management levels. Approximately 570 management personnel participate in incentive programs that may reward individuals when objectives are met, as if each of them were a partner in the organization.[9]

THE FIRST 100 YEARS: 1883–1897

1883: Joseph P. Leggett develops and patents the first successful spiral-steel coil bedspring, then forms a business partnership with his future brother-in-law, Cornelius B. Platt, a blacksmith, who operates the C. D. Platt Plow Works plant in Carthage, Missouri.

1885: J. P. Leggett receives a patent for improvements on the coiled bedspring. Leggett and C. B. Platt begin manufacturing coiled bedsprings at the Platt Plow Works plant.

1895: Harry Platt, a brother of C. B. Platt, opens a franchise factory in Louisville, Kentucky.

1897: The partners move to a building on the corner of Second and Maple Streets in Carthage.

End of a Century

In 1982, as Leggett & Platt approached its 100th anniversary, considerable changes in the management team occurred. The death of chairman Mack Cornell early in the year was an incalculable loss to his family, friends, and the company. Mack had served as a board member and a company leader for 47 years.[10] He was hired as Leggett's sales manager in 1935 and continued to direct the sales team after becoming president in 1953. He remained president until 1960, when he was elected chairman of the board, the position in which he remained until his death. Harry M. Cornell, Jr., was elected chairman after the passing of his father, while also maintaining his responsibilities as president and CEO.[11]

Leggett & Platt's division managers pose for a group photo in December 1981 at the company's National Technical Center in Carthage, Missouri.

Two important leaders also retired that year— Edwin C. Sandham, president of Leggett & Platt's EST division, and Frank Ford, senior vice president of the diversified products group. Both continued to serve on the company's board of directors.[12]

In 1982, Karl G. Glassman joined Leggett & Platt as a Western division sales representative, taking advantage of the opportunity to work alongside his father, Art Glassman. Karl already had several years of experience in the business, having worked

---

THE FIRST 100 YEARS: 1901–1921

1901: The partnership of J. P. Leggett and C. B. Platt is incorporated under the name "Leggett & Platt Spring Bed & Manufacturing Company." The initial members of the board of directors are Caffee, Hall, Leggett, McClurg, Newell, Ornduff, and Platt; there are 16 initial stockholders, including all seven directors.

1904: Pacific Spring Bed Company of Oakland, California, begins manufacture of the Leggett Patent Steel Spring Bed.

1905: George D. Leggett (brother of J. P. Leggett) joins the board of directors and serves until 1934.

1911: Plant is established in Windsor, Ontario; C. E. "Jack" Platt, son of C. B. Platt, becomes manager.

1921: Founder J. P. Leggett dies in the spring. C. B. Platt becomes president.

for De Lamar Bed Spring Corporation of Los Angeles, a company owned by his mother's family, before Leggett & Platt purchased it in 1979. "I graduated from high school on a Sunday, and my dad said, 'Congratulations. Your shift starts at 5:30 tomorrow morning, so don't be late.'"[13]

Starting on the factory floor at De Lamar, Karl Glassman eventually became the company's production manager, a job he continued into his early college years. Although Leggett & Platt was interested in retaining both father and son, at the time of the De Lamar purchase, Karl chose to return to college full time to earn a degree in management and finance. He was already on the road to a career in banking when the sales position at his father's division became available. It was the first of several positions that Glassman would hold with Leggett & Platt.[14]

Throughout 1982, Leggett expanded its production capacity for Mira-Coil®, anticipating greater

sales as the international division negotiated with manufacturers and suppliers abroad.[15]

Although the company's sales increased by 4.7 percent for the year, net earnings dropped by 23.6 percent. The company struggled to continue its past record of gains in the face of a recession. Undaunted, Harry Cornell, Jr., said in the Annual Report:

A decrease in earnings is always disappointing. Yet, there is satisfaction in the fact that in 1982, your company operated in the most difficult business environment of its 22-year history under current management and emerged with undiminished financial strength, industry position, and growth potential.[16]

That "difficult business environment" was the result of a recession that lingered beyond economists' projections.[17] Rather than the recovery in consumer spending that was predicted for the third quarter, the year ended with high unemployment, and consumer spending inhibited by credit card and installment debt.[18] As a result, household furniture expenditures, as a percent of personal consumption, reached their lowest point since the 1960s, a factor attributed in part to the postponable nature of such expenditures, as well as to the lower level of price inflation in furnishings as a whole.[19]

Above: Karl G. Glassman joined Leggett & Platt in 1982 as a Western division sales representative.

Right: An attractive brass paperweight memento was distributed to various individuals to commemorate Leggett & Platt's 100ᵗʰ anniversary in 1983.

THE FIRST 100 YEARS: 1925–1934

1925: A new, 49,500-square-foot factory is built in Carthage on West Vine Street.

1929: Founder C. B. Platt dies. J. P. Leggett, Jr., becomes president. Frank B. Williams joins the board of directors and serves until 1947.

1932: J. P. Leggett, Jr., steps down as president due to health problems, and Frank B. Williams takes the helm as interim president.

1933: George S. Beimdiek, Sr., joins the board of directors and serves until 1959. The plant in Carthage begins to manufacture innerspring units.

1934: Harry M. Cornell, Sr. (son-in-law of J. P. Leggett) joins the board of directors and serves until 1982.

THE ARRIVAL OF MIRA-COIL®

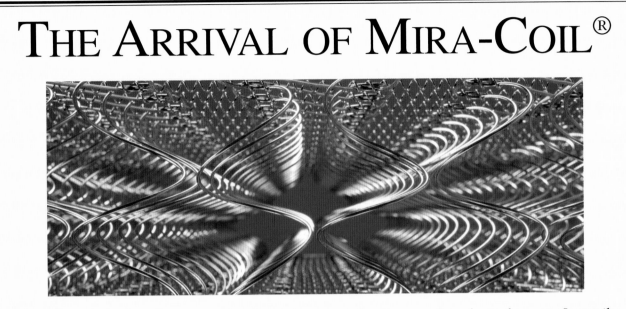

IN 1968, LEGGETT & PLATT BEGAN WORK ON A promising new continuous coil concept for innersprings. After two years and several failed designs, Leggett hired the Frank L. Wells Company of Kenosha, Wisconsin, to help develop the product and machinery.

Tom Wells, Sr., a fourth-generation family member of the Wells Company, began working on the continuous coil project and ultimately joined Leggett in 1974. The work continued until 1976, when Tom told management that "everything developed to that point had to be scrapped. It was absolutely no good and wouldn't work."[1] Costs for the project at that time had already reached into the millions.

Leggett's engineers began again and eventually invented a spring unit and machinery that are still used today.

Before they succeeded, however, the design team faced some additional complications. Wells recalled a demonstration meeting intended to convince nearly two-dozen VIPs from a major mattress company (and its parent company) to use the continuous coil unit for their best-selling mattress. In preparation for the meeting, the engineers worked nonstop for almost two days, only to find that their efforts were useless:

The machine wasn't going to work, so I sent the other four guys home. Then I went home and put on a suit and a tie because I was the ringmaster who was supposed to demonstrate the machine.

[The] contingent arrived, but after an hour of standing around and wanting to see the machine run at least one cycle, Leggett's managers had enough embarrassment for the day and called the group back to the boardroom for lunch. During that lunch, which I was not a part of, the customer's researchers and engineers told Harry Cornell that the concept was no good and would never work.

Harry called me up after they left and told me what they'd said. He asked, "Tom, will it work?" I said, "Yes," and then all he said was, "Well, get after it." No failure was ever fatal with him.

Eighteen months later, we sold an improved and fully automated product to another of the national mattress companies. It's still part of their flagship line.[2]

Wells explained that Leggett named its first continuous coil unit Mira-Coil® because the vice president of sales at the time, Ralph Johnson, said, "It's going to be a miracle if that thing ever works."[3]

Mira-Coil® proved a miracle in more ways than one: It used about 35 percent less wire than other innerspring products used at the time of its initial introduction to the marketplace, and continues today to provide the same resilience and firmness as a traditional mattress.[4]

Celebrating 100 Years

In 1983, Leggett & Platt celebrated 100 years of continuous service. In a brochure distributed to employees, customers, and family members, Harry M. Cornell, Jr.—chairman, president, and CEO—attributed the company's achievements to the loyalty of its customers and its employees:

We firmly believe that service to our industry and to our every customer is Leggett's reason for being and its opportunity. In celebrating the company's centennial year, we offer our most sincere appreciation to our loyal customers for their busi-

ness and reassure each one of them, large and small, that our commitment to unparalleled and constant customer service in every respect will continue to be our goal.

We also want to express our deepest pride and appreciation for all the loyal people of Leggett & Platt and their families, who over these 100 years have been responsible for our company's success. From inception, management and employees, too numerous to name, have continuously demonstrated a dedication to success based on the entrepreneurial spirit of partnership with which our company was founded and which today continues to be strongly encouraged.[20]

THE FIRST 100 YEARS: 1935–1942

1935: Harry M. Cornell, Sr., joins the company as a vice president and sales manager. By a narrow margin, stockholders vote against the proposed sale of Leggett & Platt to the L. A. Young Spring and Wire Corporation of Detroit.

1937: The Great Ohio River Flood swamps the Louisville plant, which ultimately moves to 25th and Maple Streets.

1938: F. B. Williams steps down as president, but continues as board chairman. George S. Beimdiek, Sr., is named president, treasurer, and general manager. A factory in Dallas is opened, and Leggett & Platt acquires the equipment of the Daltex Company, a small Dallas-area bedspring manufacturer, to use in the plant.

1942: Leggett survives World War II by working on defense contracts.

Opposite: In 1983, Leggett & Platt's centennial year, Andy Thomas of the company's marketing services department painted an oil-on-canvas mural. Now an established painter and muralist, Thomas still considers himself a member of the Leggett & Platt family. According to Thomas, the detail of the machinery in the mural was some of the most difficult imagery to capture on canvas. The original company owners, C. B. Platt and J. P. Leggett, are pictured sitting at a table. Later partners Felix E. Wright and Harry M. Cornell, Jr., are to the right holding a ticker tape. Other people include various members of the board, management, and employees. *(Painting printed by permission courtesy of Andy Thomas.)*

The company completed four substantial acquisitions in 1983. In January and February, Leggett & Platt purchased the stock of the Nachman Corporation of Des Plaines, Illinois, a competing manufacturer of bedding components. At the time of the acquisition, Nachman had seven manufacturing plants and a product lineup similar to, and in some cases overlapping, that of Leggett & Platt. Though Nachman's sales reached $24.3 million the year before the acquisition, the company was struggling to make a profit.[21] Following the purchase, Leggett & Platt began to consolidate corporate functions, plant facilities, and products to improve efficiencies in Nachman operations.[22]

By mid-summer, Leggett & Platt had purchased the operating assets of the Cyclo-Index Corporation of Cleveland, Ohio.[23] The company's Cyclo-Index® mechanical motion control system, which improved the operating performance of manufacturing machinery, had been used by Leggett & Platt in recent years,

EXCEPTIONAL SERVICE

THE NATIONAL ASSOCIATION OF BEDDING MANUFACTURERS

gratefully presents to

HARRY M. CORNELL, JR.

ITS EIGHTEENTH

AWARD FOR EXCEPTIONAL SERVICE

For his dedicated service to this Association as Vice Chairman of the Associate Membership Committees, 1968-1969, General Chairman of the Suppliers Council, 1969-1971, member of the NABM Long Range Planning Committees, 1974-1976 and 1980-1981, current membership On the Robert MacMorran Memorial Award Committee, and Many years' service on the Innerspring Constructions Committee of the Suppliers Council.

For his leadership and integrity as a key member of the Bedding industry, and for his valuable participation in numerous activities of NABM and the NABM Suppliers Council.

And for his outstanding and continuing contribution of time and talents in service to his community and its people.

Done this 19th day of March, 1983, at its 68th Annual Convention assembled.

Hubert F. Grossman
Executive Vice President

ON MARCH 19, 1983, HARRY M. CORNELL, Jr., received the "Award for Exceptional Service" from the National Association of Bedding Manufacturers (NABM), which is today known as the International Sleep Products Association (ISPA).[1]

THE FIRST 100 YEARS: 1945–1959

1945: Leggett purchases a warehouse in Winchester, Kentucky.

1947: Leggett sells its Dallas property and moves to Ennis, Texas.

1950: Harry M. Cornell, Jr. (grandson of J. P. Leggett) joins the company as a sales trainee in Louisville, and transfers to Kansas as a commissioned salesman in 1952.

1953: Harry M. Cornell, Sr., is elected president, following the retirement of George Beimdiek, Sr., while Harry M. Cornell, Jr., becomes manager of the Ennis, Texas, plant.

1958: Harry M. Cornell, Jr., joins the board of directors.

1959: Felix E. Wright is hired by Harry M. Cornell, Jr., as a sales trainee at the Ennis facility.

resulting in a 20-percent increase in the manufacture of coil springs.[24]

That summer, Leggett & Platt also acquired Parthenon Metal Works, Inc., of La Vergne, Tennessee. Parthenon was a manufacturer of welded steel tubing and a significant supplier to Leggett & Platt. The purchase of Parthenon brought Leggett & Platt a new internal source for raw materials such as steel tubing and slit coil steel.[25]

Before the year ended, Leggett purchased Bedline Manufacturing Company of Los Angeles. Bedline, which manufactured and sold steel bedding products and convertible sofa mechanisms, broadened Leggett's network of nationwide manufacturing and distribution facilities for bed frames and sleeper fixture hardware. It also accelerated the growth and development of an earlier acquisition, Signal Manufacturing, another Los Angeles–based producer of sleeper hardware.[26]

Two other major events in 1983 included a 2-for-1 stock split (resulting in the issuance of 4,040,852 new shares) and the hiring of David S. Haffner, a Carthage native, as a group vice president of operations.[27] His first responsibilities involved overseeing the company's Wisconsin-based aluminum die-casting operations. In the decades to come, he would become a pivotal member of the Leggett & Platt management team.

In 1983, both sales and earnings rebounded dramatically. Sales were up 21 percent to more than $354 million, and earnings had skyrocketed by 58 percent to $15.6 million.[28]

For the savvy few who invested in the company's initial public offering in 1967 and held the stock, the financial rewards were sensational. In 1967, one share of Leggett & Platt stock initially sold for $10; an investment of $1,000 would

Above: David S. Haffner joined the Leggett & Platt ranks in 1983, overseeing the company's aluminum die-casting operations in Wisconsin.

Right: With the 1983 acquisition of the Cyclo-Index Corporation, Leggett & Platt obtained a mechanical motion control system that improved the operating performance of manufacturing machinery. This photo shows the control system in 1989.

THE FIRST 100 YEARS: 1960–1967

1960: Harry M. Cornell, Sr., becomes chairman of the board. Harry M. Cornell, Jr., becomes president and CEO, and begins implementing a new corporate strategy to broaden the line of component products for the bedding and furniture industries, expand geographically, and offer compatible products directly to furniture stores. Felix E. Wright becomes manager of a new branch factory in Phoenix. The company acquires C. A. Bissman Manufacturing Company, a case goods manufacturer in Springfield, Missouri.

1963: The company adds a spring factory in Oklahoma City.

1967: Leggett & Platt carries out its initial public offering of 50,000 shares of stock (at $10 per share) and $1 million of convertible subordinated debentures; the stock is listed over-the-counter.

have bought 100 shares of the stock. With additional shares received from stock splits in 1969, 1973, 1978, and 1983, those initial 100 shares would have grown to 750 shares. On March 1, 1984, each share was valued at $18.75, so 750 were worth $14,063. On top of that, the investor would have received cash dividends of $2,013 over time, more than twice the cost of the original 100 shares. Thus, over those initial 16 years, investors enjoyed a compound average growth rate of approximately 19 percent per year, based on a 16-fold return of their investment from stock appreciation, splits, and dividends.[29]

Continuing to seek out complementary acquisitions, Leggett & Platt acquired Gordon Manufacturing Company of Grand Rapids, Michigan, in January 1984. Gordon manufactured chair controls and steel bases, primarily for use in office furniture, which brought Leggett & Platt opportunities for new products and markets.[30]

In 1984, Leggett & Platt also acquired the National Fibers division of National Bedding and Furniture Industries of Memphis, which made insulator pads and synthetic and cotton cushioning materials for bedding and furniture manufacturers.[31]

Leggett & Platt refocused some of its resources in September 1984 by selling its packaging division to a North Carolina company. At the time of the sale, the division consisted of five plants in North Carolina, Arkansas, Massachusetts, and Texas, and was producing flexible furniture and bedding packaging, along with a variety of unrelated items such as coin wrap, meat and poultry pads, and moving van pads.[32]

In a 1984 interview, Harry Cornell, Jr., explained the reason for the sale: "Although the packaging division has continued to be profitable, we believe we can better invest the proceeds from this sale in other operations that currently fit more closely with our long-term growth and profit objectives."[33]

Making the List

In 1985, *FORTUNE*® magazine added Leggett & Platt to its annual listing of the 500 largest industrial companies in the United States. That April, *FORTUNE*® ranked the company as the 489th-largest U.S. industrial corporation, based on its 1984 sales figures. Leggett & Platt attained top-100 status in three of the magazine's categories: in "Return on Shareholders' Equity for 1984," the company ranked

Office workers nationwide use Leggett & Platt products. The woman in this photo sits in a chair whose base and column were produced by the EST division.

THE FIRST 100 YEARS: 1968–1970

1968: Leggett & Platt acquires Motor City Spring Company in Detroit; Flex-O-Loc Corporation in Lawrence, Massachusetts; and Kenyon Manufacturing Company in Kenyon, Minnesota.

1969: Leggett & Platt and Armco Steel Corporation build a wire-drawing mill in Carthage. Leggett & Platt also constructs a sawmill in Naples, Texas. Acquisitions include the J. R. Greeno Corporation and its affiliate, Butler Manufacturing Company, both of

Cincinnati, Ohio, and the Dalpak Corporation of Dallas. Leggett & Platt announces a 5-for-3 stock split and later issues an additional 175,000 shares of common stock.

1970: Leggett & Platt acquires the Signal Manufacturing Company of Los Angeles. Factories are built in Georgia and Texas.

CORNELL CONFERENCE CENTER

Dedicated to the Memory of Harry M. Cornell, Sr., and Marjorie Leggett Cornell

IN 1991, LEGGETT & PLATT'S BOARD OF DIRECTORS DEDicated a new conference center on the company's headquarters campus in Carthage, Missouri, to the memory of Mr. and Mrs. Harry M. Cornell, Sr. A large plaque commemorating the building's dedication reads, in part:

Mack and Marjorie, as Mr. and Mrs. Cornell, Sr., were affectionately known to their hundreds of friends from all walks of life, served Leggett & Platt faithfully for many years.

Mack was an Officer and Director for 47 years, eventually serving as President of the Company for several years and then as Chairman of the Board before retiring in 1982. Marjorie—the daughter

of J. P. Leggett, who cofounded the Company in 1883—served as an active and then Honorary Director for 21 years. Through these 68 years of combined service, Mack and Marjorie, by their personal example, set standards of courtesy, fairness, and sincere concern for others that shaped the character of this Company.[1]

Harry M. Cornell, Jr., son of Mack and Marjorie, and then CEO and chairman of the board, received letters from many individuals recalling his parents' influence on their lives. Portions of a few of those letters are printed on the following page. The letters, plaque, and portraits of the Cornells are housed at the conference center that bears their name.

It is difficult for me to express, in writing, my sincere love and appreciation for your Mother and Dad. Mr. and Mrs. Cornell … gave to me … an opportunity … doing what most boys would then, as now, rebel about: yard work.

I remember your Dad … we spent many an hour and day together … trimming the lawn, pruning trees, weeding the peonies … I always looked forward to "sale day," the cattle auction at Red Oak. Mr. Johnson always had potatoes to send to Carthage with us, and we'd deliver them, along with the cherry tomatoes we'd pick from Mr. Cornell's 75-100 plants, all over Carthage to those who your Dad knew were in need. This quality of your Dad's, of caring about people and wanting to help them, was one of the most important.

Mrs. Cornell … was constantly sending goodies out to me, so I have not only my Mom, but my "second Mom," to thank for my healthy frame today.

Mr. and Mrs. Cornell were such positive, delightful, caring people to be around, and I consider the opportunity of working for them directly for five years a true blessing. I sincerely believe they both inspired, in one way or another, everyone's life with whom they came in contact.

> – From Jim Crocker, then National Accounts Manager
> for Leggett & Platt; recently retired after 41 years

It is very difficult—perhaps impossible, for me to translate my deep feelings for Mack and Marg Cornell into written words. They were truly unique—best examples of a generation that made our country great. They both exemplified qualities that I am fearful we are losing—self-reliance, love of God, respect for traditions, sanctity of marriage, cherishing of family values, patriotism, and above all, unimpeachable integrity. My life was enriched and blessed from having known them. I still love them—always will.

> – From Jim McCormick,
> board member from 1965 to 1995

That was the first time Harry Mack, Sr. and I laughed. We would laugh together many more times in the nearly five years Mack had remaining and particularly on those three or four occasions each year when he would stop by my office to "just talk." … He was a man with large doses of good humor, optimism and openness. He cared deeply about and loved family, friends and country. He was a sentimental man with enough strength to show his deep emotions. And in that aging body and in the fabric of all that he did was a rare youthfulness, gentleness and kindness of spirit.

Mack was a modest man who lived unencumbered by his material possessions. Had fate snatched away all that Mack owned, his wealth would have been little diminished and he would have remained one of the richest men I have known.

> – From Robert A. Jefferies, Jr.,
> then General Counsel of Leggett & Platt;
> 28-year employee; board member from 1991 to 2002

I am very pleased by the action of the board in naming the Cornell Conference Center in honor of Harry M. Cornell Sr. and Marjorie Leggett Cornell. Back in 1949, as young newly-weds, my wife and I moved onto the same block where Mr. and Mrs. Cornell lived. Their many acts of kindness meant a great deal to us and we soon came to know them as Mack and Marg.

Mack was the most complete "people-person" I have ever known. It was just his nature to be interested in people and to care about others. Whether it was his banker or his yardman, he was always ready to help. Of course, he had this same interest and concern for all the people at Leggett & Platt, be they executives, machine operators, truck drivers, salesmen, or custodians.

Marg was different—more reserved, dignified, always the lady. To her, courtesy and proper etiquette came naturally, and this was her way of showing respect and concern for others. She was the perfect balance and supplement to Mack's more exuberant nature.

Together Mack and Marg made a tremendous impact upon Leggett & Platt. Through their long years of service and many contacts with hundreds of Leggett & Platt people, they did much to produce this same courteous, unselfish, caring attitude throughout the company, and in this way made an invaluable contribution to this company's success. It is most appropriate that we name this fine building in their honor.

> – From Herbert Casteel,
> board member from 1960 to 2001

Mr. and Mrs. Cornell have had a major impact on my life. They changed me in ways I've only just begun to discover. … Mr. Mack was looking for some part-time help and asked me to come by after school to help him take care of his yard. … Mrs. Cornell was always feeding me and trying to keep me from overheating or freezing to death.

They constantly asked me what I intended to do after I got out of school and whether or not I had considered working at L&P. … It soon became apparent that any company run by people who cared this much, would have to be a great place to work. So, I clocked in.

Several years later, I came to realize that Mr. Mack and Mrs. Cornell were my mentors. They helped me set personal goals, showed me how to realize them and … never asked for anything in return.

> – From David Harris, a 22-year employee;
> then Sleep Quality Engineer for Leggett & Platt

I understand that in the very near future we will be dedicating the Cornell Conference Center. As you know, I knew both Marjorie and Mack very well personally and enjoyed serving with them on the Board of Directors. I believe that naming the new Center after them is very appropriate. In the future the Center will host meetings with employees, customers and shareholders. Both Marjorie and Mack were above all "people persons." They had the utmost concern for every customer and employee and in my years of knowing them it was very evident to me that others were always placed before themselves. This dedication to others began a tradition at the Company which has survived both Marjorie and Mack. Today one of the great strengths of Leggett & Platt is its loyal base of employees, customers and shareholders. This tradition works both ways and it began with Marjorie and Mack Cornell.

I hope that I can personally use the Center for years going forward and I will constantly be reminded that it was Marjorie and Mack that dug the foundation upon which the Company and this Center rests.

> – From Richard T. Fisher, board member
> from 1972 to present;
> currently Chairman

Leggett & Platt's Middletown division manufactured mechanisms that allowed a chair to recline into several positions.

84th; in "10-Year Earnings Growth," the company ranked 57th; and in "10-Year Total Return to Investors," it ranked 52nd.[34]

In January 1985, Leggett purchased Northfield Metal Products, Ltd., of Waterloo, Ontario. As a leading manufacturer of chair control mechanisms and steel chair bases for customers in the United States, Canada, and Europe, Northfield expanded Leggett & Platt's territory and product line.[35]

That year, the company also purchased Nashville-based Steiner-Liff Textile Products, a major buyer of woven textile cuttings that Leggett & Platt used as feedstock in manufacturing non-woven felt,

cushioning, padding, and automotive soundproofing. Steiner-Liff was considerably diversified when Leggett & Platt purchased it, with activities that included: the processing of textile fibers used as filler for decorative pillows, sleeping bags, stuffed toys, outdoor furniture, and sporting goods; fiber sales to manufacturers of fine writing papers, stock and bond certificates, and bank notes; and the manufacture and distribution of disposable sanitary wipes.[36]

In the spring of 1985, Felix E. Wright became president of Leggett & Platt while maintaining his responsibilities as chief operating officer. Harry Cornell, Jr., continued as chairman and CEO.[37]

That summer, Leggett & Platt announced it would acquire Kay Springs, Inc., of Syosset, New York. Founded in 1911, this privately owned company manufactured springs and wire components for the bedding and upholstered furniture industries. It employed 750 people in 11 plants across 10 states.[38] By September, however, Leggett began new discussions regarding the purchase because of the U.S. Department of Justice's disapproval of the acquisition.[39] By year's end, with the issue resolved to the government's satisfaction, Leggett & Platt acquired all assets of Kay Springs, Inc., except for the company's Los Angeles bedding operation.[40]

Gary Krakauer, a fourth-generation member of Kay Springs' founding family, joined Leggett & Platt through the acquisition and became president of

---

THE FIRST 100 YEARS: 1971–1973

1971: Leggett & Platt stock is listed on the NASDAQ stock exchange, and the company achieves more than $1 million in net earnings.

1972: The company acquires its Masterack division, which produces institutional beds and wire display racks. Other acquisitions include Kraft Converters, Inc., of High Point, North Carolina; Metal Bed Rail Company, Inc., of Linwood, North

Carolina; and the EST Company of Grafton, Wisconsin. Leggett & Platt issues an additional 175,000 shares of common stock.

1973: The company's stock splits 3-for-2. Leggett & Platt acquires Paramount Paper Products Company of Alma, North Carolina, and Middletown Manufacturing, Inc., of Simpsonville, Kentucky. Production is under way on an innerspring urethane-foam mattress core and on the Lectro-LOK® box spring unit.

bedding components for the company's Northeast division. He recalled what it was like folding his family's company into the larger corporation:

First off, we were one of the largest acquisitions that Leggett had made at that time, and they spent a lot of time integrating us into their system, working with us and exchanging information. They had a great integration team. They tried to retain as many management and sales people around the company as they could. They valued the intellectual properties we had and personnel that we had— terrific company to work with right off the bat.

We learned about their generous stock programs ... and the fact that even [then] Leggett had a very strong pay-for-performance policy, with annual incentive bonuses going right down to the foreman level in the factories, so that everybody felt that if you performed, you were rewarded as part of the team. It was a great experience. I think Leggett is a great employer.[41]

Leggett's management anticipated that the Kay Springs acquisition would contribute approximately $18 million to the company's sales the following year.[42]

Although Leggett & Platt's size was increasing every year, the company's strength did not just come from its acquisitions. According to Wayne Wickstrom, who had joined the company in 1973 as a division sales manager and served as vice president

Hired in 1973, Wayne Wickstrom served as a Leggett & Platt vice president and director of marketing and sales for the furniture components group from 1985 until his retirement in July 1999. To many furniture industry customers, Wickstrom was Leggett's recognized ambassador.

and director of marketing in the mid-1980s, retaining good people was just as important as acquiring new businesses. He explained:

I have always felt that the people Mr. Cornell surrounded himself with ... were really the strength. The growth was not [all] through acquisition, because during my entire tenure, we grew about half internally and half externally. So it took a lot of growth just internally to keep that pace. ... I think it was really the people that we had, and as we did acquisitions, we always kept the people.[43]

Full Circle

In 1986, Leggett & Platt operated in an environment similar to that of the previous year, with sluggish growth and modestly increased sales in the home furnishings industry. Even so, the stock continued to do well, and the company issued a 3-for-2 stock split in March.[44]

In May, Leggett completed its first acquisition for the year—MPI, Inc., of Fort Worth, Texas. MPI was a leading manufacturer of bonded foam carpet

---

THE FIRST 100 YEARS: 1974–1977

1974: The Texas sawmill is put up for sale. Foothills Manufacturing, Inc., of Forest City, North Carolina, is acquired. A new technology center is built in Carthage. The Masterack division begins a move across town in Atlanta.

1976: Leggett & Platt exceeds the $100 million sales mark for the first time. The company acquires the Phillips Foscue Corporation of High Point, North Carolina.

1977: Felix E. Wright joins the board of directors. Leggett & Platt takes half ownership of Globe Spring and Cushion Company, Ltd., of Toronto, and acquires Adcom Metals Company, which has operations in Jacksonville, Florida, and Nicholasville, Kentucky. Construction begins on new corporate headquarters outside Carthage.

TOGETHER, AGAIN

IN OCTOBER 1988, LEGGETT & PLATT purchased Flex-O-Lators, bringing the family of cofounder C. B. Platt back into the company. C. B. Platt's son, Jack, established Flex-O-Lators in 1942, and Jack's sons, Thomas and John, became president and chairman of the board, respectively. The company operated facilities in Carthage; High Point, North Carolina; and Azusa, California. Its product lineup included wire insulators, springs, and suspension systems; plastic and paper furniture edgings; and specialized packaging materials.[1]

The Platt brothers were second cousins of Harry Cornell, Jr. Their grandmother, Willmetta (Leggett) Platt, and Harry's grandfather, Joseph P. Leggett, were brother and sister. Over the years, Harry had maintained a relationship with them, introduced them to Felix Wright, and even arranged for the companies to co-develop a product. When the Platt brothers decided to sell their business, it was only natural that they contacted Harry and Felix.[2]

Jack Crusa, a certified public accountant, joined Leggett & Platt as a group specialist in 1986. He was responsible for the due diligence process and the integration of Flex-O-Lators. After the transition was complete, the new operation reported to him. Jack recently explained some of the history and significance of this acquisition:

Jack Platt worked for L. A. Young Spring and Wire until he retired. ... He came back to Carthage where a lot of his family still lived. ...

The Williams brothers, Harold and Frank, were part of a family-run industrial lighting business in Carthage. They held the patent for a product that would be used as a barrier between the springs in a mattress or car seat and the cotton padding material, to keep the padding from poking down into the springs.

Jack Platt worked with the Williams brothers and started Flex-O-Lators, primarily to supply that barrier product to the automotive industry. His sons—John, Tom, Muff [Robert] and Fritz [Frederick]—joined Jack at the company after the war ended.

When we acquired Flex-O-Lators in 1988, John and Tom Platt were heading the company. Other family members active in the business included four of Jack Platt's grandsons: George, Nick, and Tom Platt, and Jeff Grundy. Nick and Tom still work for Leggett today. Completing that acquisition was sort of like bringing the Platt and Leggett families back together. ... That was a great story and a great reuniting of the families who were here in Carthage.[3]

Although Flex-O-Lators was originally operated within Leggett & Platt's furniture components group, the acquisition would ultimately serve as a springboard for Leggett's growth in the automotive business. David S. Haffner, vice president of operations, and Jack Crusa had established a broader business plan that eventually blossomed into a much larger operation in the company's portfolio.

Jack Crusa has served Leggett & Platt in various capacities since 1986. In 1995, Crusa was named Leggett & Platt vice president and head of the automotive and tubular products unit. He became a senior vice president in 1999 and served as head of Industrial Materials from 1999 to 2004. Crusa became president of Specialized Products in 2004 and assumed the responsibilities for the company's procurement efforts.

cushioning, sold through a distributor network in 32 states. The company also produced polyurethane foam for bedding and furniture manufacturers. The MPI acquisition included six plants in Mississippi and Texas, with annual sales of $47 million, and brought Jack Morris, former chairman and principal owner of MPI, to the Leggett & Platt board of directors.[45]

During the year, Leggett & Platt also formed a partnership with a publicly traded Australian company, Pacific Dunlop, to create a new entity known as L&P Foam. Leggett sold its foam plants in High Point and Newton, North Carolina, and Tupelo, Mississippi, to the joint venture. This new partnership then completed a tender offer for the common stock of Crest-Foam Corporation, a polyurethane manufacturing and fabricating company located in Moonachie, New Jersey. Some two-thirds of Crest-Foam's annual $50 million in foam sales were derived from a wide variety of products sold in bedding, furniture, and carpet-cushioning markets.[46]

In 1987, Leggett & Platt rose to 427th on the FORTUNE® 500 list of the nation's largest industrial corporations. The company also made FORTUNE® magazine's list of "America's Most Admired Companies," ranking second among the nation's furniture industry corporations. This latter recognition was achieved despite Leggett's relative obscurity, as most people outside of the company's key indus-

tries had never heard of it. The "Most Admired" designation stemmed from the company's rating in eight categories: Quality of Management; Quality of Products or Services; Innovation; Long-term Investment Value; Financial Soundness; Ability to Attract, Develop, and Retain Talented People; Community and Environmental Responsibility; and Use of Corporate Assets.[47]

At the end of 1987, the company reported net sales of $649.2 million, which marked an unbroken, 20-year record of increased sales.[48]

In 1988, Leggett climbed to 406th on FORTUNE® magazine's list of the nation's largest industrial corporations.[49] The company's acquisitions that year began with Collier-Keyworth Company of Garner, Massachusetts. This family-owned operation was a leading manufacturer of chair controls and metal bases for office and institutional furniture.[50]

Leggett next acquired the Berkshire Furniture Company and its manufacturing affiliate, Allegheny Steel and Brass Corporation, both located in

Leggett & Platt's acquisition of MPI, Inc., brought the company six plants that produced bonded foam carpet cushioning and polyurethane foam for bedding and furniture makers.

THE FIRST 100 YEARS: 1978–1980

1978: The company settles two civil antitrust lawsuits, which requires the sale of the J. R. Greeno facility in Cincinnati and the Hominy, Oklahoma, plant, as well as restrictions on future acquisitions. The stock splits 3-for-2.

1979: Felix E. Wright, executive vice president, becomes chief operating officer. Leggett & Platt is listed on the New York Stock Exchange. The company's purchases include shares of the Missouri

Rolling Mill Corporation of St. Louis and assets of the De Lamar Bed Spring Corporation, based in Los Angeles.

1980: A patent infringement over the Wall Hugger® mechanism is resolved in Leggett & Platt's favor. The long-awaited Mira-Coil® is now in limited commercial production.

Chicago. Berkshire was a leading supplier of brass and white iron beds and wood and metal daybeds to retail businesses. Allegheny manufactured Berkshire's products and supplied related components and semi-finished products to other home furnishings manufacturers.[51]

An interesting acquisition in 1988 was Wilcox Industries, Inc., dba Indiana Chair Frame (ICF), which made chair assemblies, and later office panel systems, for federal and state prisons. These seating and panel systems, assembled by inmates, provided safe and meaningful work for those who qualified for work programs. Their pay served as restitution for victims or was used to offset prison-housing costs in addition to saving the federal and state governments untold sums of taxpayer dollars.[52]

Atypical of previous acquisitions, ICF reported directly to Lance Beshore, a member of the corporate staff. With a doctorate in political science, Beshore had joined Leggett & Platt in 1980 as the company's first manager of public affairs. In that role, Beshore pursued the company's legislative aims, building strong relationships with legislative leaders at the state and federal levels. Following the acquisition of ICF, Beshore guided the development of Leggett & Platt's governmental sales, expanding those sales in the United States and into the United Kingdom.

End of a Decade

In the spring of 1989, Leggett & Platt purchased one of its longtime suppliers, Culp Smelting &

Lance Beshore joined Leggett & Platt in 1980, establishing the company's first public affairs function. He is currently vice president of public affairs and government relations.

Refining Company of Steele, Alabama. The smelting operation produced aluminum ingot (from aluminum scrap), which was sold to a wide variety of customers who used the material to make die-cast, sand-cast, and permanent-mold aluminum products. The acquisition was a natural fit for Leggett & Platt, providing it with an additional resource for raw materials and substantial purchasing leverage in secondary aluminum ingot.[53]

Also, in the spring, Leggett & Platt acquired Webster Spring Company, Inc., and Webster Wire, Inc., of Oxford, Massachusetts. Webster Spring produced wire components used by mattress and box-spring manufacturers. In addition to its Oxford facility, the company made bedding components at plants in South Carolina, Pennsylvania, Texas, California, and Kentucky. Webster Wire was the drawing mill component of the company's operations, supplying wire to Webster Spring plants as well as other wire fabricators.[54]

Sandy Levine, a son of Webster's founder and the leader of the business, approached Leggett & Platt with the acquisition idea. Levine had known Harry Cornell, Jr., for many years, and the two enjoyed a cordial relationship. Leggett & Platt and Webster served territories that only slightly overlapped. In fact, according to Levine, the idea to create

---

THE FIRST 100 YEARS: 1981–1983

1981: Leggett forms an international division to pursue opportunities overseas.

1982: Harry M. Cornell, Jr., president and CEO, becomes chairman following the death of his father, Harry M. Cornell, Sr. Karl G. Glassman joins the company as a sales representative.

1983: Leggett & Platt celebrates 100 years of operation. The company sells 313,500 shares of common stock from its treasury and later issues a 2-for-1 stock split. Acquisitions include the Nachman Corporation of Des Plaines, Illinois; the Cyclo-Index Corporation of Cleveland, Ohio; Parthenon Metal Works of La Vergne, Tennessee; and the Bedline Manufacturing Company of Los Angeles. Harry M. Cornell, Jr., and Felix E. Wright hire David S. Haffner, who joins the company as a group vice president of operations.

the Webster Wire mill to serve the Webster Spring plants grew out of a visit he made to Leggett & Platt's wire-drawing mill in Carthage.[55]

At the end of the decade, *FORTUNE*® magazine listed Leggett & Platt as the 371st-largest industrial corporation in the United States. Leggett's acquisitions in the 1980s exposed it to new markets and greatly broadened its operations, but the coming decade would bring greater expansion than ever before.

In 1995, Leggett & Platt placed a larger-than-life version of its Partners in Progress® cast bronze sculpture in a specially designed garden in front of the company's corporate offices in Carthage, Missouri. Artist and longtime employee–partner Everette Wyatt created the sculpture in an attempt to capture the spirit of two people pulling together to accomplish a task—a spirit that many employee–partners feel makes Leggett & Platt a special place to work.

CHAPTER SEVEN

A DECADE OF DIVERSIFICATION

1990–1999

Success is founded on a constant state of discontentment interrupted by brief periods of satisfaction on the completion of a job particularly well done.

—A favorite quote of CEO and Chairman
Harry Cornell, Jr.[1]

LEGGETT & PLATT GREW GEOGRAPHICALLY in the 1990s as never before. New ventures at home and abroad began to bring unfamiliar competition and new challenges.

The company's first acquisition of the decade, in February 1990, was Young Spring & Wire, a subsidiary of the Wickes Manufacturing Company in Archbold, Ohio. This subsidiary was all that remained of L. A. Young Spring and Wire Corporation, the company that attempted to purchase Leggett & Platt in December 1935. The acquisition operated as part of the Flex-O-Lators division and expanded Leggett & Platt's capabilities in manufacturing automobile seating systems.[2]

In March, Leggett & Platt acquired Gribetz International, Inc., a designer and builder of quilting and fabric-cutting machinery sold primarily to manufacturers of bedding, furniture, home textiles, and apparel.[3]

Due to successful growth in its Berkshire division, Leggett & Platt formed the Fashion Bed Group in 1990. To complement the division, Leggett acquired J. B. Ross Manufacturing, Inc., of New Brunswick, New Jersey. This business manufactured high-end brass and white-iron fashion beds that it sold to fine furniture stores, department stores, specialty sleep shops, and interior designers.[4]

Leggett acquired another line of fashion bed products by purchasing Dresher, Inc., and its subsidiary, Harris-Hub. These firms manufactured and distributed brass, white iron, wood, and other specialty beds, in addition to steel beds and frames. Although Dresher's annual sales were approximately $80 million, it had reported losses for six quarters, including all of 1989.[5]

The Dresher acquisition was initiated by Dresher's management, in part to help fend off growing competition from overseas. "Both companies believe that improvements in operating efficiencies can be achieved by combining operations," said Dresher Chairman and CEO A. Barry Merkin at the time of the acquisition. "This combination provides Dresher the best opportunity to combat imports, which have made serious inroads into our markets in recent years. It will also help us sustain and build upon the long-established, quality reputation of our products, our service, and our people."[6]

Leggett & Platt's 1997 Annual Report cover reflected the company's effort to diversify its product line and to provide *"engineered products for everyday use … nearly everywhere."*

The team at the Berkshire subsidiary would manage the Fashion Bed Group, which consisted of the Berkshire, J. B. Ross, and Dresher companies.

In July 1990, Leggett & Platt also acquired five facilities from the No-Sag Division of Lear-Siegler. The operations in this transaction included three foam plants in West Chicago, Illinois, and Dubuque, Iowa; a wire products facility located in Kendallville, Indiana; and a wire and steel bedding products

The Paragon, the world's most advanced multi-needle chain stitch quilting machine, was produced by Gribetz International of Leggett & Platt's Global Systems Group. The Paragon featured several patented technologies that have become industry standards for mattress production. The quilting was performed on mattress panels used as the primary sleep surface and on the border sections that formed the sides of the mattress. High-quality styling and high-speed production established the Paragon as the mattress industry's leader among quilting machines.

manufacturing plant in London, Ontario, Canada. These facilities added to Leggett & Platt's capacity in wire components and other wire products for the home furnishings and automotive industries.[7]

Business was strong in early 1990, but consumer confidence in the United States steadily deteriorated during the long, deliberate, and public build-up of allied military forces preceding the Persian Gulf War. Leggett & Platt's sales fell along with the sales of its customers. War-related increases in raw material costs, which the company initially declined to pass along to customers, affected profitability. As some of Leggett's financially weaker customers suffered, receivables and bad debt expense grew.

Trucking and delivery prices also surged due to rising oil prices. Commenting on the severity of the situation, Felix Wright told management:

Higher energy costs … specifically fuel price increases, can cost us hundreds of thousands of

dollars in a month. Most of our products are priced on a delivered basis. When fuel costs increase, as they did in the second half of 1990, we can't effectively pass the increased costs on to our customers. These increased fuel costs cut into our narrow margins. Of course, we take a double hit sometimes because it costs more to buy and transport our raw materials, too.[8]

The Coriander (left), the Silhouette (center), and the Adobe (right) were three models that the Fashion Bed Group produced in the 1990s.

Wright went on to explain, however, that unpredictable and rising fuel costs were not new. The company worked to limit the cost increases by analyzing systems, using reliable shipping methods, reviewing handling and packaging methods, and continually assessing the most effective ways to ship goods.[9]

Perhaps the war's greatest impact on Leggett & Platt was that it led to a 1990 analysis of the weak performance of certain urethane foam-producing operations, and ultimately to the restructuring of the urethane division.[10] In 1991, Leggett & Platt decided to sell, close, or consolidate several facilities in the Northeastern states and North Carolina.[11] This business segment had been especially hard-hit by the increase in raw material and operating costs, reduced demand, and lower production. However, by restructuring the operations to concentrate on limited product lines, the company expected to resolve these problems.[12]

As the year ended, Leggett & Platt raised the rate on its cash dividend to shareholders, making 1990 the 19th consecutive year of dividend increases. The company's strategic prowess was serving it well as it entered a new decade.[13]

Tough Decisions

In February 1991, Leggett & Platt rose to 72nd out of the 306 companies on *Fortune*® magazine's list of "America's Most Admired Companies." It also ranked second out of the nation's nine furniture companies.[14]

Although restructuring of the urethane foam operations and a lingering recession caused a 1 percent drop in net sales, earnings in 1991 increased, due partly to improved consumer confidence after the war.[15] Paul Hauser, senior vice president of Leggett & Platt and head of Residential Furnishings, joined Leggett & Platt in 1980 as a product manager for the bedding group. He explained that the company had always encountered cyclical market conditions, but that it monitored economic indicators in order to prepare for changes in demand:

Consumer spending is key. ... As a company in the United States, I think the overall economy ... will dictate a lot of your growth or non-growth. If you're in somewhat of a recession, you're going to feel it regardless of your market share. Housing starts certainly are something we look at and track, along with consumer spending, obviously. Advertising that's done by our customers has an effect on us. ... All those things are dynamic; we track and analyze them all.[16]

As part of the restructuring of its foam business, Leggett & Platt sold five of its urethane foam operations, including four plants in North Carolina and Mississippi in June and July 1991.[17] The company also sold the Moonachie, New Jersey, portion of its Crest-Foam Corporation. Remaining operations in Edison, New Jersey, and Newburyport, Massachusetts, focused on manufacturing carpet cushioning materials and flexible urethane foam for the bedding and furniture industries.[18]

In 1991, Leggett & Platt also consolidated the product lines, facilities, and personnel of its Fashion Bed Group. The consolidations, which were more

MAKING A FORTUNE

IN 1985, LEGGETT & PLATT JOINED THE PRESTIGIOUS ranks of the *FORTUNE*® 500, the list of America's largest companies, determined by revenues.[1] At that time, *FORTUNE*® magazine had two separate 500 lists—one for industrial firms and another for service companies. Based on Leggett's 1984 revenues, it ranked 489th among the industrial firms. The companies on the *FORTUNE*® listings were also evaluated on three other measures: i) Return on Shareholders' Equity, ii) 10-Year Earnings Growth, and iii) 10-Year Total Return to Investors. In these categories, Leggett & Platt ranked 84th, 57th, and 52nd, respectively.[2]

The company remained on the list of industrial firms through 1994, when it reached its highest ranking ever at 275th place, with revenues of $1.53 billion. Then in 1995, *FORTUNE*® merged its two 500 lists and reduced the total number of companies from 1,000 to 500. For the next three years, Leggett was not included in the new list, but the company continued to grow and reclaimed a place on the list in 1998. It rose as high as 380th in 2003, but in recent years has ranked among the 400 to 500 largest corporations in the country.[3]

Beginning in 1987, Leggett was included on another *FORTUNE*® magazine list, "America's Most Admired Companies." Remarkably, it achieved this status as a little-known company with few recognizable brand names.

While *FORTUNE*® determines the 500 list by business revenues, it selects "America's Most Admired Companies" through a survey conducted by the Hay Group. The survey is administered to executives, directors, and analysts of companies within specific industries, and the questions concern eight attributes: management quality; quality of products and services; innovation; long-term investment value; financial soundness; the ability to attract, develop, and retain talented people; social responsibility; and the use of corporate assets. Described as a "report card on corporate reputations," the "Admired Companies" list ranks businesses by their scores in the eight categories.[4]

For Leggett & Platt, the principle that unites and supports these attributes is the company's long-standing commitment to ethics. Leggett's leaders are convinced that ethical business practices are necessary to ensure quality in management; to attract, develop, and retain talent; to wisely manage resources; and to achieve excellence in all the other categories.

Ethics, Integrity, and Partnership

Ethics are so woven into the corporate culture that even the strict structural changes dictated by the Sarbanes–Oxley Act of 2002 barely affected the company's governing body. Felix Wright said:

Our culture is different. I don't think you're going to find very many $5.5 billion companies in the

challenging than originally anticipated, were complicated by severely depressed demand for fashion beds in 1991.[19]

In a management newsletter published after this restructuring, Harry Cornell, Jr., told readers how difficult the process had been:

We've always tried to consolidate operations and be more efficient, but in 1991, we made some really tough decisions. In a few of our businesses, we simply haven't produced consistently acceptable profits. We have stayed with most of these operations a good long time. We were in these businesses for all the right reasons ... they fit, and we could see other companies making money in similar businesses. But we couldn't, and that was terribly frustrating.

Once we made our restructuring decision, we moved quickly and successfully. ... We strengthened L&P's margins in the process, but we also found other rewards. We'd been spending tremendous time and

---

FORTUNE® 500 that have the exact culture as ours. Maybe ours is not perfect, but it sure has a lot of integrity to it, and it has a lot of other principles that I believe will keep us driving forward for a long time to come.

Sarbanes said, "Yes, you should have outside independent directors." Been doing that from day one. So it's not a bunch of insiders that are trying to do things that might not be totally in the best interests of the shareholders, but we've never had that problem, either. So, the mix, the complexity of the board has changed ... but the changes that we had to make from the primary structure of board committees, or the board itself, to the primary structure of our finance and accounting, were miniscule compared to anybody else in the FORTUNE® 500 as far as I'm concerned.[5]

Duane Potter joined Leggett & Platt in 1968 as an assistant manager and eventually became a senior vice president and member of the board of directors. He was known as a champion of the company culture among new executives in the field. Duane explained that Leggett is a more successful company because it treats employees as partners and encourages them to become stockholders:

It's comfortable to know that through our strategy and through our culture ... people enjoyed coming to work here in the morning knowing

that ... they're working for themselves. We try to keep the equity within the company all the way down through the ranks, and so it gives them that pride of ownership.[6]

Harry Cornell agreed, adding that this spirit of partnership will make the company successful in the future:

One of the reasons we decided to produce this book is to share with our employee–partners the story of where the company has been, and how it got to where it is today. We hope that an understanding of the company's history, spirit, and background helps our ... partners gain a sense of ownership, and realize that the company is theirs to grow. I'd like to say to them, "Now it's your company. Take what is there, and work hard to grow it profitably from here." Those of us who've been around for a while—we're just passing the baton, passing along the company, and bringing on new partners. We hope they will grow and improve the company for our employee–partners and shareholders, and then, when they leave Leggett, pass it on to others who will make it even better.[7]

Duane Potter, former senior vice president, served on the board of directors from 1996 to 2002. He was an advisory member of the board from 2002 to 2008.

*energy on those inconsistent operations
... and had too little to show for the
effort. The restructuring has given us
time—time to strengthen and work with
our better performing businesses. This
has been a big shot in the arm.*[20]

To see Leggett & Platt successfully face the challenges of restructuring was encouraging to investors. Even more exciting to investors, employee–partners, and customers was the growing popularity and acceptance of several innovative products. Many designers, engineers, and technicians played a part in these inventions. Three important individuals—Larry Higgins, Henry Zapletal, and Tom Wells, Sr.—led a variety of efforts in innovation at Leggett & Platt, including continuously designing and redesigning innerspring and box spring products, as well as improving and retrofitting the machinery used to manufacture those products. The company's steady flow of new, often patentable, products and near continual development of faster, more efficient production machinery created a challenging market for competitors.

Among the bedding components growing in popularity were the Superlastic® innerspring units, generations of innerspring products spawned from

Mira-Coil®, the LOK-Fast® grid and modules for box springs, and the Semi-Flex® box spring. These latter two were derivations of the popular Lectro-LOK® unit.[21]

Malcolm Marcus joined Leggett & Platt when the company acquired 50-percent equity of Globe Spring in 1977. He recalled the impact of the Semi-Flex® unit:

The Semi-Flex® product revolutionized the box spring industry in North America. It was a one-piece, welded grid top that was a wonderful product and allowed the bedding people to save a lot of money because there was only one piece that they had to deal with rather than three or four different parts that they had to assemble. So this saved the bedding people a fortune. It was a wonderful product, still in existence today.[22]

Above, center, and right: Leggett & Platt's extensive wire capabilities allow it to draw wire to suit any client's need. Galvanized wire, for example, is produced by the wire group and used for a wide variety of applications.

Looking Up

Over the course of 1992, the company's profit margins and earnings improved substantially. Net sales increased by 8 percent to $1.2 billion, and the company's return on average equity increased from 12.4 percent to 14.5 percent. Although profit margins were still below expectations, the company's long-term debt-to-capitalization ratio was down to 18 percent, and it had no short-term debt outstanding at the end of 1991 or 1992.[23]

The turnaround was attributed to four key factors: improved operating efficiencies as sales and production volumes increased, constant attention to costs after the restructuring in the previous year, lowered debt and interest rates, and a decline in bad debt expense as economic conditions improved.[24]

Midway through 1992, Leggett declared a 2-for-1 stock split, issuing shareholders one additional share of stock for each share already owned.[25] The company was again favorably ranked in *FORTUNE®* magazine's list of "America's Most Admired Companies."[26]

The company made two major acquisitions in 1993 by forming a merger agreement with the Hanes Holding Company and its subsidiary, VWR Textiles and Supplies.[27]

Hanes was based in Winston-Salem, North Carolina, and operated three facilities. The Hanes Converting Company in Conover, North Carolina, was a converter and distributor of woven and non-woven industrial fabrics used by bedding and home furnishings manufacturers to make seat decking, dust covers, insulators, and lining materials. The Hanes Fabrics Company in Hackensack, New Jersey, was a converter of woven, non-fashion fabrics used as drapery lining and quilt backing. The Hanes Dye & Finishing Company in Winston-Salem was one of the nation's largest commission dye finishers of industrial fabrics for home furnishings and apparel. (The apparel fabrics were primarily used to make pockets and waistband linings.) Together, these three operations generated annual sales of about $150 million.[28]

VWR Textiles and Supplies of Hickory, North Carolina, was a converter and distributor of woven and non-woven industrial fabrics for bedding and furniture manufacturers. It generated annual sales of about $70 million.[29]

In the third quarter of 1993, Leggett & Platt acquired Armco Steel's interest in the wire mills the two companies had jointly owned for 24 years.[30]

Harry Cornell said: "Leggett's purchase of Armco's interest will allow Leggett greater flexibility in growing our wire-drawing business. ... This association is being amicably brought to a close as a part of Armco's announced strategy of concentrating on specialty steel and prudently scheduling divestment of non-strategic assets."[31]

By year's end, Leggett & Platt employee–partners saw their company's net sales increase by 16 percent, while earnings rose 27 percent to $2.09 per share. In charting its 10-year growth rate, from 1983 to 1993, the company reported average growth of annualized net sales, earnings, and dividends of 14.6 percent, 14.8 percent, and 15.3 percent, respectively.[32]

International Expansion

Some 16,000 people throughout the United States and Canada were considered Leggett & Platt employee–partners by the end of 1994. That year, the company completed several more acquisitions and increased its product lineup.[33]

In April, Leggett & Platt purchased Vantage Industries of Atlanta, Georgia, which manufactured non-skid pads used primarily to hold area rugs in place. In June, it acquired U.S. Wire Tie Systems of Woodridge, Illinois, which sold galvanized wire and bale tie machinery and parts, primarily to customers who compacted, baled, and recycled solid waste. It also purchased the Pullmaflex group, a leading manufacturer of wire grid, seating suspension systems, and lumbar supports for the furnishings and automotive industries in Europe. This acquisition was a perfect fit with the company's Flex-O-Lators division, which was the leading producer of

equivalent components in America. Pullmaflex expanded Leggett & Platt's interests well into the European market through its plants in Belgium, Great Britain, and Sweden, and produced annual sales of approximately $20 million.[34]

Also in 1994, Leggett & Platt formed a joint venture with a company in Mexico to produce innersprings there. This brought Leggett into Mexico's bedding market. Today, the company operates two spring plants in Mexico, supplying the country's industry with innerspring and box spring components.[35]

In the fall of that year, Leggett & Platt added two businesses to its Masterack division: Talbot Industries of Neosho, Missouri, and Southeastern Manufacturing Company (SEMCO) of Ocala, Florida. Talbot fabricated display racks for items such as snack foods and bakery goods, and also produced commercial fixtures and formed wire products for

Left: In the 1990s, Leggett & Platt's aluminum group became North America's leading independent supplier of non-automotive die castings. This small gasoline engine component is a good example of the group's capabilities.

Center: The Leggett & Platt aluminum group also produced housings for highway lighting and other outdoor light fixtures.

Right: In the mid-1990s, Leggett & Platt made its largest acquisition to date with the purchase of Pace Industries, a Fayetteville, Arkansas, company with plants in seven U.S. states and Mexico, and sales approaching $250 million. The acquisition doubled Leggett & Platt's capabilities in engineered aluminum die-cast components, such as the engine casing below.

industrial applications. SEMCO specialized in manufacturing and marketing metal shelving, displays, and commercial furnishings. When acquired, Talbot generated $40 million in annual sales, and SEMCO generated $15 million.

The largest acquisition of 1994 was Super Sagless Corporation of Tupelo, Mississippi. The company was a major producer of furniture components such as recliner chair hardware, sofa sleeper mechanisms, and related motion hardware, as well as fabricated wire and metal products for the furnishings industry. Super Sagless produced annual sales of more than $70 million.[36]

Above: Talbot Industries of Neosho, Missouri, a 1994 acquisition, was a fabricator of displays for snack food, bakery items, and other store products.

Right: Leggett & Platt's largest 1994 acquisition was the Super Sagless Corporation of Tupelo, Mississippi, which complemented Leggett & Platt's production of furniture components and systems, such as recliner chair hardware, sofa sleeper mechanisms, and related motion hardware.

As Leggett & Platt continued to grow and acquire new operations, it remained committed to providing excellent customer service. Eloise Nash served as one of Leggett's finest customer service teachers, conducting seminars for employees throughout the country. She joined the company in 1951, working as a customer service representative in the sales department, and eventually became a company officer and Leggett's first female vice president. Eloise said:

[In the beginning], I was a troubleshooter. At that time, [I was] taking care of some of the national accounts. ... I even scheduled the trucks. But if something else needed to be done, and if you had the time to do it, you did it. ...

But it's not always just doing what [the customers] want. ... [It's also] doing what you tell them that you're going to do. ... Once you have proved yourself to them, that you are going to do those things, they don't worry about giving you the orders. ...

I taught customer service seminars all over the United States, and that's one of the things that I stressed so much. You know that customer, and you take care of that customer. You need to know his wife's name. You need to know how many kids he's got and even his dog's name. ... Of course, [a customer may] say, "Well, my wife's been sick" or something, and I'd always make a little note on

ARTISTIC SPIRITS

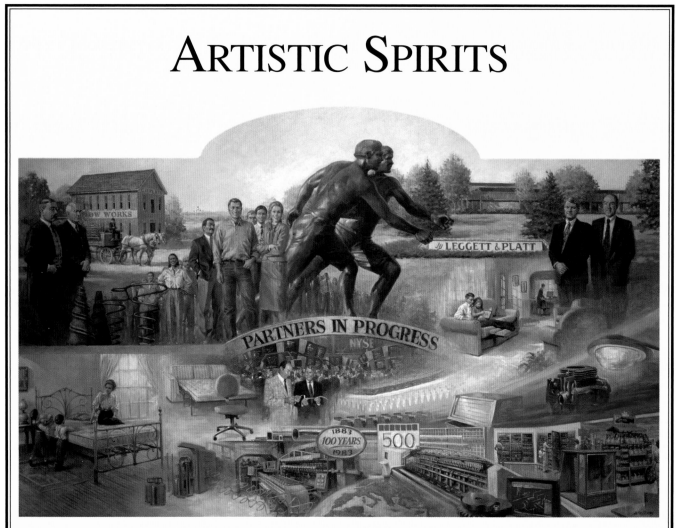

FOR YEARS, HARRY CORNELL, JR., AND FELIX Wright have enjoyed and collected fine art, especially works depicting nature and the American West. Many of these original oil and watercolor paintings, pastels, and bronze sculptures grace the facility and grounds of Leggett & Platt's corporate headquarters.

Among the oil paintings are several works by Andy Thomas, an accomplished professional artist and a former 16-year Leggett & Platt employee and director of marketing services. Andy's carefully researched, action-filled paintings of events in American history have been commissioned and acquired by state and national parks around the country. He has also produced several vivid murals depicting major events in Leggett's history. In addition, Leggett &

An updated version of the company's historical mural, painted by Andy Thomas, reflects many important people and events that have made a significant impact on the history of Leggett & Platt. *(Printed by permission, courtesy of Andy Thomas.)*

Platt is fortunate to own and display a dozen or more of his earlier paintings.[1]

Everette Wyatt, an artist and former manager of engineering for Leggett's wire division, sculpted Partners in Progress®. This cast bronze statue depicts two individuals pulling together to accomplish a task, representing Leggett's spirit of teamwork.

Another of Everette's widely admired works is the image of Reverend Asbury, a circuit-

Right: Everette Wyatt, an artist and former manager of engineering for Leggett & Platt's wire division, is shown holding one of his bronze sculptures, "Tsali." He also sculpted the life-size Partners in Progress® statue that stands in front of Leggett & Platt's corporate offices.

Inset: One of Everette Wyatt's famous works is the statue of Reverend Francis Asbury, a circuit-riding Methodist minister, which he sculpted for Asbury College in Wilmore, Kentucky.

Below left: Marcia Cooper (standing) and Libby Peck have each worked faithfully as administrative assistants to Leggett & Platt's executive team for more than 30 years. They are dedicated "artists," especially skilled at working with others. The painting behind them, "Texas Hill Country" by William Slaughter, is a favorite of employees and visitors.

Below right: Artist Andy Thomas, a former 16-year Leggett & Platt employee–partner, stands next to one of his paintings titled "Retribution Party," which hangs in a hallway at Leggett & Platt's corporate offices in Carthage. *(Printed by permission, courtesy of Andy Thomas.)*

The art at Leggett & Platt is intended as more than decoration—it's meant to rouse the artistic spirit that Harry Cornell and Felix Wright encouraged in others. In essence, many Leggett & Platt partners are seen as "artists." From accountants and engineers to production workers and corporate employees, each individual works diligently to delicately sculpt Leggett into a successful company that will endure for many generations to come.

riding Methodist minister, which he sculpted for Asbury College. A smaller version of that sculpture was displayed in the Oval Office during Ronald Reagan's administration.[2]

that, and the next time I talked to him, I'd always check my notes to make sure, and I'd say, "How's Sue getting along?" or something like it. ... People appreciate things like that. I didn't do that just for the business standpoint. ... But I was interested in their family, too, because I had grown to like them as friends.[37]

According to Nash, servicing competitive customers such as Sealy and Serta was both fun and challenging. As the company grew internationally, gaining and retaining market share in unfamiliar and competitive new regions presented even greater challenges.

By the end of 1994, Leggett & Platt succeeded in raising its net sales 22 percent and its earnings per share 33 percent—both record figures. The company's shareholders had now enjoyed 24 straight years of dividend increases.[38]

Increased Diversification

Leggett acquired seven companies in 1995, primarily manufacturers and distributors of components to the furniture industry.[39] During the year, sales in the company's office, institutional, and commercial furnishings markets grew, while residential furniture sales softened due to weakening retail sales. After three consecutive years of above-average growth, demand for bedding products outpaced demand for other residential furniture, although both markets saw a slowdown at year's end.[40]

Over the years, Leggett & Platt has attempted to describe itself in an understandable manner that allows room for it to grow. By the mid-1990s, the company's leaders found that they had grown beyond the company's reliable and well-known reputation as a provider of components to the furnishings industry. The company was headed toward the expansion of its aluminum die-casting operations, fixture and display business, and other operations. In company and investor publications, management began to present the company in terms that would be better suited for a more diversified enterprise. Thus, Leggett & Platt began to describe itself publicly as a company that engineered products to create value, building on its considerable strengths in people, financial flexibility, technology, and market franchise, and on its unique network of manufacturing and distribution facilities.[41]

Center: With the 1994 acquisition of the Southeastern Manufacturing Company (SEMCO) of Ocala, Florida, Leggett & Platt expanded its ability to serve customers with finished products for their metal shelving, display, and furnishings needs.

Below (left and right): Leggett & Platt's finished products are engineered to complement its other products. For customers ranging from retailers and resellers to dealers and distributors, Leggett & Platt makes point-of-purchase displays, commercial shelving, and fixtures.

Right: Executive management team members (left to right): Michael Glauber, senior vice president of finance and administration; David Haffner, executive vice president; and Robert Jefferies, senior vice president of mergers, acquisitions, and strategic planning.

Below: Herbert C. Casteel served as a member of Leggett & Platt's board of directors from 1960 to 1995. He was an advisory member from 1995 to 2001.

Partners in Progress

Everette Wyatt, a sculptor and longtime Leggett employee, was challenged by the company's leaders to create a work of art depicting Leggett's spirit of partnership. He fashioned Partners in Progress®, a small sculpture of two individuals pulling together to accomplish a task. In 1995, the company commissioned Everette to render a larger-than-life version to be displayed at the corporate headquarters. In May of that year, the handsome cast bronze sculpture was placed in a special garden near the office's main entrance. As part of the dedication ceremony, longtime board member, Herbert Casteel, said:

> *Everette Wyatt, the artist who designed and hand-crafted this beautiful sculpture, well understood the spirit of partnership that makes Leggett & Platt such an outstanding company, and he did a superb job of capturing this spirit in bronze. In Everette's words, "It makes no never-mind what it is these ol' boys are doin'. Point is, they're pullin' together to get it done."*
>
> *The thousands of men and women who are Leggett & Platt bring to this company a wide variety of talents and a great range of abilities. Yet throughout this company there is a spirit of partnership, an attitude of mutual respect, a cooperative effort toward common goals. People count at Leggett & Platt, and therein lies the secret of our success.*[42]

Harry Cornell, Jr., concluded the dedication ceremony with these words:

> *We extend our gratitude and dedicate this sculpture to every Leggett*

> *partner ... to those who lived before us, are with us now, and to those who will be in future generations ... the people of Leggett & Platt who are our greatest asset and share a special partnership spirit.*[43]

In the late summer of 1995, Leggett & Platt announced a 2-for-1 stock split and increased the quarterly dividend for pre-split shares to $0.20 per share, a 25 percent increase over the previous year's dividend.[44]

At year's end, the company announced an 11 percent increase in sales, a 14 percent increase in earnings, and a 23 percent increase in cash dividends.[45] Approximately 75 percent of the sales and earnings growth had come from acquisitions.[46] In its 29 years as a public company, Leggett & Platt's sales had grown from $13 million to $2.06 billion, and its net earnings had increased from $351,000 to $134.9 million.[47]

Still Room to Grow

In 1996, Leggett employed approximately 21,000 people in facilities throughout the world.[48] Part of that figure came with the company's largest acquisition to date—Pace Industries, a Fayetteville, Arkansas, company with plants in seven U.S. states and Mexico, and with sales approaching $250 million.[49] Like Leggett & Platt, Pace was a leader in engineered aluminum die-cast components, and the acquisition doubled Leggett & Platt's business in this area.[50] As a result of the merger, Leggett & Platt began to produce aluminum

FELIX E. WRIGHT

CEO, 1999 TO 2006

WHEN FELIX WRIGHT SPEAKS TO LEGGETT'S EMployee–partners about going the extra mile for customers, he isn't talking about an abstract idea. Wright joined the company in 1959 in customer service at the Ennis, Texas, operations. To paraphrase Felix's words, here is a description of his initial duties:

> *My job was to load a truck and deliver products to our customers in the Dallas area. If one of the customers wasn't paying his bills, it was my job to pick up a check and bring it back with me.*
>
> *When I got back to the plant, I'd check to see which customers had called and who I needed to call back. ... Once that work was finished, I'd start loading again for the next day.*
>
> *Sometimes, pretty late in the afternoon, a customer would call and tell me they needed something and couldn't wait until tomorrow. So, I'd pull a few things off the back of the truck, load up what they wanted, and make a run back to Dallas. Those days I got home pretty late.*
>
> *We're always willing to go that extra mile for the customers, and we expect that same kind of performance from our people today. Going the extra mile has never been more important.*[1]

Felix was born and raised near Ennis, Texas, where he attended high school. After graduating, he earned a bachelor's degree in business from East Texas State University in 1958 before accepting a job with Leggett & Platt.[2]

In 1961, Wright was sent from Ennis to manage a new facility in Phoenix, Arizona. While there, he was promoted to general manager of sales and marketing west of the Rockies, a position he held until 1967.[3]

That year, Wright was appointed vice president and general manager of operations at Winchester, Kentucky, where he relocated. Wright was also entrusted with the responsibility of creating and building Leggett & Platt's Eastern division. He successfully led the Eastern operations, built relationships with potential acquisition partners, completed acquisitions, and integrated them into the newly formed division.

In 1975, Wright was promoted to senior vice president and group manager of bedding components, and relocated to Carthage, Missouri. A year later, he received another promotion, assumed responsibilities for additional operations, and was asked to guide Leggett's research and development of new products.[4]

By 1979, Wright was executive vice president and chief operating officer. In those capacities, he directed the company's recently restructured operating management that included multiple groups, led by corporate vice presidents who reported to him. In May 1985, he became president and continued as chief operating officer. In May 1999, Wright succeeded Harry Cornell, Jr., as CEO and also became vice chairman of the board of directors. In 2002, he was elected chairman of the board, retaining his other responsibilities. Then, upon David Haffner's promotion to CEO in 2006, Wright continued his service as chairman of the board until May 2008.[5]

A year before he became the chief executive, in an interview in Leggett's Management Information

Bulletin, Wright expressed an eagerness to perpetuate the company's culture in his upcoming job and took the time to describe that culture. He prepared a list of 14 statements (shown below) that began with the importance of honest, ethical behavior and outstanding customer service. The list ended with the value of long-term relationships with partners, customers, and shareholders. About Leggett's culture, Wright appropriately said, "We can put a description of our culture in writing, but that won't ensure it continues. It is something which has to be observable ... our

managers have to live it, demonstrate it, and encourage it in others."[6]

The transition in leadership from Harry Cornell, Jr., to Felix Wright was carefully planned and smoothly completed. Wright became only the second chief executive in 40 years.

"I never set out in my career to be the CEO of this company," he said. "My father always taught me, whatever you try to do, you try to do to the best of your ability with the God-given talents that you have. That's what I attempted to do every day I worked at Leggett."[7]

LEGGETT CULTURE—ACCORDING TO WRIGHT

1. *We are ethical business people. Illegal, immoral, or unethical behavior is unwelcome. We value honesty.*

2. *We are customer service zealots. We go the extra mile for our customers. Each of us, in every job, is expected to do our very best to ensure our customer will be pleased and want to buy from us again and again.*

3. *We sincerely care about our partners and the world we live in. We care about safety and the environment.*

4. *We desire an entrepreneurial spirit in our operations. Each operation is a separate profit center to encourage this spirit.*

5. *We strongly prefer doing a job correctly, the first time.*

6. *We stress good strategic direction and an intense focus on details.*

7. *We are glad to share the company's history and our business strategy with all our employee–partners. It is difficult to feel affiliated with a business if you don't know where it has been and where it is going.*

8. *We are discontent with the status quo. We do not believe we are ever as good as we are going to be. We want to continuously improve every product, service, and process in our business.*

9. *We encourage employees to become shareholders. Partners don't have to be*

shareholders to take personal responsibility for their work and the company's success ... to act like owners ... but it helps.

10. *We can't prosper and grow without having a continual flow of new ideas, improved products, and machinery. Research and development is vital, but we'd like everyone to contribute to the flow of ideas. One of our unique strengths has been our ability to provide proprietary products for our customers—to give them something unique or special.*

11. *Almost everything we buy and use can be bought and delivered for less than the asking price. We must shop, compare, and ask for a better deal. We want the best for less, always.*

12. *We dislike bureaucracy and playing politics ... avoid both. We value genuine friendliness and concern for others, and we like to laugh.*

13. *We will always outwork our competition. We willingly work long hours ... but we also "work smart."*

14. *We value long-term relationships. We like long-term partners, long-term customers, long-term suppliers, and long-term shareholders. These relationships add joy to our work lives.*[8]

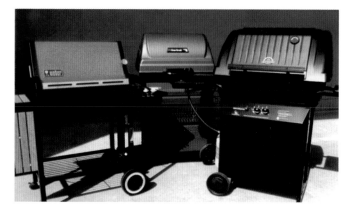

components for gas barbecue grills, motorcycles, small- to mid-sized gasoline engines, clean-room floorings for silicon chip factories, and other commercial and consumer products. The deal also brought with it several tool and die operations serving the castings industry; these businesses were further vertically integrated into Leggett & Platt's operations.[51]

The Pace facilities included a plant in Mexico that operated under a joint venture with Emerson Electric, a major consumer of aluminum die castings used in the production of electric motors and many other electrical tools and small appliances.[52]

Daniel R. Hebert, senior vice president and head of the aluminum group, who came to Leggett & Platt with Pace, explained the impact of the acquisition:

Pace, at that time, had grown significantly, starting as about an $8 million business in the late 1970s; by the mid-1990s, they had grown that to $130 or $140 million. It had significant growth potential in the future, but lacked the capital. That was one of the reasons, the main driving reason, for seeking additional infusion of capital, either through an IPO or through a partnership with someone like Leggett. So

Above: The Pace Industries acquisition of 1996 complemented the barbecue grill–producing capabilities of Leggett & Platt's EST division.

Right: Daniel R. Hebert joined Leggett & Platt in 1996 as corporate vice president at Pace Industries, later called the Aluminum Products segment. He was appointed senior vice president of Leggett & Platt and head of the aluminum group in 2002.

Leggett's infusion of capital and its very strong balance sheet have been significant factors in our ability to grow the casting business.[53]

The acquisition of two related companies, Excell Store Fixtures and Slot All Limited in Toronto, Canada, significantly expanded Leggett & Platt's commercial fixture and display business. These companies—expected to add about $50 million to Leggett & Platt's annual sales—produced and sold custom-designed metal and wood display cases, shelving, counters, and other fixtures. Wooden bookshelves for Barnes & Noble were an increasingly important portion of Excell's production.[54]

In October 1996, Leggett & Platt acquired the Steadley Company of Carthage, a longtime competitor in bedding components. Like Leggett & Platt, Steadley had been founded as a privately owned company in Carthage around the turn of the 20th century. Both companies began as manufacturers of steel coil springs.[55]

When acquired, Steadley was a producer of springs and other components for furniture and bedding manufacturers, and had seven manufacturing and distribution facilities and 800 employees in Missouri, Texas, Florida, North Carolina, Tennessee, and California.[56]

The Steadley acquisition followed the settlement of a lawsuit that Leggett & Platt filed against Swiss-owned Spühl AG and that Steadley had joined. The suit alleged that Spühl breached a contract with Leggett & Platt by selling to Steadley certain inner-spring manufacturing equipment that Spühl had contracted to sell exclusively to Leggett & Platt.[57]

Although the suit caused some discomfort at the time, Ernest Jett, senior vice president, general counsel, and secretary, explained the company's growing need to protect its interests:

Intellectual property is an area that has become increasingly important to Leggett & Platt. ... Over a period of time, it became more and more evident that our company was not only going to be the low-cost producer, but we also found that we were making our margins on products that could not be easily duplicated—products that had IP protection. So gradually, IP became more and more important.[58]

A federal judge in Kansas City mediated a settlement of the lawsuit. Leggett's representatives at the mediation suggested one way to settle the matter might be for Leggett to buy Steadley (that way the machinery promised exclusively to Leggett would soon be in Leggett's ownership). The judge included that option in the settlement arrangements, and Leggett proceeded to buy Steadley. A year after that, Leggett also bought Spühl.[59]

In the news release announcing the Steadley acquisition, the company stated:

Management of both companies has told employees and customers that they intend to make the integration of facilities and operations as smooth as possible. Management further stressed their beliefs that the acquisition should result in improved customer service, production, and distribution efficiencies, and attractive opportunities for long-term growth of the combined businesses.[60]

Leggett & Platt made a dozen acquisitions in 1996, including the November purchase of Latrobe Plastic Company and Airo Die Castings, two Loyalhanna, Pennsylvania, die-casting firms specializing in components for telecommunications and consumer electronics equipment. At that time, a growing trend toward outsourcing by makers and users of

die-cast components was affecting the market. The Latrobe/Airo acquisition allowed Leggett & Platt to capitalize on this trend, as well as to expand its die-casting product line.[61]

Other acquisitions during the year included the purchase of two divisions of A. J. Gerrard and Company of Des Plaines, Illinois, a producer and seller of specialty wire products; Cameo Fibers, Inc., of Conover, North Carolina, a maker of cushioning materials; Oconto Metal Finishing, Inc., of Oconto, Wisconsin, a finisher of cast aluminum products; and Fairmont and Pacific Fairmont Corporations of Chicago and San Diego, respectively, both in the carpet underlay business.[62]

International expansion continued, as well, with the acquisition of Gateway Holding, Ltd., of Essex, England, a manufacturer of mattress finishing and conveyor equipment, and Les Bois Blanchet, Inc., of Quebec, Canada, a specialty lumber manufacturer. Additionally, Leggett & Platt continued to expand its presence in Mexico, opening bedding component manufacturing facilities in Guadalajara and Mexicali.[63]

Stepping It Up

For 1997, Leggett & Platt reported double-digit growth in both sales and earnings, and annualized sales approached $3 billion.[64]

Among its acquisitions that year was Rodgers-Wade Manufacturing Company of Paris, Texas, a firm that manufactured and marketed custom and semi-custom laminated wood display cases, shelving, and storage fixtures for video stores and retail outlets. Leggett & Platt also acquired Amco Corporation of Chicago, a manufacturer of high-end, customized shelving and storage fixtures for food service, material handling, and office use.[65]

In 1997 and through the first 10 weeks of 1998, Leggett & Platt acquired 20 businesses.[66] The company added nine businesses to its

Above: Ernest C. Jett joined Leggett & Platt in 1979 as the company's assistant general counsel. Jett added to his duties in the legal department over the years, working his way to company vice president in 1995. Today, Jett serves Leggett as a senior vice president, general counsel, and secretary.

Right: With the 1999 acquisition of Nagle Industries, Inc., came automotive cable manufacturing capabilities.

THE STUDENT LEARNER PROGRAM

LEGGETT & PLATT'S STUDENT LEARNER PROGRAM IS A fine example of the company's positive involvement with the community. Leggett formed this partnership with the Carthage public school system in July 1999 to help previously underperforming sophomores, juniors, and seniors complete their high school education while learning valuable skills that could be readily applied in the workforce.

In addition to Precision Machining courses at the Carthage Technical Center, students receive a wealth of hands-on training in disciplines such as pneumatics and hydraulics; basic power mechanics; stick, metal inert gas (MIG), and gas welding; basic electrical skills (residential, electronics, and industrial); blueprint reading and home maintenance; and computer maintenance.

Although the curriculum emphasizes mechanical training, the program's primary goal is to encourage students to complete their high school education successfully. For this reason, each student learner is provided with a Leggett & Platt mentor. Grades and attendance are monitored, and tutoring is available with an honors student hired by the company.

The application process is rigorous enough to ensure that the students who are selected have a strong desire to participate despite their less-than-perfect credentials. Applicants must complete the freshman-level Engineering Technology course at Carthage High School and obtain a nomination from the school. Nominees are then required to write an essay describing why they want to join the program, submit a Leggett & Platt job application, and participate in an interview with the selection committee. In previous years, as many as 30 applicants have been nominated; however, no more than 13 students are selected and welcomed into the program each year.

Tom Wells, Sr., former vice president of machinery and technology, created the program, through which he tangibly expressed his Christian faith and abiding concern for others. Some of the Student Learner training has taken place at Leggett's Zapletal Education and Development Center (ZED Center), which, at Wells' suggestion, was named in honor of longtime employee–partner and exceptionally talented engineer Henry Zapletal.

The Leggett & Platt Student Learner Program is unique in that participants are actual company employees. Students work in Leggett's Carthage-area locations, including Machine Products, Porter International, Flex-O-Lators, and the IDEA Center. They are paid to learn technical and life skills, which allow them to focus on the objectives of the program without needing to be employed at other part-time jobs.

The program has earned recognition at both state and national levels. In 2000, Leggett & Platt's machine products division was recognized as the "Missouri Industry of the Year," largely because of its commitment to enriching the community's youth and families through the Student Learner

---

fixture and display division, seven of which were located in the United States and two in Canada.[67] Three businesses based in the United States joined Leggett & Platt's aluminum die-castings operations that year. And, lastly, in materials and technology, the company acquired eight businesses: six in the United States, one in England, and one in Switzerland. The latter of these was Spühl AG, acquired as part of the arbitration of the patent lawsuit settled a year earlier.[68]

Together, these companies expanded Leggett & Platt's annualized sales by $560 million, sending revenues over the $3 billion mark.[69]

At that time, Robert Jefferies, senior vice president of mergers, acquisitions, and strategic planning,

Left: Junior William Guerra adjusts the mill for a new setup for his nut and bolt machining project.

Center: In 1999, Vern Mason (left), Gared Fleishman (standing), and David Boatright successfully completed the Student Learner Program. All three continued to work for the company after graduation.

Right: Sophomore Danely Flores turns down a metal shaft as part of her plumb bob project on a metal lathe.

Program.[1] The following year, the program earned Leggett & Platt Machine Products the "Exemplary Worksite Learning" award from the National Tech Prep Network.[2] In 2003, the program received the prestigious "Friends of Education" award from the Southwest Center for Educational Excellence (a consortium of more than 40 schools in Southwest Missouri).

Individually, students have put their learning to the test in competitions organized by SkillsUSA, a partnership of students, teachers, and industry working to ensure a skilled U.S. workforce. Students have performed well at the state-level competitions and have often placed among the top 10 nationally. All these collective and individual achievements are very satisfying to the students and leaders, but David Rice, the program director, explained, "The greatest reward is watching students mature through our program."[3]

Sixty-seven students have graduated from the program from its inception in 1999 through 2008, and Leggett & Platt has hired more than 70 percent of the graduates as full-time employees. Vern Mason, who completed the Student Learner Program in 1999, was named Leggett & Platt Machine Products "Employee of the Year" for 2006. Another 1999 program graduate, Chance Newman, operated the Student Learner Shop for several months in the absence of the shop supervisor. Newman was recently named the Machine Products "Employee of the Year" for 2007. Lastly, another recent graduate from the Student Learner Program, John Burns, went to work after graduation for Leggett & Platt's Porter International facility. He has done an outstanding job, and in 2007, Burns was named "Employee of the Year" at Porter.[4]

Some program graduates choose to attend college or to pursue job opportunities elsewhere. Although their career choices differ, the program provides all student learners with practical knowledge, skills, and work experience that will help them to succeed and strengthen their communities.

and Michael Glauber, senior vice president of finance and administration, were deeply involved in the company's extraordinary acquisition program. A discussion between them describes their experiences:

Jefferies: *The due diligence ... was more of a nuts and bolts thing that was not too difficult to deal with.*

The only difficulty was that sometimes we would have five and six and seven of these going on at once, and we were very thinly staffed at all levels, and it was more of a time constraint rather than a proficiency constraint or an expertise constraint. How long does it take to become profitable? That varied. One of the things I'm proud of is that while we wanted to become profitable quickly, Harry and his team were very long-range oriented and were prepared to be patient, and we bought things that we knew weren't going to contribute probably as quickly as we would have liked. ...

Glauber: *Most of our acquisitions were accretive the first year.*

Jefferies: *Particularly in springs. There were greater synergies.*

Glauber: *We paid for some of the synergies that we envisioned, particularly in innersprings, because we knew what we could do with them when we acquired them. I remember I was always shaking my head at Harry paying some of the prices, but they were very good acquisitions.*

Jefferies: *We paid based on intuition as well as financial models.*

Glauber: *Yes, to see what some of those things could do for us; and of course, Harry had the insight. Knew where he wanted to go in a lot of those cases.*

Jefferies: *The irony over the years is that some of the things that I thought going in were very expensive turned out to be dirt cheap, and some of the things I thought were dirt cheap turned out to be very expensive. When you do 200 or 300 of these, you just don't always know.*[70]

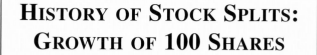

HISTORY OF STOCK SPLITS: GROWTH OF 100 SHARES

MARCH 1967	IPO	100 SHARES
MAY 1969	5-FOR-3	167 SHARES
JANUARY 1973	3-FOR-2	250 SHARES
SEPTEMBER 1978	3-FOR-2	375 SHARES
AUGUST 1983	2-FOR-1	750 SHARES
MARCH 1986	3-FOR-2	1,125 SHARES
JUNE 1992	2-FOR-1	2,250 SHARES
SEPTEMBER 1995	2-FOR-1	4,500 SHARES
JUNE 1998	2-FOR-1	9,000 SHARES

That year, on the *FORTUNE*® list of "America's Most Admired Companies," Leggett & Platt ranked 48th—in the top 11 percent—of 431 companies in American industry.[71]

Ending an Era

Early in 1998, as part of a carefully planned succession, Harry Cornell, Jr., announced that he would retire as CEO in May 1999, although he would continue to serve as chairman of the board of directors. Felix Wright would become the new CEO; he would, however, continue to serve as president and chief operating officer until May 1999.[72]

In a special message released in 1998, Harry announced his successor with great pleasure: "Felix's excellent performance, coupled with his talent, experience, and a strong management team, has led us to a seamless transition point, naturally and with great confidence."[73] As part of the announcement, Harry anticipated that

A formidable team was formed in 1999, when Felix E. Wright (center) moved to the position of CEO as Harry M. Cornell, Jr. (left), retired from the post, although he remained Leggett & Platt's chairman of the board. David S. Haffner (right) advanced to executive vice president and chief operating officer.

David Haffner, executive vice president, would succeed Wright as chief operating officer. Haffner, who had joined Leggett & Platt in 1983, was already responsible for more than 75 percent of the company's operations.[74]

Before the leadership transition took place, John Hale, senior vice president of human resources, interviewed Wright for Leggett's internal publication, the Management Information Bulletin (MIB). Hale recalls:

John Hale began his Leggett & Platt career in 1979 as manager of employment and training. For several years, he was also the manager of employee benefits. Beginning in 1987, Hale became the head of human resources and was made an officer of the company in 1995. He is currently the senior vice president of human resources. During his 29 years with the company, John has helped hire, train, and assimilate many of Leggett's employees, and has served as the de facto company historian and custodian of the culture.

In 1998, when Harry was passing the [CEO] baton to Felix, Felix said he was looking forward to preserving the company's culture. ... Frankly, I was a little uncertain how this would be accomplished. ... So I asked Felix how, given that we're buying 10 or 20 businesses a year, he was planning to preserve this culture? ... He came in on Monday with a piece of notebook paper on which he had written a "baker's dozen" worth of items ... and we still review those items with every one of our new employees at the corporate office.[75]

Throughout 1998, Leggett & Platt acquired 16 businesses. The company's rank on *Fortune*® magazine's "Most Admired" list placed it in the top

Cornell's Closing Statement
Upon Retirement as CEO (1960–1999)

*L*EGGETT'S ACCOMPLISHMENTS HAVE BEEN *substantial since 1960, when at $7 million in yearly revenues, we began to build the framework for our continuing growth strategy. Did we dream then that the company would cross the $3 billion mark in annualized sales and have a total market value of more than $5 billion early in 1998? No, not specifically. However, we did foresee great opportunities to expand our business, while enhancing prospects for profitable growth and shareholder wealth. With ongoing refinements and assessments, these cornerstones of our strategy will guide us.*

Long-term shareholders, employee–partners, customers, and many of their families know of my absolute commitment to Leggett and its continued success. My personal rewards in leading our management team for nearly 40 years are immeasurable. They extend far beyond financial terms and investment returns on Leggett stock to countless business relationships and priceless personal friendships ... worldwide. It has been particularly gratifying to see so many employee–partners succeed and benefit from the financial success of the company as shareholders.

My service with Leggett will forever be an unforgettable experience for me. Leggett's long-term outlook is brighter today than ever. We have a proven strategy, substantial capital resources, and a group of employee–partners second to none ... all in place and dedicated to making it happen, day-in and day-out. Together, we will keep our expectations high and anticipate an exciting future.[1]

The Leggett & Platt board of directors in 1998 included (seated, left to right): Herbert C. Casteel (Advisory) and Alice L. Walton. Standing, left to right: R. Ted Enloe, III; Maurice E. Purnell, Jr.; Frank E. Ford, Jr. (Advisory); Alexander M. Levine; Raymond F. Bentele; Jack B. Morris (Advisory); Richard T. Fisher; Harry M. Cornell, Jr. (Chairman); Thomas A. Hays; Felix E. Wright; Bob L. Gaddy; Richard L. Pearsall; Duane W. Potter; and David S. Haffner. Robert A. Jefferies, Jr., is not pictured.

6 percent of nearly 500 major corporations. In June, Leggett & Platt announced another 2-for-1 stock split; in the 31 years following the 1967 initial public offering (IPO), one share of initial stock expanded to 90 post-split shares. Investors who held their IPO shares for those 31 years would have received a compound average growth rate of approximately 19 percent on their initial investment.[76]

Some of the most exciting news of 1998, however, was Leggett & Platt's entry into China through its agreement to produce proprietary innerspring units for bedding manufacturers in that country. Also in China, Leggett opened a facility for machinery pro-

duction and machinery parts sourcing, followed by a furniture mechanism plant.[77]

Dennis Park, senior vice president and head of the Commercial Fixturing & Components segment, recalled how the company was initially able to penetrate the Asian market:

Our initial venture into Asia was actually an acquisition that we made in the late 1990s in Australia. ... At the same time as we were looking at the Australian market, we recognized that they had long-established trading activities with the Asian market—Indonesia, Singapore, Malaysia, and just beginning in China. ...

So once we made that acquisition, it allowed us to develop customer relationships in many other Asian countries, and again, that was ultimately what allowed us to be extremely well-positioned when we were ready to take a physical presence into the Chinese market, and we already had a number of pre-established customers there.[78]

From that point forward, Leggett & Platt began actively pursuing more international opportunities with a strategy that international growth, like that achieved in North America, would be methodical and carefully planned to complement existing operations.

New Leader, International Growth

In May 1999, after nearly 40 years of leadership, Harry Cornell transferred the CEO responsibilities to Felix Wright. In parting, Harry reminded Leggett & Platt employee–partners of one of his favorite quotes that had hung in his office for many years—a saying that he had often used to guide and inspire others during his tenure: "Success is founded on a constant state of discontentment interrupted by brief periods of satisfaction on the completion of a job particularly well done."[79]

Under Wright's leadership, Leggett & Platt accelerated its acquisition program on both the domestic and international fronts, acquiring 29 companies in 1999 that specialized in residential and commercial furnishings, industrial materials, and other specialty products.[80] The foreign acquisitions took place in Australia, Brazil, China, Italy, Mexico, Spain, and the United Kingdom.[81]

At the close of market trading on October 15, 1999, Standard & Poor's added Leggett to the S&P 500 Index, one of the primary standards for measuring performance of the stock market.[82] Leggett was further honored that year as it climbed to the top 5 percent of *Fortune* ® magazine's "America's Most Admired Companies." It ranked 23rd out of 469 companies.[83]

Leggett & Platt has been rightfully admired for several reasons—its successful growth and profitability, the ethical behavior of its leaders, and its positive influence on communities. One fine example of Leggett's community involvement is its award-winning Student Learner Program, started in 1999 as a partnership with the Carthage public school system. The program has helped previously under-performing students improve their prospects for completing their high school education while acquiring technical skills, gaining job experience, and earning money as Leggett & Platt student employees.[84]

Leggett & Platt ended the millennium with another positive year of performance. The company announced net sales of $3.7 billion in 1999, up 12.1 percent over the previous year. Net earnings increased to $290.5 million, up 17.1 percent. For eight consecutive years, the company had achieved record sales and earnings, and for 29 consecutive years, it had raised dividends.[85] Leggett & Platt entered the 21st century as a thriving, confident, and profitable company.

Leggett & Platt 2004 Annual Report *Leggett & Platt*

Everyday, Everywhere.

Although its products were used in everyday activities and in every walk of life, by the new millennium, Leggett & Platt had become a regular member of the *FORTUNE®* 500 list without ever becoming a household name.

CHAPTER EIGHT

EMBRACING THE GLOBAL MARKET

2000–2008

As we go forward internationally, and as we find ways to differentiate ourselves from other competitors and grow into businesses in which we don't currently participate, we're going to need significant technical competency.

—President and CEO David S. Haffner[1]

LEGGETT & PLATT ENTERED THE NEW millennium as a time-tested, diversified, and growing enterprise. Excerpts from the company's 2000 Annual Report describe its leading market positions at that time:

- *Today we are the worldwide leading supplier of components to the bedding and furniture industries.*
- *We are the market leader in design and manufacture of a broad suite of retail store fixtures.*
- *We are the leading independent producer of components for office furniture manufacturers.*
- *Our aluminum group is the leading independent producer of non-automotive die castings in North America.*
- *We are North America's leading supplier of drawn-steel wire.*
- *We are the leading worldwide supplier of automotive seating and lumbar systems, and a leading supplier of control and power train cable systems.*
- *We have a premier global position in wire forming equipment, industrial quilting and sewing machinery, and other specialized machinery we design, patent, and manufacture.[2]*

For the first half of 2000, Leggett experienced strong sales growth that boosted the year's sales volume to a record high of $4.3 billion. During this time, the number of employees also grew substantially.[3] In January, Leggett employed approximately 31,000 people worldwide. By June, that number increased to more than 34,000.[4]

Unfortunately, consumer demand declined dramatically in the second half of the year. The company promptly responded to the decline by initiating production cutbacks at operations with decreasing sales, but the combination of fewer sales and underutilized plants amplified overhead costs and reduced profit margins. Additional factors, such as higher medical and energy expenses, also lessened the year's profits.[5]

In September, Leggett & Platt released a statement concerning the earnings decline:

Unanticipated developments in several business segments contribute to the reduced earnings. Continuing problems in the company's Aluminum

---

Leggett & Platt's IDEA Center opened in 2007 and was part of the company's renewed emphasis on research and new product development.

Felix E. Wright, president and CEO (left), and Harry M. Cornell, Jr., chairman of the board (right), were at the head of the leadership team that made some tough decisions about cutbacks and divestitures in the early years of the new millennium.

Products segment produced the largest portion of the shortfall. Both sales and margins in the Aluminum Products segment will be down significantly from last year's levels as a result of reduced demands in several product lines, plant inefficiencies, and higher raw material and energy costs. In the Commercial Furnishings segment, reduced demand for some products will result in sales that are considerably lower than anticipated. In addition, margins remain below year-earlier levels due to integration inefficiencies at some recently acquired businesses. Finally, in the Residential Furnishings segment, the company is experiencing softening demand, reduced production, and lower margins.[6]

To combat the earnings decline, Leggett implemented a four-point tactical plan. First, the company would correct operational problems in underperforming facilities. Second, operations with irreparable problems would be consolidated, closed, or sold. Third, acquisitions and capital spending would be reduced, primarily in the aluminum and commercial segments. Fourth, the company would repurchase up to 10 million shares of its stock, approximately 5 percent of the current share base.[7]

CEO Felix Wright assured the shareholders that the tactical plan only temporarily shifted the focus of the company's goals:

This is not a strategic change in our long-term growth plans. This is a tactical shift to accomplish two things. First, it gives management of underperforming operations time to devote their full attention to correcting problems, without the demands that additional acquisitions bring. Second, it frees up cash

to repurchase what we believe are extremely undervalued shares, without requiring that we significantly leverage the balance sheet. Strategically, we plan to return to our traditional level of acquisition expenditures, and the resultant top and bottom line growth, once operational performance improves.[8]

Matthew C. Flanigan joined Leggett & Platt in 1997 after a successful banking career. Before becoming a senior vice president and chief financial officer, he oversaw Leggett's office and contract furniture components operations. Flanigan described the weakened sales of these operations early in the decade, providing one example of the overall decrease in demand Leggett experienced at that time. He concluded with some positive remarks about the company's tactical plan:

In 2000, some of our markets softened. I was responsible for the office furniture components group, and from 1999 and 2000 to within about 18 months later, that market demand, as defined by shipments of office furniture, dropped 33 percent, which is unheard of in the history of that industry.

In the late 1990s, you had the dot-com activity—a lot of these exciting Internet companies went public. They were flush with IPO proceeds. One of the first things they needed to do was hire people to take their newly public companies to greatness. They needed to get the work environments that would attract talent, and it so happened that a lot of those work environments had seating that Leggett had a whole bunch of components going into.

Well, once you get to 2000–2001, that bubble burst. Not only did you have a significant contraction of demand because there weren't those companies out there anymore buying that product, but lo and behold, suddenly there weren't those people sitting in those chairs. So you put those two forces together, and you have a 33 percent drop in the business.

Now here's the good news: Dave [Haffner] and Harry [Cornell] and Felix [Wright] pulled together

Right: Matthew C. Flanigan, a former banker, joined Leggett & Platt in 1997 to oversee the company's office and contract furniture components operations; he later became senior vice president and chief financial officer.

Below left: Leggett & Platt's motion mechanisms are found in some of the finest upholstered furniture in the world today.

Center: Leggett & Platt's power lift recliner mechanism is engineered for strength and durability, offering convenience and comfort.

Below right: Using its aluminum die-casting capabilities, Leggett & Platt made jugs, or piston holders, for Harley-Davidson motorcyles.

as a team. They weren't caught terribly off-guard by what happened and were able to right-size and bring the operations to a level of equilibrium given what the market was allowing them to sell at that point in time. The company continued to make very good returns, profit margins, and returns on the assets deployed, even that very next year and the year after, well above the corporate average [despite] that drop in market demand because they had done such a good job.[9]

The tactical plan limited acquisitions in the second half of 2000,

but by year-end, Leggett had purchased 21 companies. The 2000 Annual Report refers to them as "bolt-on additions," businesses that attached easily to existing operations. New companies were added to each of Leggett & Platt's five market segments: Residential Furnishings, Commercial Furnishings, Aluminum Products, Industrial Materials, and Specialized Products.[10]

By the end of the year, net sales reached a record $4.3 billion, but earnings decreased 9.1 percent to $264.1 million. Despite this decrease, the tactical plan was already producing good results. The company increased its free cash flow to $271 million, 28 percent higher than the previous record achieved in 1999. Long-term debt was at 33 percent of total capitalization.[11]

Streamlining Operations, Searching for Opportunities

In 2001, a difficult year for the U.S. economy, Leggett & Platt continued to apply the tactical plan. It consolidated or sold 20 facilities, restructured operations, eliminated overhead, and reduced full-time–equivalent employment by 3,700. The company decreased capital spending to its lowest level in four years and acquired just 10 new businesses. These were

Success is founded on a constant state of discontentment interrupted by brief periods of satisfaction on the completion of a job particularly well done.

purchased primarily to enhance Leggett's best-performing operations.[12]

The weakened economy of that time was further stressed by the terrorist attacks of September 11, 2001. Members of the Islamic militant sect, Al Qaeda, hijacked four U.S. commercial airliners. Two were flown into the World Trade Center towers in New York; one was flown into the Pentagon in Arlington, Virginia; and the last airplane crashed in a rural field in Pennsylvania. In addition to the passengers and crew, thousands were killed in the wreckage of the Pentagon and in the collapse of the Twin Towers, as the structural supports gave way from the intense heat of the burning aircraft fuel.

Economic turmoil ensued immediately after the tragedy. All airline flights were grounded; military forces were placed on high alert; and Wall Street trading was suspended in the face of plummeting futures and falling stock prices on a global scale.

Matt Flanigan recalled the emotional impact of the attacks on the nation and the subsequent financial impact on Leggett & Platt's operations:

It struck a chord with the confidence of corporate America. ... As companies are making a lot of money, they tend to expand, hire, and need to provide office environments for additional resources. Consumer confidence in general is a big driver of whether there is demand.

So after 9/11, you had companies, with the airline industry being the most dramatic example ... [that]

suddenly did not only know where things were going, but the costs to compete had gone up, whether it was security or what have you. [So many said], "We're just not going to do any expansion. We're not going to do any hiring. We're going to lay low here for a year or so." And that's what happened to a lot of the customer base. [While the] Internet boom or bubble burst had been a major hit, with 9/11 shortly thereafter, it became a double whammy on corporate confidence, and it really caused the downturn to last all the way from 2000 into 2003.[13]

Like all U.S. businesses, Leggett & Platt experienced the trying financial effects of September 11. However, the company not only weathered the difficult downturn, but functioned remarkably well in spite of it.

In December 2001, Leggett operated 29 business units and employed 31,000 people in more than 300 facilities located in 18 different countries.[14] The more internationally focused company developed three strategies for further expansion in foreign markets. First, if one of Leggett's manufacturing customers established an operation abroad, Leggett would, at the customer's request, open a factory there to supply components.[15]

Second, Leggett & Platt would seek out opportunities for deverticalization. The company would demonstrate its ability to produce components more cost-effectively than foreign manufacturers. The prospect for deverticalization was especially strong in Europe, where bedding and furniture manufacturers produced many of their own components, much like U.S. manufacturers of the 1960s and 1970s.[16]

Third, Leggett would simply purchase or build a factory to establish a presence in a foreign market.[17]

Leggett & Platt's 2001 sales and earnings reflected the year's economic downturn. Net sales decreased 3.8 percent to $4.1 billion, and net earnings decreased 29 percent to $187.6 million.[18] Despite these decreases, the company achieved a record high cash flow, $535 million, and increased its annual dividend to shareholders for the 30th consecutive year.[19] Leggett & Platt has consistently ranked as one of the top five companies in the *FORTUNE* 500 list with regard to the number of consecutive annual dividend increases and the high rate of average compound annual dividend growth. (As of 2008, the company had increased its dividend for 37 consecutive years.)[20]

Opposite: In celebration of his 50th anniversary with Leggett & Platt in 2000, Harry M. Cornell, Jr., was presented with this oil-on-canvas mural, commissioned by Felix Wright from local artist Andy Thomas. The mural portrays Harry with his hand on a globe; directly behind him on the left is his father, Harry M. Cornell, Sr., along with his grandfather, company cofounder J. P. Leggett. Directly behind them, Harry is depicted at a much younger age in front of the Carthage, Missouri, factory where he worked as a youth (and later). The building on the upper right is the Ennis, Texas, facility, which he managed. Under that is the old corporate office in Carthage, the New York Stock Exchange, and a corner of the present corporate office. A reproduction of the Partners in Progress® bronze is shown bottom center. At the time of this writing, Harry had served Leggett & Platt in various capacities for 58 years. *(Printed by permission, courtesy of Andy Thomas.)*

In 2002, Leggett & Platt's leadership included (left to right) Karl Glassman, executive vice president of operations and president of Residential Furnishings; Felix Wright, chairman and CEO; and David Haffner, president and chief operating officer.

In 2002, Leggett & Platt completed the tactical plan. In total, the company had sold or consolidated 27 facilities and restructured other operations. It had reduced overhead, decreased full-time–equivalent employment by around 3,700, and bought back 9 million shares of company stock. Leggett trimmed capital spending to its lowest level in five years and brought working capital to its lowest level in seven years.[21]

Since the tactical plan limited acquisitions, Leggett purchased only seven more "bolt-on" businesses in 2002. They were expected to raise annual revenue by about $70 million.[22] In addition, in an important asset acquisition, the company purchased a steel mill in Sterling, Illinois, that had been closed due to bankruptcy.

New Leadership, New Direction

In May 2002, Leggett completed another long-planned succession of management. Harry Cornell, who had retired as CEO in 1999 and smoothly passed the CEO's responsibilities to Felix Wright, now also retired from his duties as chairman of the board. Cornell, who had served nearly 40 years as CEO and 21 years as chairman of the board, was appointed chairman emeritus and continued to serve as an active member of the board as well as a consultant to the company. Leggett & Platt's CEO, Felix Wright, became the company's new chairman. David Haffner was promoted to president and also remained as chief operating officer. Similarly,

Karl Glassman was appointed executive vice president of operations and remained president of the Residential Furnishings segment.[23]

On July 30, 2002, in response to the recent string of corporate and accounting scandals, the Sarbanes–Oxley Act was signed into law. It imposed stricter regulations on companies' financial practices and governance. The legislation caused relatively minor operational changes for Leggett & Platt, a company with a long history of high ethical standards. The company addressed this integral part of its culture in its 2002 Annual Report:[24]

Companies are known by the reputation their employees earn. Through the years Leggett's employee–partners have earned a reputation and set a high standard for honesty and integrity. Those are deeply held, fundamental values of our firm—tenets we will adhere to even if they somehow prove disadvantageous in the marketplace. Because of this, it distressed us last year to learn of management misdeeds perpetrated on investors by a small number of corporations. We are encouraged to see investors more closely scrutinizing all firms' accounting practices and governance policies.

Leggett shines under the light of close examination. First, our pension plans remain over-funded in the aggregate despite three years of stock market decline. Few FORTUNE® 500 firms can make that statement. We have consistently applied, and will continue to employ, conservative pension assumptions. Second, we are in compliance with all new corporate governance rules. Indeed, we were already following good governance practices and therefore found it easy to conform to the new rules. We have had a majority of independent directors on our board for several years, and all of our key board committees consist solely of independent directors. Third, we issue stock options to a broad group of employee–partners each year, and in 2003, we will begin recording those options as an expense item. In addition, a large group of

THE STERLING STEEL MILL

IN MAY 2002, LEGGETT & PLATT PURCHASED AN INACtive steel rod mill in Sterling, Illinois, from the bankrupt Northwestern Steel & Wire. Since 2003, this facility, now named Sterling Steel, has supplied at least half of the steel rod for Leggett's operations each year. Today, the mill produces in excess of 500,000 tons of rod annually using a 400-ton electric arc furnace, an eight-strand billet caster, and a single-strand rod mill.[1]

The milling process begins with scrap or by-product steel that is melted in the arc furnace and combined with other elements. The molten steel is poured through a tundish (a reservoir in the top of the mold) to form billets (semi-finished, cast products) that are rolled into rod. The rod is then shipped to Leggett & Platt's wire mills, where it's drawn into smaller dimensions, suitable for various wire products made in Leggett's plants.[2]

"Owning Sterling Steel has assured Leggett & Platt of a reliable supply of quality rod," said Joseph D. Downes, Jr., senior vice president of Leggett & Platt and head of the Industrial Materials segment. "Having a consistent source of raw materials enables our wire-drawing machines to run more efficiently, which in turn leads to higher-quality wire products. Sterling has been a great investment for the company."[3]

Left: Joseph D. Downes, Jr., has worked for Leggett & Platt's wire group in several capacities since 1980. Downes became a company vice president and head of the wire group in 1999. He was named president of the Industrial Materials segment in 2004 and became a senior vice president in 2005.

Below: These photos illustrate the process by which steel rod is produced. First, scrap or by-product steel is loaded into the electric arc furnace and melted (left). Hot molten steel is then poured through a tundish to mold billets (center), which are then rolled into rod (right). The rod is then drawn into wire at the company's wire mills.

executives collectively forfeits about $5 [million] to $7 million of cash salary each year to acquire additional stock options (through a company sponsored plan). And fourth, we have a long history of high-quality earnings, financial transparency, and conservative accounting practices. We emphasize GAAP-based [Generally Accepted Accounting

Principles] earnings, include restructuring costs as a normal part of doing business (not as non-recurring costs), have recorded only two special charges in the last 25 years (for a total of $31 million), and, in contrast to most acquisitive firms, we took no goodwill write-down for implementation of FAS [Federal Accounting Standard] 142. [25]

DAVID S. HAFFNER

CEO, 2006 TO PRESENT

ORN IN 1952 AND RAISED IN CARTHAGE, MISSOURI, David S. Haffner grew up in close proximity to Leggett & Platt. His grandfather's house was only a block from the company's Mound Street offices. As a young man, however, Haffner never intended to work for the local business.

After high school, Haffner attended Missouri Southern State University and then transferred to the University of Missouri–Columbia where he earned a degree in industrial engineering and received the Top Senior Industrial Engineering Award.

After college, Haffner's father suggested he interview with Leggett & Platt. Haffner recalled:

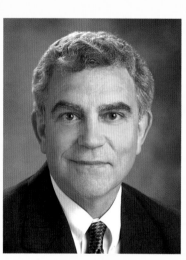

Out of respect for my father, I went for an interview with Leggett & Platt, but I had a number of good job offers pending and really couldn't imagine going to work for a very small company. I remember my interview with Frank Ford. ... He told me the company didn't have an opportunity for me. At the time, it seemed like a relief. [1]

David accepted a job as a project and design engineer for Schreiber Foods, Inc., a major dairy products company based in Green Bay, Wisconsin. The job provided the opportunity to thoroughly

apply his education and to travel. "So I had this fabulous job going all around the world, designing processing plants and systems, and working with international governments and individual companies," said Haffner. "And that's what got me to Australia and Europe and Asia and South America and all over the place. In fact, I spent quite a bit of time in the Middle East back in the 1970s." [2]

While working for Schreiber, Haffner earned a master's degree in business administration from a branch of the University of Wisconsin, and in 1977, he was promoted to director of engineering.

Due to the untimely death of his father-in-law and the deteriorating health of his own father, Haffner transferred to a Schreiber operation in Missouri where he and his wife, Connie, could be closer to family.

In 1983, Schreiber asked Haffner to return to Wisconsin to fill a senior executive position at the company's headquarters. Haffner faced a difficult decision, and Felix Wright helped him with it. Haffner recalled, "Maybe it was divine intervention." He continued:

Felix was on his way to Cassville, Missouri, to pick up some parts for one of his tractors. He had his mother, his father, and his wife

Steel Rod Mill

In 2002, with the nation still climbing out of the economic downturn, Leggett & Platt made a giant leap "backward" with the purchase of an idle rod mill and melt furnace from the former Northwestern Steel and Wire Company of Sterling, Illinois. This move into rod production further advanced the company's vertical supply strategy through backward integration, ensuring a consistent supply of quality raw material for Leggett & Platt's wire mills. When fully operational, the Sterling rod mill began generating 450,000 tons of steel rod per year, supplying roughly half of Leggett's wire mill requirements.[26]

---

with him. ... He'd read in the paper that I intended to go back to Wisconsin, and he stopped by my house to congratulate me. He told me that it disappointed him somewhat. He was pleased and excited for me personally, but it disappointed him because he thought Leggett offered an awfully good opportunity. At that time, I told him, "My friends in Green Bay don't know, but I think I'm staying in Missouri." It turned out to be one of the best decisions I've ever made.[3]

Haffner accepted a position with Leggett & Platt as a group vice president of operations. Within three years, he acquired a thorough knowledge of several Leggett businesses. Ironically, his first assignment included responsibility for the company's aluminum die-casting operations in Wisconsin, and he often traveled there.[4]

Shortly thereafter, Haffner was reassigned to learn the company's wire mill operations and was made subsequently responsible for expanding Leggett's office components business. In 1985, Haffner was appointed as vice president and officer of the company, and president of the furniture components group. In that capacity, he was responsible for all nonbedding furniture operations. With his technical background, his interests in design and development, and his administrative abilities, he mastered each position and was soon promoted.

In 1995, Haffner was elected to the board of directors. The same year, he became Leggett's executive vice president; he served in that capacity until he became president in 2002. Additionally, from 1999 to 2006, Haffner served as the company's chief operating officer. On May 10, 2006, he was promoted to CEO.[5]

Haffner discussed his responsibility to Leggett's shareholders as CEO:

We genuinely respect the expectations shareholders have, not just for the fiscal well-being and financial performance of the company, but for its integrity and culture.

There are thousands of shareholders effectively wagering that you and the team around you are going to make the right decisions. It can be very humbling. To me, it's more important than the value of the stock or stock equivalents any one of us may own.

The thousands of people who work in our plants and own a few hundred shares are banking on us to make the right decisions. It's a responsibility that can certainly keep you awake at night.[6]

Haffner also considers the continuance of Leggett's corporate culture a high priority:

Perpetuating Leggett's unique culture is a huge responsibility—something I keep high on my list of priorities.

Because of my experience in a cheese-making business, culture has a special meaning to me. In that environment, if you modify the culture, you don't get the same end result. ... As Leggett grows internationally, we'll inevitably be influenced by different governments and customs. Some changes in our culture are predictable and desirable.

On the other hand, there are elements of our culture we want to be certain to preserve—ethical business practices, great customer service, and a relatively non-political environment. ... These things are critical to our people and success.[7]

Much of the credit for this purchase went to Mike Glauber, Leggett's senior financial officer at the time. For 25 years, Glauber was a member of Leggett's wire committee, and he participated in quarterly reviews of steel rod costs in Kansas City, Missouri, home of Armco Steel. Due to his knowledge of the industry, he recognized the benefits of purchasing the Sterling facility. Felix Wright recalled:

A number of us ... said that there was one thing we didn't want to do. We didn't want to be a steel business. ... We stuck by that because it's been a roller coaster market, and obviously people can't get any kind of return on their investment. ...

[The] steel industry [had] gone through a horrendous cycle and [was] in the down cycle, and a good old company ... Northwestern Steel and Wire, couldn't make it. But they had been a totally integrated steel company making everything from 24-inch bar joist to all kinds of galvanized products to rods to anything you want to make in steel. ... They got themselves in a mess to where they couldn't stand it. The bank finally pulled their loan.

So Mike Glauber gets a big bunch of the credit for continuing to beat on my door and say, "Felix, I think there's a great opportunity here for a vertical play, not a steel play." ...

[Looking] at what happened, it's still strange when you start talking about a vertical play. ... But as things culminate, you continue to think about it, and they take it from Chapter 11 to Chapter 7. So when they take it to Chapter 7, it means it's going to be broken apart.

So, at that point, you have to go through all the environmental deals and so on. ... You can imagine our boardroom conversations about an 1879 steel mill on 200-some acres. But anyway, you get the opportunity maybe to look at a melt furnace, which is the most modern melt furnace in North America.

Left: Mike Glauber, who joined Leggett & Platt in 1969, worked his way through the ranks as controller, treasurer, and finance vice president, ultimately becoming senior vice president of finance and administration.

Center: John Reynolds, conference center coordinator at the corporate offices in Carthage, stands in front of the entrance to the Cornell Conference Center. Reynolds is a longtime employee who has worked for Leggett & Platt for more than 30 years.

Right: Karl Glassman, who has been with Leggett & Platt since 1982, added the title of executive vice president of operations to his responsibilities in 2002.

They had spent $24 million putting a melt furnace in two years before they took it into Chapter 7. So we knew what that was. The rod mill was pretty antiquated, but they were making rod that we were buying. We were a pretty good customer.

So the concept became what was okay for Leggett. What about a vertical play? What if you go in and only buy a caster, a 400-ton melt furnace, and a rod mill, and everything else goes away, and you're a vertical rod supplier of 50 percent of your needs? So that's what we were able to come to grips with and buy, and we were able to buy those assets. All the rest of the assets on the property were eventually cut up by either ourselves or other steel scrap people and run back through our furnace, and were melted into products that we would make rod for ourselves during that first 18 or 24 months.[27]

Before purchasing the mill, it was determined that the facility's energy expenses could be greatly reduced by operating the melt furnace only Friday through Sunday, when electrical costs were lower,

OSCAR "BUD" HOUGLAND

ALTHOUGH SOME COMMENTATORS CLAIM THAT LOYALTY between employees and their companies is dead, examples of such loyalty are abundant at Leggett & Platt. Consider, for example, Oscar "Bud" Hougland, who was hired January 1, 1930, and retired July 25, 2003—after more than 73 years of service.

Gene Woestman, a former general manager at Leggett's Winchester, Kentucky, facility, provided information about Bud's career, which is paraphrased below:

Oscar "Bud" Hougland began working as a laborer for Leggett & Platt in 1930, at the Louisville, Kentucky, plant, unloading the angle iron used to manufacture bedsprings. Bud was the son-in-law of Fred C. Bouser, who started with Leggett in 1903 and was one of the original superintendents of the Louisville factory. While in Kentucky, Bud also worked in the bottom wire and top bending department, ran bedspring coilers, and assembled bedsprings until 1934, when he was promoted to foreman of the assembly department. In 1938, Bud was again promoted to general foreman, a position he held until 1941.

In March 1941, Bud transferred to the Dallas, Texas, plant, working as superintendent until the plant closed in 1944. For two months after the Dallas plant closed, Bud returned to work as general manager of the Louisville plant. Then, Bud took an opportunity to move to Winchester, Kentucky, to open a bedspring factory, which he operated as general manager, all the while still holding the same position at the Louisville plant. In 1967, Bud became operations manager of the Winchester facility, a position he held for many years.[1]

Bud officially retired from Leggett & Platt in 1978, but management asked him to continue working as an advisor, which he did until he left the company in 2003. Bud said he could not imagine what life would have been like if he had stopped working. "I probably would have went nuts, or my wife would have," he said.

Saundra Snowden, the office manager in Winchester, recalled the last couple of decades of Bud's career:

We had the first retirement for Mr. Bud in 1978, but he never quit coming to work ... usually at 6 A.M., and he always had coffee made for the girls. He would go home around 2 or 3 P.M., unless there was something going on in the plant— new machinery or some type of a major problem. He continued to be productive; he did paperwork for Gene [Woestman] and was always there for good advice.[2]

In 2000, Leggett & Platt executives honored Bud Hougland for his 70 years of service to the company. Pictured left to right: Gene Woestman, former general manager of Leggett & Platt's Winchester, Kentucky, operations; Felix Wright; Bud Hougland; and Harry Cornell, Jr.

but Glauber said it was difficult to convince others that this was a good idea.

"You lower your power rates, but the disadvantages to doing that are you're going to have to realign your facilities a little more often, and that might eat up your $10 a ton savings you got over here," he said. "But we could run it three days. We could turn it on and turn it off. ... It was not an easy sell even at that point. I guarantee you it was not an easy sell. [Some people] thought we were crazy."[28]

It was finally confirmed that the furnace would produce sufficient volumes of steel if only operated Friday through Sunday. Initially, there was a concern that turning the furnace on and off every week might decrease the life span of critical parts by 50 to 60 percent, but Leggett & Platt determined by experience that the longevity of these parts would only decrease by 10 percent. This was acceptable considering the energy savings that would result from shutting down the furnace.[29]

Prior to the purchase, Leggett & Platt required the completion of successful negotiations with the mill's former labor union. The company also had to meet several Environmental Protection Agency requirements. With these issues settled, Leggett purchased the property at auction for the astonishingly low price of $5 million—a bargain considering the owners had invested an estimated $150 million in refurbishing

LOOKING TO THE EAST

WHEN LEGGETT & PLATT ENTERED THE CHINESE market in 1998, the company encountered challenges it had not previously experienced.[1]

"One thing we realized in the last couple of years is one size does not fit all," said Paul R. Hauser, senior vice president of Leggett & Platt and head of Residential Furnishings. "Asia is a different model with a different market than Europe, which is a much more mature market versus an emerging market. So you have to treat those differently in terms of your strategies."[2]

Leggett was quick to adapt its strategies in the emerging Chinese market, and by 2007, the company's holdings included 20 profit centers in China. Felix Wright summed up the strategy:

Patience. We wanted to own the majority of our Asian operations outright. We wanted to run them with Chinese nationals. We didn't want to run it with a bunch of ex-pats. ... We were very blessed to have had a great Chinese national that arrived with an acquisition, a fellow named Philip Shen.

We've tried to mitigate some of the risks, but we understand we're operating in a Communist country. We'll never mitigate all of them.

[We've also] tried to set up our operations and send the technical expertise to help train the Chinese in "lean manufacturing" and many other areas. ... We're not just throwing bodies at those operations, but we're trying to set them up, structure them, and run them in the most efficient manner possible ... thinking we could even be the low-cost producer in Asia. And once [we become] the low-cost producer in Asia, as that economy grows, we want to be able to service it, or if more of those components come back over here,

Paul R. Hauser joined Leggett & Platt in 1980 as product manager for the bedding group, of which he became president in 1999. Since then, Hauser has moved up through the ranks to become senior vice president of Leggett & Platt and head of the Residential Furnishings segment.

the property prior to the bankruptcy.[30] After buying the mill, Leggett & Platt invested an additional $20 million to improve and adapt the facility to the company's particular needs.

Concerning the success of this acquisition, Mike Glauber commented:

The Sterling mill turned out to be an absolute grand-slam home run for Leggett. Demand for rod in the market increased dramatically, and we had our own protected, high-quality supply. Not only that, but the price we paid for the mill and the low depreciation costs, in addition to the favorable energy and labor costs, helped us to be the low cost supplier downstream in the marketplace. Leggett & Platt and our customers benefited tremendously from this deal.[31]

The rod mill provided greater market leverage than any previous acquisition. "That's the best purchase that Leggett has ever made in its corporate history," said Ted Enloe, a company board member since 1969. "The scrap prices just went through the roof, but the rod prices coming out of the mill increased even more. So the spread between scrap and rod was the greatest in history. ... It was just incredible."[32]

To meet its longstanding goal of 15 percent profitable growth per year, Leggett continued to expand

---

obviously we want to make the best return on our investment.[3]

Dennis S. Park, senior vice president of Leggett & Platt and head of Commercial Fixturing & Components, discussed the difficulties of implementing U.S. business processes in some overseas facilities:

Oftentimes ... you are going into a company that really does not have a lot of formalized processes in place. They do not have operating systems that allow you to properly track the activities the way that we, as a public company, need to and want to for our shareholders. So you have to be able to bridge the position that the company was operating under with where we know we need to take the company. ... We want to do that in such a way that no one feels threatened by the additional amount of activity, but they recognize the value in it.[4]

Wright provided a major reason why Leggett would expand its Asian operations in the years to come:

We don't believe that everything is going to wind up in Asia. ... We do think that there will probably be more components that we'll make in Asia over the next five years, and that's not

Dennis S. Park, senior vice president and head of Commercial Fixturing & Components, joined Leggett & Platt in 1977. Over time, his roles at the company have included president of Home Furniture Components and president of Home Furniture and Consumer Products.

because of the labor in our product or the pressure on the cost of our product, but it is the pressure of our customer moving their product and the labor associated with it to a low-cost labor environment. ... And we have to go with him if we're going to still service the components that go into the products.[5]

Whether in Carthage, Missouri, or in plants near Shanghai, Leggett maintains and extends its ethical corporate culture. According to Park:

Regardless of where we're operating in the world ... the focus is on doing the right thing—being ethical, being focused on the customer, being focused on creating a safe work environment, and making sure our employees are treated like partners. ... We find that those conditions exist [in Leggett's operations] in all other parts of the world.[6]

Through its Saint Paul Metalcraft division in Michigan, a maker of zinc and aluminum die castings, Leggett & Platt produced components for Arctic Cat.

domestic operations, acquire businesses, and vertically integrate production (as with the rod mill) and further internationalize its operations.

In 2002, the company owned three major production plants in China. Two of these facilities manufactured innerspring units for sale within the country. The third produced machinery and sourced machine parts. Leggett & Platt was also constructing a new plant, located in Jiaxing, to manufacture furniture mechanisms.[33]

By the end of 2002, despite the continuing lackluster economy, Leggett's net sales had risen 3.8 percent to $4.3 billion, and net earnings had increased 24.3 percent to $233.1 million. The company also raised its dividend to shareholders for the 32nd consecutive year.[34]

Headed to New Heights

Refurbishments to the Sterling rod mill were completed by March 2003, and production began. The facility operated profitably in its first year, supplied half of Leggett's annual demand for steel rod, and buffered the company from the escalating costs of rod that resulted from increased worldwide demand and tight supply.[35]

The launch of the Iraq War on March 20, 2003, altered the economic and political environment of the time. The United States led a multinational coalition force into Iraq to topple the regime of Saddam Hussein. This significant war in the Middle East, however, had limited effects on the continued expansion of Leggett & Platt's businesses in Asia.

The company added several facilities in China. Early in the year, it completed the construction of its new furniture mechanisms plant in Jiaxing and purchased the assets and machinery of a local supplier. In June, Leggett acquired the Guangzhou Veihe facilities, which manufactured small electric motors used mainly in automobile seat lumbar systems, and in October, the company acquired Pangeo Industries in Changsha, which produced automobile cable, also for seat lumbar systems. By the end of the year, Leggett operated eight Chinese facilities.[36]

At home and abroad, the company purchased a total of 15 businesses in 2003.[37] One of these, RHC Spacemaster, was the fourth-largest acquisition in Leggett's history. Before RHC declared bankruptcy early in 2003, it ranked as one of the top five store fixtures manufacturers, serving widely recognized customers such as Sears, Wal-Mart, Target, and JCPenney. The company's financial difficulties resulted largely from an 80-percent reduction in store openings by its largest customer and from the bankruptcy of Kmart, another major customer. Other factors such as the slower retail environment, excess capacity in the industry, and higher steel tariffs also reduced RHC's revenues.[38]

Bill Weil, corporate controller for Leggett, recalled the risks and challenges of the RHC acquisition:

We bought it cheap, but they had starved it for working capital; we had to add a fair amount to get it going, which increased our cost of the acquisition. Then we closed a lot of their facilities. … It turned out Spacemaster was really a mess, and it diverted a lot of our attention to get that acquisition integrated. … Time will tell if it's a good deal for us. It did give us some pretty good customers.[39]

In the press release announcing the RHC acquisition, Leggett & Platt acknowledged the financial difficulties facing fixtures manufacturers, but affirmed the soundness of its own financial position and remained confident concerning its future in the fixture and display business:

The bankruptcy of RHC provides further evidence of the store fixture industry's continuing financial struggles. Due to a lackluster economy and uncertain consumer sentiment, retailers have been postponing both new store openings and existing store refurbishments for almost three years. This depressed demand is taking its toll on the industry. In the past two years, four of the top 10 manufacturers … declared bankruptcy.

In contrast, Leggett's financial position is notably sound, and the company is well situated to benefit from the eventual increase in store fixture demand. Leggett expects that, once the economy turns, the recovery in fixture demand should be robust. Small, thinly capitalized, or inexperienced manufacturers may not be able to respond to the rapid rise in demand. Leggett's financial stability, breadth of operations, economies of scale, project management skills, and broad product offerings position the company to respond quickly to, and capitalize significantly on, the eventual economic recovery.[40]

Although Leggett & Platt was confident of its future in fixtures and displays, the company recognized the need to improve operating efficiencies and margins in this strategic area of business. Leggett had acquired 30 fixtures companies between 1996 and 2000 and was attempting to mold them into a cohesive, well-coordinated group. While decreased market demand was certainly part of the reason for their unimproved profitability, the company expected better performance from these operations.[41]

In the third quarter of 2003, Leggett announced a focused management effort to improve the fixture and display operations. The company expected greater efficiencies, better adherence to standard costs, tighter inventory control, and enhanced staff skills.[42]

At the end of 2003, Leggett reported record sales of $4.39 billion and a substantial increase of cash flow to $444 million. Earnings, however, declined 11.6 percent to $206 million.[43] This was the result of higher energy prices—natural gas prices rose 80 percent—and a weaker U.S. dollar.

Roaring Back

The year 2004 was a highly successful year for Leggett & Platt. Net sales increased 16 percent to $5.1 billion. Net earnings rose an impressive 38 percent to $285 million. Investors were heartened by the company's robust 12-percent internal sales growth and by its ability to pass on higher raw material costs to a loyal customer base. As a result, the price of company stock climbed 31 percent during the year, and in December, shares traded at an all-time high of $30.68.[44]

Leggett generated more cash than it needed to fund internal growth, acquisitions, and dividends. It maintained a strong balance sheet, further reduced its debt, and increased dividends by 7 percent.[45]

These accomplishments were achieved despite numerous challenges, in particular, the unsettling turbulence in the global steel industry. Leggett & Platt's steel expense increased more than $200 million over the amount it paid in 2003. This was a significant concern as the company now used roughly 1.3 million tons of steel annually, accounting for

In 2003, Leggett & Platt made the fourth-largest acquisition in its history with the purchase of a major store fixture competitor, RHC Spacemaster. Although the purchase was made at a time when this industry sector was plagued by a reduction in retail store openings and the bankruptcy of one of RHC's major retail clients, the acquisition significantly enhanced Leggett & Platt's existing store fixture manufacturing business.

approximately 17 percent of the total cost of goods sold at that time.[46]

The rapid increase of steel prices again confirmed that the Sterling rod mill had been a wise investment. Because of its success, Leggett planned to expand the mill's production by 20 percent in 2005.[47]

The company acquired nine businesses in 2004. These enlarged the Residential Furnishings, Commercial Fixturing & Components, and Specialized Products segments. Leggett also finalized an agreement with the world's largest manufacturer of engines for outdoor power equipment, Briggs & Stratton Corporation. Under the terms of the agreement, Leggett would construct a 140,000-square-foot die-casting facility to supply components to the Briggs assembly plant in Auburn, Alabama. The deal was expected to increase the Aluminum Products segment's annual revenue by $45 million.[48]

In the fall of 2004, members of Leggett & Platt's executive team visited the New York Stock Exchange (NYSE) to ring the closing bell on September 13 in celebration of the company's 25th anniversary on the exchange. When first listed in 1979, Leggett's annual sales were $214 million, and earnings were just under $7 million. At that time, the stock closed at a split-adjusted price of 46 cents per share. In the 25 years since, the company's sales, net earnings, dividends, and stock price had experienced compound annual growth rates of 13 to 18 percent.[49]

The 2004 Annual Report included a series of colorful, entertaining pictures identifying Leggett & Platt components in many recognizable, everyday products present in most American homes and businesses. Though Leggett & Platt is part of the daily life of millions of people, the company is generally not the maker of the finished products, so, ironically, it is not a household name.

Ups and Downs

For Leggett & Platt, 2005 was a year of significant accomplishment. It achieved record sales of $5.3 billion, up 4.2 percent, and increased cash flow to $448 million. The company repurchased 5 percent of its stock and raised shareholders' dividends for the 35th consecutive year.[50]

Leggett acquired 12 businesses, which were expected to yield $320 million in annual revenue collectively. Two of the new acquisitions were in China, bringing the company's count of operating facilities in that country to 11.[51]

The most substantial acquisition of the year and the third-largest in Leggett & Platt's history was America's Body Company (ABC), with revenues of $150 million. ABC designed, manufactured, and distributed equipment for light- and medium-duty commercial trucks. Its products included racks, cabinets, and shelves for van interiors, as well as auto bodies for cargo vans, flatbed trucks, service trucks, and dump trucks. Leggett added ABC to its other van interiors operations and formed the new commercial vehicle products group as part of the Specialized Products segment. This established Leggett as the second-largest supplier in the $1.5 billion truck equipment market.[52]

Two additional large acquisitions in 2005 were Ikex, Inc., and Jarex Distribution, LLC, whose combined revenues totaled $65 million. These companies enhanced Leggett's production and distribution of geotextiles, silt fencing, erosion control, and

COMMUNITY OUTREACH

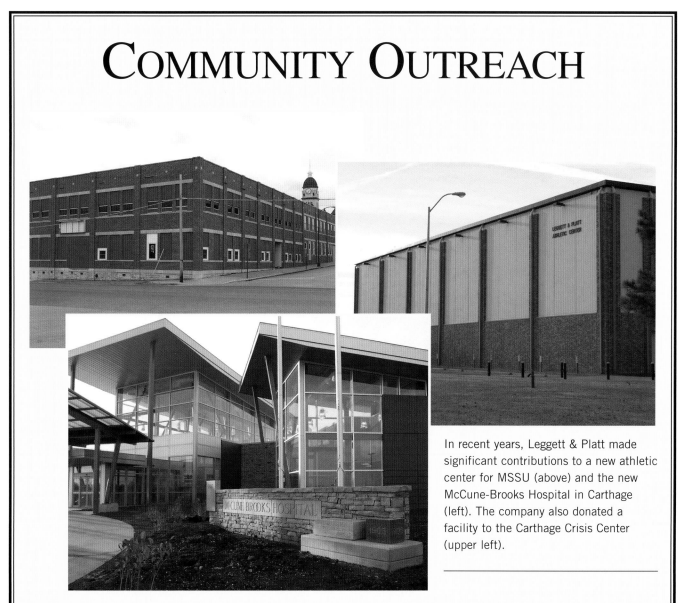

In recent years, Leggett & Platt made significant contributions to a new athletic center for MSSU (above) and the new McCune-Brooks Hospital in Carthage (left). The company also donated a facility to the Carthage Crisis Center (upper left).

FOR YEARS, LEGGETT & PLATT HAS GIVEN BACK TO the communities of Carthage and its neighboring cities.

In 1997, the company contributed to the construction of the Leggett & Platt Athletic Center at Missouri Southern State University (MSSU) in Joplin.[1] The university serves many people from the community, as well as students from outlying areas. In addition, Leggett & Platt regularly recruits people from MSSU and has more than 150 of its graduates employed around the country. Over the years, many Leggett & Platt employees—including the current CEO David S. Haffner—have served on committees and advisory boards at the university.[2]

In 2006, Leggett donated its former National Technical Center building to the Carthage Crisis Center, which provides food and shelter to homeless individuals and assists them in finding jobs.[3]

Also in 2006, construction began on the new McCune-Brooks Hospital in southwest Carthage.[4] Since Leggett & Platt made a generous financial pledge to this healthcare foundation, the hospital's Wellness Center—where patients undergo physical therapy and outpatient rehabilitation—has been named after the company.

Left and inset: TerraTex SD Non-woven Geotextile (inset) from Hanes Geo Components aids in the filtration of water in highway edge drain applications, while TerraTex SD Woven Geotextile (left) separates native soil from pavement material to improve road stability and durability.

Below: The 2005 acquisition of America's Body Company brought Leggett & Platt greater capability in the fabrication of racks, cabinets, and shelves for van interiors.

soil stabilization products for the construction, landscaping, and agricultural markets.[53]

That year, the company completed the improvements to the Sterling rod mill, increasing its capacity by 20 percent. This expansion enabled Leggett to produce more than 500,000 tons per year and to internally supply a greater percentage of the steel rod used by its operations.[54]

In contrast to the many achievements of 2005, Leggett's leaders expressed disappointment with an 11.9-percent decrease in net earnings, resulting mainly from the expenses of a formal restructuring plan launched in September.[55] The plan focused on improving several operations and reducing excess plant capacity. Previously, Leggett intentionally maintained the excess capacity, expecting market demand to rebound to the high levels of the late 1990s, but it had not, so the company identified 36 underperforming or underutilized facilities for closure or consolidation.[56]

The company also expressed disappointment with the unimproved profit margins in the fixture and display operations, and with the decreased price of company stock. Though the price was improving by the end of the year, it had not regained the record high level of 2005.

Karl Glassman discussed the company's slowed growth during this time period and explained that future acquisitions would be more closely evaluated for long-term viability:

A lot of it [the slowed growth] is a by-product of our significant market share in some of our mature industries, a growing sophistication on the part of our customers and our customers' customers. The

consolidation of our customers has made it more difficult for us in many cases to make the profits that we used to. Include external forces like Chinese imports and an increasing U.S. cost base, and we have to take a world view as opposed to a North American manufacturer view. So it's all become very complex, and the rate of change is probably quicker. ...

Today, it's a different set of circumstances. There are competitive forces that we haven't yet fully understood. So the shift is important. We have been historically a collector of businesses. If it was bedding and furniture related, then we needed to be in it. We have to shift away from that way of thinking, and we're in the process of doing so.

We tended to be collectors—emotional collectors—of businesses, and while it's not fair to say that we're not emotional, because we certainly are

*human, we can't afford to be as emotionally con-
nected with things in the future as we have been in
the past. We have to do a true analysis of what
the long-term viability of a business unit is, three
to five years out. We used to know intuitively that
they would be good, successful businesses because we were in them.*[57]

Innovation Redefined

In 2006, in another smooth leadership succession, Felix Wright transferred the CEO's responsibility to David Haffner. Haffner became only the third
chief executive in 46 years.[58] The seamless successions
and continuity of leadership at Leggett's senior level
are remarkable. Harry Cornell, Jr., served as president and then as CEO for nearly 40 years. His successor, Felix Wright, had been with the company for
40 years when he became CEO in 1999, and David
Haffner had worked with both these men for 23 years
when he succeeded Wright in 2006.

Leggett & Platt's board of directors in 2005 included (standing,
left to right) Karl Glassman; Raymond Bentele; Phoebe Wood;
Ralph Clark; Richard Fisher; Ted Enloe, III; Felix Wright;
Maurice Purnell, Jr.; David Haffner; and (seated) Joseph
McClanathan; Harry Cornell, Jr.; and Judy Odom.

Wright remained chairman of the board, and
Haffner, in addition to his new responsibilities, continued as president. Karl Glassman became the
chief operating officer and continued as executive
vice president.

That year, Leggett & Platt closely examined its
operations and revised its strategic plan for the future.
The company targeted annual sales growth of 8 to 10
percent. It also planned to increase its margin on
earnings before interest and taxes (EBIT) from
8.5 to 11 percent.[59]

To achieve its targeted growth, Leggett & Platt
devoted a greater percentage of its cash flow to finding

INVESTOR RELATIONS

I N 1979, UPON THE DEPARTURE OF G. LOUIS Allen, vice president and treasurer, Leggett & Platt initiated a formal investor relations program. J. Richard "Rich" Calhoon (below left) began this endeavor and served as vice president of investor relations for more than 20 years until his retirement. David M. DeSonier (below right) was hired in 2000 in preparation for Calhoon's departure and has since led the company's investor relations efforts. DeSonier's role has expanded over time to also include strategy, investments, and financial communications.[1]

new profitable growth opportunities. Part of this growth would result from a renewed emphasis on product development and technological advancement. "For the last few years, I've been of the opinion that Leggett needed to strengthen its technical competency," said David Haffner. "We're very technically competent, but as we go forward internationally, and as we find ways to differentiate ourselves from competitors and grow into businesses that we don't currently participate in, we're going to need significant, additional technical competency."[60]

Leggett created new executive positions devoted exclusively to growth and development. Vincent Lyons, an accomplished mechanical engineer, was hired as vice president of engineering and technology to coordinate and augment company-wide research and development (R&D). Leggett also appointed a business development director for each segment. The directors possessed substantial experience in mergers and acquisitions, as well as business development, and were commissioned to ensure profitable growth in their segments through both internal expansion and external acquisitions.[61]

Concerning these new positions, David M. DeSonier, vice president of strategy and investor relations, said:

> We aren't just pursuing revenue growth—we want the profit that comes along with it. It's profitable growth that we're seeking. We are changing—trying to put more effort into profitable growth—and that requires dedicating a few people solely toward that effort. While all of us are involved in the search for growth, everybody also has a full plate of other activities to manage, and often long-term growth gets pushed aside for more urgent priorities. The new team has the luxury of dedicating 100 percent of its effort toward seeking profitable growth.[62]

In June 2006, Leggett & Platt broke ground on a new research facility, the IDEA Center. IDEA stands for Innovation, Design, Engineering, and Acceleration—the purposes of this R&D operation.[63] In keeping with Leggett's ongoing positive contributions to the community, the company donated its previous research facility, the National Technical Center, to the Carthage Crisis Center. The 45,000-square-foot building was in excellent repair and greatly expanded the Crisis Center's ability to provide food, shelter, and other services to the disadvantaged.[64]

In the latter part of 2006, Leggett continued to reinvigorate R&D efforts by conducting its first annual "technology summit." The company's key managers from around the world gathered to brainstorm, share ideas, and develop plans. Leggett also formed an engineering council to evaluate innovative ideas and identify opportunities for synergy throughout its operations. In addition, the company purchased knowledge management software to enhance collaboration and research.[65]

Vincent Lyons spoke of one of the changes in Leggett's R&D—a renewed emphasis on the end consumer:

We are concentrating on understanding—much more than ever before—our customers' needs and even the end consumers' needs. Before, we did not try to understand as much the end consumers' needs. We relied on our customers to tell us what they needed. We developed product to solve that, but we realized that it's very important for us to better understand the needs of our end consumer, and from that, we are working on quite a few developments.[66]

As a result of examining its end markets, Leggett & Platt developed one of the most innovative products ever introduced into the bedding market: Semi-Fold®, the world's first folding box spring.

"What we found through research is, in the Northeast especially, because of the way houses are designed, you have a tough time getting a mattress upstairs," said Lyons. "So [an inflexible] box spring is almost impossible. Well, this will solve that need. When it's folded up, it's almost flat, and it's much easier to manage. You can get it upstairs, and then it's very easy to fold out."[67]

Lyons also spoke of a new innovation strategy called WIN 70/30. WIN stands for Worldwide Innovation Network, a Web page where anyone can submit product ideas to Leggett & Platt, and 70/30 describes the company's goal to generate 70 percent of new product ideas internally while receiving 30 percent from external sources. Lyons explained:

Anyone who is visiting the Leggett & Platt Web site can click on a link that will take them into our innovation Web site, where they can submit ideas to

us. … We will evaluate that idea. … They could be a customer. They could be a supplier. They could have some affiliation with Leggett & Platt, but it could be just anyone familiar with Leggett & Platt.

For all the people within Leggett & Platt with great ideas, this gives them an avenue to submit those ideas, and we can evaluate them. It also provides an opportunity for external people [external to Leggett & Platt], to submit ideas to us, [which] we normally would not think of because they may not be related to anything that we currently do today.

There will be a monetary reward for ideas [used], and … the [creators of the] top innovations throughout the year will be recognized as recipients of the J. P. Leggett Innovators Award, and those awards will be presented to the individuals on the eve of our [annual] technology forum. … The recipients of that

Left: In January 2007, Leggett & Platt started a new chapter in product development with the opening of the IDEA Center, which serves as the company's research and development headquarters.

Above: In 2006, Leggett & Platt embarked on a new product and technology development strategy. Leading the charge was Vincent Lyons (center), vice president of engineering and technology, flanked by Leggett & Platt's five business development directors (left to right): Joe Harris, residential; Steffan Sarkin, aluminum; David Brown, industrial; Mitch Dolloff, specialized; and Jay Thompson, commercial.

Far left: Leggett & Platt produces a wide range of racks and shelving for retail customers around the world. Along with much of the fixtures industry, the company has struggled to remain satisfactorily profitable in this area of business.

Immediate left: Leggett & Platt is the recognized leader in carpet cushion and pad for hard and soft floor-covering materials, offering rebond, premium, rubber, synthetic fiber, and laminate underlayment.

Below: Through its Parthenon Metal Works subsidiary, Leggett & Platt makes steel tubing that is used in many of its own furniture component manufacturing processes.

award will be inducted into our Inventors Hall of Fame. These innovative programs will continue to create excitement and bring out the creative juices in all of our employees throughout the years.[68]

Ironically, though Lyons works daily to engineer better products such as sleep systems, sleep is the farthest thing from his mind.

People ask me how I sleep at night, and I can't sleep. There's no time to sleep. It's so much fun. It's such a great opportunity to come to a company that's been successful for 125 years and to chart a new path from an innovation and technology standpoint. The opportunity to create is extremely exciting, and we're doing some things today that we have not done in the past.

"Innovation Redefined" is our new corporate logo, and it certainly represents what we're doing from an innovation, product development standpoint.[69]

The End of an Era

In 2007, Felix Wright remained chairman of the board, but reduced his involvement in the day-to-day business of the company. He began to serve as a consultant to senior management. When announcing the change in Wright's daily activities, the company discussed its succession practices:

At the most senior levels of the company, our management has long believed that openly communicated succession plans promote understanding and teamwork and help avoid the divisive and unpro-

ductive jostling for position that can occur when it isn't clear who will lead the organization.

Orderly succession, as we have tried to practice it, also provides for continuing access to the experience and institutional knowledge of former leaders. That's possible at [Leggett & Platt] because our retiring leaders have not dishonored themselves or the company—the opposite— they have done excellent work and helped select and coach the next generation of leaders. By their good work and active support of the new leaders, they have retained our affection and earned our continuing thanks.[70]

Keeping with the succession tradition, in February 2008, Felix Wright, chairman of the board, and Harry Cornell, Jr., chairman emeritus, announced that they would not be seeking reelection to the board of directors that year. Leggett & Platt's bylaws stated that directors must retire at age 72 unless they received a waiver. Since both men had exceeded the age limit, they decided not to request the waiver. In a Special-Edition Management Information

WORLDWIDE LOCATIONS

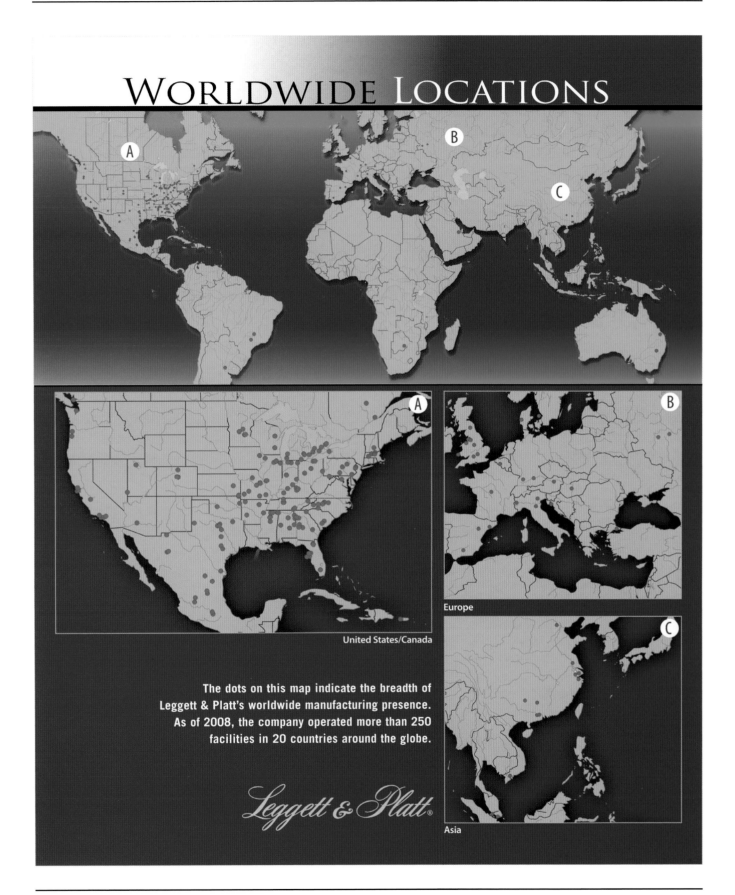

United States/Canada

Europe

Asia

The dots on this map indicate the breadth of
Leggett & Platt's worldwide manufacturing presence.
As of 2008, the company operated more than 250
facilities in 20 countries around the globe.

Leggett & Platt

Bulletin, Cornell and Wright expressed their reasoning behind the decision:

> *Hence, simply put, it is time for us to leave the Board and for Leggett & Platt's leaders to take the company in new directions and to new heights. ... We are grateful for the opportunity to have served our partnership over all these years and are gratified with our company's profitable growth and shareholder value. ... As continuing major shareholders, you can be sure we are as interested as ever in Leggett & Platt's success, and we will continue to be available for counsel whenever needed.[71]*

In a press release announcing the decision, David Haffner commented:

> *Together, Harry and Felix have served Leggett & Platt for 107 years. To a large degree, though they would be reluctant to take the credit, they have been the architects of our company's success and growth over the last five decades. Their legacy of partnership and teamwork, as both employees and board members, characterizes well the culture of our company. They will be greatly missed.[72]*

The board of directors' nominating committee recommended the election of Richard T. Fisher as an independent chair. Fisher had served on Leggett's board for 36 years, having first been elected in 1972. "We are excited to have an individual of Mr. Fisher's caliber become Leggett's next chairman," said Felix Wright. "A seasoned board member, Richard has served as our Presiding Director since 2003. He has performed admirably, and we have high expectations of what he will accomplish as he leads our board of directors."[73]

Divest and Acquire

Reflecting the renewed focus on profitability, Leggett & Platt sold its Prime Foam business in the first quarter of 2007. Prime Foam chiefly produced commodity foam cushioning for upholstered furniture and bedding manufacturers. The business generated nearly $200 million in revenues in 2006 and ranked as the largest divestiture in company history, but it represented only a portion of Leggett's foam operations. (The company retained the foam operations that manufactured carpet padding.)[74] David Haffner said:

> *This divestiture is consistent with our previously stated intention to actively manage our portfolio of businesses. We will continually evaluate the strategy and competitive positions of our individual businesses, and plan to participate only in markets in which we can be a market leader and generate an attractive cash-flow return on investment. The*

SUPPLIER OF THE YEAR

*F*URNITURE TODAY, A WEEKLY JOURNAL PUBLICAtion for the bedding and furniture industries, honored Leggett & Platt by presenting the company with the Supplier of the Year award for 2007. The company received its award at the annual *Furniture Today* Leadership Conference in Florida that November. *Furniture Today* Executive Editor David Perry said, "While Leggett & Platt may not be a familiar name to consumers, it's a well-known and highly respected name in the trade, producing components for sleep sets and upholstered furniture, as well as offering a full line of metal beds in its Fashion Bed Group."[1]

The award serves as a tribute to the hard work of Leggett employees both in Carthage, Missouri, and around the world. "*Furniture Today* is truly the premier publication serving the furniture and bedding industry, so it's certainly focused on two of our key industries," said Karl Glassman, Leggett & Platt executive vice president and chief operating officer. "We're certainly honored to receive what truly is a prestigious award, and we view it as a testament to our many employees who are dedicated to serving not only the manufacturer and retailer, but the end consumer."[2]

IN OCTOBER 2007, FELIX E. WRIGHT WAS INDUCTED into the American Furniture Hall of Fame (AFHF) in High Point, North Carolina. The AFHF is an all-industry effort organized to honor those individuals whose outstanding achievements have contributed to the continued growth and development of the American furniture industry and to research, collect, and preserve the industry's cultural, economic, and artistic history.[1]

Believing a person's integrity to be his most valuable attribute, Wright ingrained the principle of business integrity into his management style throughout his long career at Leggett & Platt. Under his direction, the company has multiplied its product offerings and expanded its distribution network.

At the induction ceremony, Wright spoke of the many challenges and changes the furniture industry has faced during his nearly 49 years in the business. Although today's markets are difficult, Wright offered words of encouragement for the future:

I believe that our industry still provides great opportunities for servicing the home furnishings market. Demand may ebb and flow with market conditions, but it is not going to go away. We need good business leaders committed to doing the right things ... [and] to develop[ing] the business strategies and business plans that can service a somewhat different consumer ... in a different market environment. With every challenge there becomes a greater opportunity for somebody to survive and develop a company that is a shining star. I certainly believe those opportunities are still here, and with honesty, integrity, impeccable customer service, and products that meet our consumers' needs, success will certainly continue to be ours.[2]

---

sale of the Prime Foam operations reflects this portfolio approach. Although the business is performing well and has some opportunity for growth, our market position is small, and the business is not strategic to Leggett.[75]

Leggett & Platt completed three sizeable acquisitions in 2007. On March 6, the company purchased Gamber-Johnson, LLC, of Stevens Point, Wisconsin, a leading designer and manufacturer of work surfaces and docking stations for computers, screens, printers, and communication equipment in service vehicles. Gamber-Johnson's customers included local and state police, the U.S. military, emergency medical services, utilities, telecommunications companies, and other mobile repair and service professionals.[76]

Gamber-Johnson joined the commercial vehicle products group of the Specialized Products segment. Leggett began to distribute Gamber-Johnson's products through its fleet, ship-through, and upfitting operations. Jack Crusa, senior vice president of Leggett & Platt and head of the Specialized Products segment, said:

The Gamber-Johnson acquisition extended our reach for servicing the market for commercial vehicle fleets' needs for functional interior components. It added a new product group and allowed us to touch a whole new base of customers, those demanding rugged vehicle installations for on-board computers. We were also very impressed with the management team, and a deciding factor was their willingness to stay on long term and continue to lead the business with the same level of enthusiasm. To date, we have been extremely pleased with this business.[77]

On March 23, Leggett & Platt acquired Nestaway, LLC, with facilities in Cleveland, Ohio; McKenzie,

Tennessee; Beaver Dam, Kentucky; and Clinton, North Carolina. Nestaway designed, produced, and supplied complex coated wire forms. It primarily manufactured residential dishwasher racks, or baskets, for major customers such as Maytag, GE, Bosch, Electrolux, and Whirlpool. Nestaway also produced other coated and painted wire forms such as vending machine racks, golf cart baskets, and dryer racks. It became part of Leggett's Industrial Materials segment.[78] "This acquisition presents Leggett & Platt with significant cross-segment selling opportunities," said Joe Downes, senior vice president of Leggett & Platt and head of the Industrial Materials segment. "Nestaway also enables the Industrial Materials segment to move further up the value chain with our rod and wire."[79]

A dishwasher rack manufactured at Leggett & Platt's Nestaway facility in Clinton, North Carolina.

On November 30, Leggett acquired a Chinese manufacturer of office chair components, Chieng Yeng. It was founded in Taiwan in 1977, but relocated to China in 2002. The company's primary products were casters, glides, and aluminum and plastic chair components. These were sold in China and exported to the United States, Japan, and Europe.[80]

Through Chieng Yeng, Leggett & Platt established a low-cost Chinese manufacturing plant for office chair components. Leggett's U.S. customers operating in China could now receive these products from an in-country Leggett operation.

Looking Ahead ...

The Prime Foam divestiture and the three sizeable acquisitions in 2007 were constructive, well-executed moves for Leggett & Platt. However, the company's growth, profitability, and performance for its investors continued to be below expectations for the third year. In mid-2006, the company had launched a series of internal strategy discussions concerning the company's recent performance and its future direction.

In February, 2007, Leggett's senior executives and board of directors hired a premier strategy consulting firm to provide an independent, thorough assessment of the company's business units. Though

Leggett had recently completed the formal restructuring plan begun in 2005, David Haffner emphasized that the outcome of the strategic review would be "broader in scope, more strategic in nature, and more long-term oriented than any of our previous activities."[81]

In mid-November 2007, Leggett & Platt announced the outcome of the review and a dramatic alteration of its strategy. Commenting on the changes, David Haffner said:

We are making significant, necessary changes to the way we assess our portfolio of businesses and how we manage our asset base. We intend to be better stewards of shareholders' capital, generate significantly more free cash, and return a larger amount of that cash to our investors. Our shareholder returns have suffered for the past few years, as part of our portfolio has dragged us down. We are correcting that by divesting several of our businesses. These are tough decisions we don't make lightly because they affect many of our employee–partners; however, these actions are required to bring about a stronger, better performing, and more focused Leggett & Platt.[82]

The company's new, primary objective was to increase total shareholder return (TSR), the total benefit an investor receives from owning a share of stock. Revenue growth, previously Leggett's primary aim, was now only one method of improving TSR. To reinforce the importance of TSR to its executives and managers, the company modified annual bonus calculations to include a return on assets component.[83]

Leggett & Platt decided to view its business units as a portfolio, arranging them in four categories—Grow, Core, Fix, and Divest—based on their competitive advantages, strategic positions, and financial health. To aid in the regular assessment of a business unit's category, rigorous strategic planning processes would be implemented across the company.[84]

BOARD OF DIRECTORS TIMELINE

1901 TO PRESENT

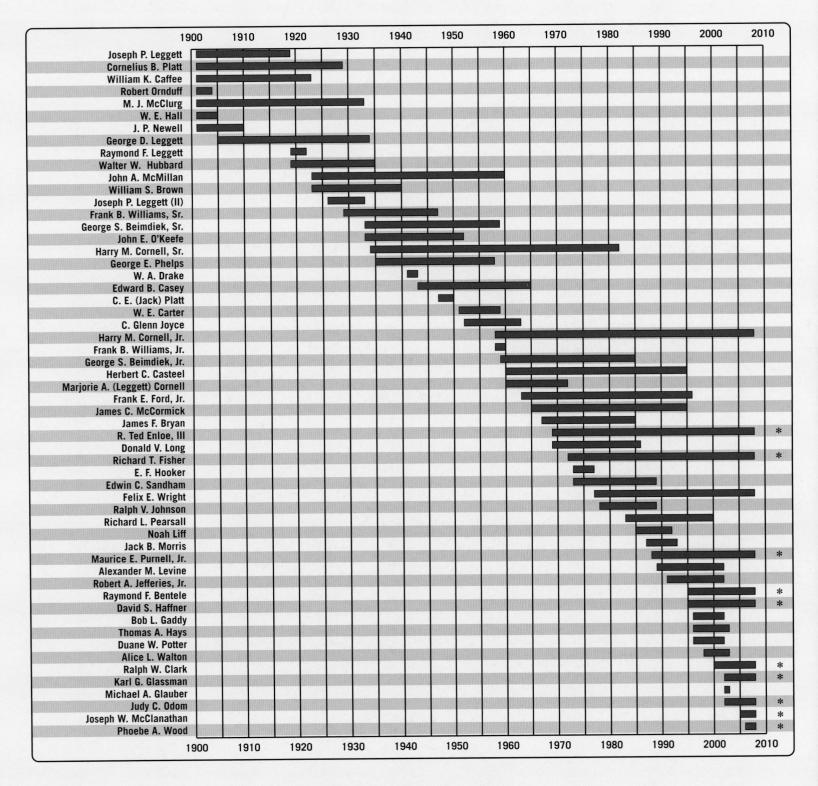

Currently serving, as of June 2008

Businesses assigned to the Grow category were expected to capitalize on competitive market positions and emphasize proprietary product development, and were allocated appropriate financial resources. Core businesses were expected to enhance productivity, maintain market share, and generate free cash flow with only minimal future capital investment. Businesses assigned to the Fix category were given a limited period of time to improve performance, or they would be moved to the Divest category.[85]

Leggett & Platt planned to divest its entire Aluminum Products segment and six additional business units. To remain in the company's portfolio, business units needed to generate after-tax returns on assets greater than the company's cost of capital. Those not meeting or exceeding the required level of returns would be transferred to the Fix or Divest categories.[86]

The company expected the new strategy to further bolster one of its longtime strengths, a healthy free cash flow level. To return more of that cash to shareholders, in November 2007, Leggett increased the annual dividend 39 percent to $1 per share. The company also intended to repurchase a significant amount of its stock.[87]

Given the considerable task of implementing the new strategic plan, management expected minimal sales growth for the next two years. Over the long term, with growth efforts focused on a narrower set of higher quality opportunities, the company anticipated collective revenue growth of 4 to 5 percent

This aerial photo shows Leggett & Platt's corporate offices near Carthage, where approximately 600 people work.

per year. Leggett would acquire fewer businesses, but would continue to look for opportunities to enter new, higher-growth businesses that meet strict criteria.[88]

Through the expected 4 to 5 percent revenue growth, the higher dividend to shareholders, and the commitment to repurchase shares, the company anticipated annual TSR of 12 to 15 percent over the long term. By comparison, the average TSR of the S&P 500 for the next five years was expected to be around 10 percent. In a press release outlining Leggett's future strategy, David Haffner concluded:

Our shareholders deserve the benefits that we expect will result from these actions. Longer term, I'm convinced we will reestablish Leggett & Platt as a growing and substantially more profitable enterprise, a company that consistently generates above-average total shareholder return. The current management team is absolutely dedicated to rapid implementation and precise execution on this change in strategy and focus.[89]

The dramatic changes within the company's strategy reflect Leggett & Platt's commitment to a successful future for shareholders and employee–partners. The company's willingness to redefine itself and adapt to inconsistent economic and business environments has been a critical reason for its continuation and success for 125 years. It has demonstrated the resilience and flexibility to survive wars, fires, the Great Depression, and numerous recessions, successfully meeting the challenges of fierce competition and changing markets.

Throughout the company's history, however, some aspects have remained consistent. Leggett has remained steadfastly committed to honest, ethical business practices, building itself on a foundation of hard work, ingenuity, and teamwork. The company strives to treat its employee–partners with fairness and respect, and it seeks the best interests of its shareholders. Leggett & Platt's leaders have also been diligent in preparing their successors and smoothly transferring responsibilities, ensuring that the company maintains the requisite talent and management required to meet continuing challenges.

Leggett & Platt's ability to adapt to new markets and economic dynamics, yet remain constant in the value it places on people and management practices, seems to be the very characteristic that will ensure the company's future success.

Acquisition History*

1960 – 2007

Springs & Box Springs (55 deals)

Company	Year	Country
Oklahoma City	1963	U.S.A.
Englander Co.	1965	U.S.A.
Flex-O-Loc Corp.	1968	U.S.A.
Kenyon Manufacturing Co.	1968	U.S.A.
Motor City Spring Co.	1968	U.S.A.
Butler Manufacturing	1969	U.S.A.
Dalpak Corp.	1969	U.S.A.
J. R. Greeno Corp.	1969	U.S.A.
Globe Spring & Cushion Co. (50%)	1977	Canada
De Lamar Bed Spring Corp.	1979	U.S.A.
Missouri Fabricators, Inc.	1980	U.S.A.
Pride Box Spring	1982	U.S.A.
Nachman Corp.	1983	U.S.A.
Kay Springs, Inc.	1985	U.S.A.
Red Springs	1985	U.S.A.
Karr Manufacturing	1987	U.S.A.
Multilastic Limited	1987	U.K.
Dream Makers, Inc.	1988	U.S.A.
International Spring Corp.	1988	U.S.A.
Hoover Group	1989	U.S.A.
Webster Spring Co., Inc.	1989	U.S.A.
Olympic Spring	1992	U.S.A.
Carriero (50%; 25% in 1996)	1993	Mexico
Maxwell Spring	1993	U.S.A.
Oxford Metal Products	1994	U.S.A.
Hoover	1995	U.S.A.
M&M	1995	Germany
Mississippi Spring	1995	U.S.A.
Resortes Monterey	1995	Mexico
Chesterfield Wood Products	1996	U.S.A.
Steadley	1996	U.S.A.
Bilbao	1997	Spain
Family Frames	1997	U.S.A.
Paris Spring	1997	Canada
Tiffany	1997	Mexico
American Innerspring Co.	1998	U.S.A.
Toledo Fjederindlaeg	1998	Denmark
Option Spring Products	1999	U.S.A.
Spring Flex	1999	Brazil
Wellhouse Wire	1999	U.K.
Heplast/Hespo	2000	Croatia
Ilma Srl	2000	Italy
Industrias Subinas	2000	Spain
Elson & Robbins	2002	U.K.
Siddall & Hilton Products	2002	U.K.
Ningbo	2003	China
Saval Spring & Wire	2003	U.S.A.
Xiang Yang	2003	China
Askona	2004	Russia
Veneza Espumas	2005	Brazil
ZSP Wire Industries	2005	S. Africa
Atlas Spring Manufacturing	2006	U.S.A.
Elson & Robbins Pocket Coil	2006	U.K.
Probel Spring	2006	Brazil
Samson Spring	2006	Australia

Fabric Converting (17 deals)

Company	Year	Country
Tiffany Textile Co. (50%)	1979	U.S.A.
Hanes Holding Co.	1993	U.S.A.
VWR Textiles	1993	U.S.A.
Lenrod	1997	Canada
Marsh Fern	1997	U.K.
Yarborough	1997	U.S.A.
Falcon Industries	1998	U.S.A.
Western Textile Co.	1998	U.S.A.
Jute Exports Limited	1999	U.K.
Mount Hope Finishing	1999	U.S.A.
Yarborough-Ind. Fabrics Div.	1999	U.S.A.
Coinse SA de CV	2000	Mexico
Edmund Bell & Co., Ltd.	2000	U.K.
Synthetic Ind. F&B Converting	2001	U.S.A.
Vitaweb Division of Vitafoam	2001	U.K.
Union Wadding	2004	U.S.A.
Sani-Line Sales	2005	U.S.A.

Fibers (16 deals)

Company	Year	Country
Kraft Converters	1972	U.S.A.
Paramount Paper	1973	U.S.A.
Quality Pad Co.	1981	U.S.A.
National Fibers Division	1984	U.S.A.
Steiner-Liff Textiles	1985	U.S.A.
O'Neill Brothers	1986	U.S.A.
Buffalo Batt & Felt Corp.	1988	U.S.A.
Hobbs Pad	1991	U.S.A.
Cameo Fibers	1996	U.S.A.
Guilford Fibers	1997	U.S.A.
Sealy Pad Line	1997	U.S.A.
Cumulus Fibers	1998	U.S.A.
Bonded Fiber Products	1999	U.S.A.
KLM Industries	2001	U.S.A.
Johnston Ind. Fiber Unit	2003	U.S.A.
Stearns Technical Textile	2003	U.S.A.

Foam (17 deals)

Company	Year	Country
Phillips-Foscue Corp. (92%)	1976	U.S.A.
Crest-Foam Corp.	1986	U.S.A.
Echota Cushion, Inc.	1986	U.S.A.
MPI, Inc.	1986	U.S.A.
Pacific Dunlop (L&P Foam)	1986	Australia
Custom Foam Fabrication	1988	U.S.A.
Hood Industries	1989	U.S.A.
E-K Novelty	1995	U.S.A.
Fairmont	1996	U.S.A.
Hi Life Product	1997	U.S.A.
Iredell Fibers	1997	U.S.A.
Southwest Carpet Pad, Inc.	1999	U.S.A.
General Foam – Durabond Plant	2000	U.S.A.
Padco/Molded Urethane	2000	U.S.A.
Foamex Rubber & Felt	2005	U.S.A.
Mary Ann Industries	2005	U.S.A.
Sponge Cushion, Inc.	2006	U.S.A.

Wood Products (7 deals)

Company	Year	Country
C. A. Bissman Manufacturing Co.	1961	U.S.A.
Bois JLP	1984	Canada
National Frame	1992	U.S.A.
Bois Aise	1994	Canada
Les Bois Blanchet	1996	Canada
Miller Manufacturing	1997	U.S.A.
Spruceland Forest Products, Inc.	1999	Canada

Consumer Products (16 deals)

Company	Year	Country
Metal Bed Rail Company, Inc.	1972	U.S.A.
Missouri Rolling Mill Corp. (MRM)	1979	U.S.A.
St. Croix	1981	U.S.A.
Bedline Manufacturing Co.	1983	U.S.A.
Allegheny Steel & Brass	1988	U.S.A.
Berkshire Furniture Co.	1988	U.S.A.
Dresher, Inc.	1990	U.S.A.
J. B. Ross Manufacturing	1990	U.S.A.
Beauti-Glide	1991	U.S.A.
Duro Metal	1991	U.S.A.
Continental Silverline	1992	U.S.A.
Harvard Manufacturing	1992	U.S.A.
BC Products	1996	U.S.A.
Western Bed Products	1997	U.S.A.
STS Linens, Inc.	2004	U.S.A.
Westex International	2005	Canada

Coated Fabrics (4 deals)

Company	Year	Country
Vantage Industries	1994	U.S.A.
Rug-Hold	2003	U.S.A.
American Non-Slip	2005	U.S.A.
Griptex Industries	2005	U.S.A.

Furniture Hardware & Other Furniture Products (23 deals)

Company	Year	Country
Signal Manufacturing Co.	1970	U.S.A.
Middletown Manufacturing, Inc.	1973	U.S.A.
Pontiac Furniture	1979	U.S.A.
Foster Brothers	1982	U.S.A.
C. S. O'Brien	1986	U.S.A.
Stylelander	1993	U.S.A.
Super Sagless Corporation	1994	U.S.A.
Waterloo Furniture Components	1994	Canada
Wiz Wire	1994	Canada
Matrex	1995	U.S.A.
Bell Spring	1997	U.S.A.
Ark-Ell Springs, Inc.	1999	U.S.A.
Omega Motion LLC	1999	U.S.A.
Superior Products	1999	U.S.A.
Wyn Products	1999	Australia
Southern Bedding	2000	U.S.A.
TechCraft Operations	2000	U.S.A.
Jiaxing	2003	China
Sackner	2003	U.S.A.

RESIDENTIAL	COMMERCIAL	ALUMINUM	INDUSTRIAL	SPECIALIZED

Furniture Hardware & Other Furniture Products (continued)

Company	Year	Country
Everwood Products	2005	U.S.A.
Jinshajiang Sofa Components	2005	China
Fulda	2007	China
Knitmasters JV	2007	U.S.A.

Adjustable Beds (2 deals)

Company	Year	Country
Maxwell Products, Inc.	1999	U.S.A.
Orthomatic Adjustable Beds	2003	U.S.A.

Geo Components (4 deals)

Company	Year	Country
Ikex/Jarex	2005	U.S.A.
Webtec	2005	U.S.A.
Attilla Enterprises	2006	U.S.A.
Lone Star Products	2006	U.S.A.

Fixture & Display (33 deals)

Company	Year	Country
SEMCO	1994	U.S.A.
Talbot Industries	1994	U.S.A.
ISS	1995	U.S.A.
Excell	1996	Canada
Amco	1997	U.S.A.
Hodges	1997	U.S.A.
PMI Purchase Mktg.	1997	Canada
Rodgers-Wade	1997	U.S.A.
Tarrant Interiors	1997	U.S.A.
Wichita Wire	1997	U.S.A.
American Woodworks	1998	U.S.A.
Syndicate Systems	1998	U.S.A.
Universal Stainless, Inc.	1998	U.S.A.
Wilson Display	1998	Canada
Arc Specialities	1999	U.S.A.
Beeline Group, Inc.	1999	U.S.A.
Dann Dee Display Fixtures	1999	U.S.A.
De Todo en Alambre	1999	Mexico
Design Fabricators, Inc.	1999	U.S.A.
Jarke Corporation	1999	U.S.A.
Met Displays, Inc.	1999	U.S.A.
Sensible Storage, Inc.	1999	U.S.A.
Toledo Store Fixtures	1999	U.S.A.
Zell Brothers, Inc.	1999	U.S.A.
Dillmeier Group	2000	U.S.A.
EDRON Store Fixtures	2000	U.S.A.
Genesis Fixtures	2000	U.S.A.
Gillis Associated Industries	2000	U.S.A.
KelMax Equipment	2000	U.S.A.
DisplayPlan, Ltd.	2001	U.K.
MZM SA de CV	2001	Mexico
RHC Spacemaster	2003	U.S.A.
China Display Fixture Co.	2005	China

Office Furniture Components (14 deals)

Company	Year	Country
Gordon Manufacturing Co.	1984	U.S.A.
Northfield Metal Products, Ltd.	1985	Canada
Collier-Keyworth Corporation	1988	U.S.A.
Indiana Chair Frame	1988	U.S.A.
Warterloo Spring	1992	U.S.A.
Faultless Doerner	1993	Canada
Hamilton Wire	1993	Canada
Northeastern Components	1995	U.K.
Davidson Plyforms	2001	U.S.A.
Miotto International	2001	Italy

Office Furniture Components (continued)

Company	Year	Country
Sterling & Adams Bentwood, Inc.	2002	U.S.A.
Hickory Springs/Hammer Metals	2004	U.S.A.
Chieng-Yeng	2007	China
Intes JV	2007	China

Plastics (10 deals)

Company	Year	Country
Foothills Mfg.	1974	U.S.A.
Futron Plastics (50%)	1979	U.S.A.
Weber Plastics Co., Ltd.	1987	Canada
Technical Plastics Corp.	1998	U.S.A.
K. W. Precision Metal Products	1999	Canada
Pulsar Plastics	1999	U.S.A.
SCP Plastics	2003	U.S.A.
Unique Molded Products	2003	U.S.A.
Conestogo Plastics	2004	Canada
Shepherd Products	2004	Canada

Aluminum (14 deals)

Company	Year	Country
EST	1972	U.S.A.
MetalCraft	1979	U.S.A.
Assured Castings	1987	U.S.A.
Culp Smelting	1989	U.S.A.
Latrobe	1996	U.S.A.
Oconto	1996	U.S.A.
Pace	1996	U.S.A.
Cambridge Tool	1997	U.S.A.
Die Cast Products	1997	U.S.A.
B&C Die Cast	1998	U.S.A.
Mo-Tech Corporation	1998	U.S.A.
Saint Paul Metalcraft	1998	U.S.A.
Product Technologies	2000	U.S.A.
Saltillo, Mexico JV	2002	Mexico

Wire & Rod (15 deals)

Company	Year	Country
Adcom Metals Company	1977	U.S.A.
Webster Wire, Inc.	1989	U.S.A.
Armco Wire partnership	1993	U.S.A.
Laclede Oil Tempering Lines	1994	U.S.A.
U.S. Wire Tie Systems	1994	U.S.A.
A. J. Gerrard	1996	U.S.A.
Belton	1997	U.S.A.
Metrock Steel & Wire	1998	U.S.A.
John Pring & Sons	1999	U.K.
Laclede Mid America	2000	U.S.A.
Shaped Wire, Inc.	2000	U.S.A.
Insteel – Andrews	2002	U.S.A.
North American Wire Products	2002	U.S.A.
Northwestern Steel	2002	U.S.A.
Nestaway	2007	U.S.A.

Steel Tubing (3 deals)

Company	Year	Country
Parthenon Metal	1983	U.S.A.
Blazon	1993	U.S.A.
Excaliber	2001	U.S.A.

Commercial Vehicle Products (7 deals)

Company	Year	Country
Masterack	1972	U.S.A.
Gor-Don	1995	Canada
Crown North America	2000	U.S.A.
Team Fenex, Ltd.	2001	U.S.A.
Tailgater, Inc.	2003	U.S.A.
America's Body Company	2005	U.S.A.
Gamber–Johnson	2007	U.S.A.

Automotive (15 deals)

Company	Year	Country
Flex-O-Lators	1988	U.S.A.
No-Sag	1990	U.S.A.
Young Spring & Wire	1990	U.S.A.
Pullmaflex	1994	Belgium
Phoenix Metal	1997	U.S.A.
Nagle Industries, Inc.	1999	U.S.A.
Bergen Cable Technology, Inc.	2000	U.S.A.
Schukra Group	2000	Canada
ByTec, Inc.	2002	U.S.A.
Guangzhou Veihe	2003	China
Kwang Jin Co., Ltd.	2003	S. Korea
Pangeo Cable Industries	2003	China
Idomrugo Kft.	2004	Hungary
Modern Industries	2004	U.S.A.
Huaguang Parts	2005	China

Machinery (17 deals)

Company	Year	Country
Cyclo-Index Corporation	1983	U.S.A.
Gribetz International	1990	U.S.A.
Alexander Machine	1992	U.S.A.
Gribetz Threads	1993	U.S.A.
WBSCO	1994	U.S.A.
Gateway	1996	U.K.
Pathe	1997	U.S.A.
Porter	1997	U.S.A.
Spühl	1997	Switzerland
Steppex/Quiltex	1997	U.K.
Syd-Ren	1997	U.S.A.
Kaybe Machines	1998	U.S.A.
Vertex Fasteners, Inc.	1998	U.S.A.
Agimex S.A.	2000	France
Jentschmann AG	2000	Switzerland
Innovatech International S.A.	2001	Greece
Nahtec	2004	Germany

Summary of Acquisition Totals

	1960s	1970s	1980s	1990s	2000s	Total
• Residential	9	11	29	65	47	161
• Commercial	–	2	5	31	19	57
• Aluminum	–	2	2	8	2	14
• Industrial	–	1	2	8	7	18
• Specialized	–	1	2	18	18	39
Total	9	17	40	130	93	289

* This appendix reflects all significant acquisitions to the best of Leggett & Platt's knowledge; may exclude some smaller acquisitions.

Notes to Sources

Chapter One

1. Leggett & Platt Spring Bed and Manufacturing Company, "The Beds of Kings," 1923, page 23.
2. Investor Relations Department, *Leggett & Platt Fact Book* (Leggett & Platt, Inc., 2006), pages I–14.
3. Ibid.
4. Ibid., I–15.
5. Ibid., BG–2.
6. Ibid., BG–3.
7. Ibid., BG–4.
8. Ibid., BG–7.
9. Ibid., BG–9.
10. Ibid., BG–12.
11. Ibid., BG–13.
12. Ibid., BG–14.
13. Ibid., BG–15.
14. Lawrence Wright, *Warm & Snug ... The History of the Bed* (Gloucestershire, England: Sutton Publishing, Ltd., 2004), page 31.
15. The Better Sleep Council, "The Bed in History," 2007, http://www.bettersleep.org/.
16. Ibid.
17. Ibid.
18. The National Sleep Foundation, "The Importance of Sleep," 2007, http://www.sleepfoundation.org/.
19. Ibid.
20. United States Patent and Trademark Office, *Bed-Spring*, Patent No. 319758, 26 May 1885, http://www.uspto.gov/.
21. Ibid.
22. "Obituary of Joseph Palmer Leggett," *The Carthage Press*, May 1921.
23. Ibid.
24. "Obituary of Catherine T. Platt," Jasper County Records and Research Center, Missouri.
25. "The Story of Leggett and Platt ... The Main Springs of Rest," 1950, page 3.
26. Carthage Missouri Convention and Visitor's Bureau, *Through the Years ... Carthage, Missouri*, page 11.
27. Ibid.
28. Ibid.
29. "The Story of Leggett and Platt ... The Main Springs of Rest," 3–4.
30. Harry M. Cornell, Jr., telephone conversation with Ron W. Marr, 11 January 2007.
31. "The Story of Leggett and Platt ... The Main Springs of Rest," 3.
32. Ibid., 4.
33. Ibid.
34. United States Patent and Trademark Office, *Spring Bed Bottom*, Patent No. 553412, 21 January 1896, http://www.uspto.gov/.
35. United States Patent and Trademark Office,

Manufacture of Spring Bottoms, Patent No. 611131, 20 September 1897, http://www.uspto.gov/.

36. United States Patent and Trademark Office, *Machine for Attaching Bed-Springs to Cross-Wire Braces*, Patent No. 611132, 20 September 1898, http://www.uspto.gov/.

37. United States Patent and Trademark Office, *Sectional Bed Bottom*, Patent No. 656411, 21 August 1900, http://www.uspto.gov/.

38. "The Story of Leggett and Platt ... The Main Springs of Rest," 7.

39. Michele Hansford, Archives of the Powers Museum (Carthage, Missouri).

40. Ibid.

41. *1900 Carthage City Directory*, Archives of the Powers Museum (Carthage, Missouri).

42. "The Story of Leggett and Platt ... The Main Springs of Rest," 7–8.

43. Ibid., 8.

44. Ibid.

**Chapter One Sidebar:
Carthage, Missouri:
The Maple Leaf City**

1. Carthage Missouri Convention and Visitor's Bureau, *Through the Years ... Carthage, Missouri*, page 5.

2. Ibid., 6.

3. Ibid., 7.

4. The Road Wanderer, "Historic Carthage, Missouri," http://www.theroadwanderer.net/.

5. Phyllis Rossiter, *A Living History of the Ozarks* (Pelican Publishing Company, 2001), page 126.

6. Ron W. Marr, *The Ozarks, An Explorer's Guide* (Countryman Press, 2006), page 169.

Chapter Two

1. Leggett & Platt Spring Bed and Manufacturing Company, "The Beds of Kings," 1923, page 2.

2. Ibid., 7.

3. Ibid., 1.

4. Ibid., 9–22.

5. Ibid., 23.

6. Ibid., 7.

7. Ibid., 8–20.

8. Ibid., 6–7.

9. "The Story of Leggett and Platt ... The Main Springs of Rest," 1950, page 8.

10. Ibid.

11. "C. B. Platt Dies Today in St. Louis Hospital," *The Carthage Press*, 22 March 1929, page 5.

12. "The Story of Leggett and Platt ... The Main Springs of Rest," 8.

13. "C. B. Platt Dies Today in St. Louis Hospital," 5.

14. "Obituary of Joseph Palmer Leggett," Harry M. Cornell, Jr., personal archives.

15. "The Story of Leggett and Platt ... The Main Springs of Rest," 8.

16. Ibid., 10.

17. Ibid.

18. "C. B. Platt Dies Today in St. Louis Hospital," 5.

19. "J. P. Leggett New Head," *The Carthage Press*, 27 March 1929, page 1.

**Chapter Two Sidebar: The
Inventive Mind of J. P. Leggett**

1. United States Patent and Trademark Office, *Bed Spring*, Patent No. 318758, 26 May 1885.

2. United States Patent and Trademark Office, *Manufacture of Spring Bottoms*, Patent No. 611131, 20 September 1898.

3. United States Patent and Trademark Office, *Machine for Attaching Bed Springs to Cross-Wire Braces*, Patent No. 611132, 20 September 1898.

4. United States Patent and Trademark Office, *Sectional Bed Bottom*, Patent No. 656411, 21 August 1900.

5. United States Patent and Trademark Office, *Spring Bed Bottoms*, Patent No. 553412, 21 January 1896.

6. United States Patent and Trademark Office, *Spring Bed Bottom*, Patent No. 1089233, 3 March 1914.

7. United States Patent and Trademark Office, *Machine for Bending and Cutting Coiled Springs*, Patent No. 1094076, 21 April 1914.

8. United States Patent and Trademark Office, *Spring Bed Bottom and Manufacture of the Same*, Patent No. 1313902, 26 August 1919.

9. United States Patent and Trademark Office, *Target Trap*, Patent No. 804143, 7 November 1905.

10. Harry M. Cornell, Jr., interview by Jeffrey L. Rodengen, digital recording, 22 November 2006, Write Stuff Enterprises, Inc.

11. United States Patent and Trademark Office, *Carrier for Target-Traps*, Patent No. 852123, 30 April 1907.
12. United States Patent and Trademark Office, *Lid for Tea-Kettles*, Patent No. 535252, 5 March 1895.
13. United States Patent and Trademark Office, *Endless Necktie*, Patent No. 771163, 27 September 1904.
14. Ibid.
15. United States Patent and Trademark Office, *Railway Car*, Patent No. 1073429, 16 September 1913.
16. Ibid.
17. United States Patent and Trademark Office, *Vehicle Propelling Mechanism*, Patent No. 1093277, 14 April 1914.
18. Ibid.
19. United States Patent and Trademark Office, *Motor-Vehicle Transmission System*, Patent No. 1117582, 17 November 1914.
20. United States Patent and Trademark Office, *Automobile Propelling Mechanism*, Patent No. 1482017, 29 January 1924.

**Chapter Two Sidebar:
An Emotional Farewell**

1. John Hale, Sr., Vice President for Human Resources, Leggett & Platt, *Speech to the Carthage Area Chamber of Commerce*, 14 March 1983.
2. Ibid.
3. Ibid.
4. Ibid.

Chapter Three

1. "Missionaries' Letters Praise Bed Springs of Leggett & Platt Firm," 10 August 1931.
2. M. J. McClurg, "Leggett & Platt Spring Bed and Manufacturing Company, Board of Directors Meeting Minutes," 18 December 1929.
3. "Missionaries' Letters."
4. Ibid.
5. Ibid.
6. M. J. McClurg, "Leggett & Platt Spring Bed and Manufacturing Company, Board of Directors Meeting Minutes," 18 August 1930.
7. M. J. McClurg, "Leggett & Platt Spring Bed and Manufacturing Company, Board of Directors Meeting Minutes," 19 July 1932.
8. Harry M. Cornell, Jr., notes supplied to publishing house, 2007.
9. "The Story of Leggett and Platt ... The Main Springs of Rest," 1950, page 10.
10. National Association of Bedding Manufacturers, *Bedding Manufacturer*, November 1933.
11. International Sleep Products Association, "About ISPA," http://www.sleepproducts.org/.
12. "The Story of Leggett and Platt ... The Main Springs of Rest," 14.
13. George S. Beimdiek, Sr., Leggett & Platt, Inc.; "Board of Directors Meeting Minutes," 18 April 1935, page 2; Harry M. Cornell, Sr., Leggett & Platt, Inc.; "Board of Directors Special Meeting Minutes," 23 April 1995.

14. Harry M. Cornell, Jr., interview by Jeffrey L. Rodengen, digital recording, 22 November 2006, Write Stuff Enterprises, Inc.
15. Cornell, Jr., notes.
16. Ibid.
17. George S. Beimdiek, Sr., "Letter to Stockholders," 15 April 1937, Carthage, Missouri; Leggett and Platt Spring Bed and Manufacturing Company, Annual Report, 31 December 1936, page 5.
18. Ibid., 1.
19. "The Story of Leggett and Platt ... The Main Springs of Rest," 11.
20. George S. Beimdiek, Sr., "Letter to Stockholders"; Leggett and Platt Spring Bed and Manufacturing Company, Annual Report, 31 December 1936, page 1.
21. George S. Beimdiek, Sr., "Letter to Stockholders," 26 March 1938; Leggett and Platt Spring Bed and Manufacturing Company, Annual Report, 31 December 1937, page 1.
22. George S. Beimdiek, Sr., "Letter to Stockholders," 17 March 1939; Leggett and Platt Spring Bed and Manufacturing Company, Annual Report, 31 December 1938, page 1.
23. George E. Phelps, Leggett & Platt Spring Bed and Manufacturing Company, "Board of Directors Meeting Minutes," 19 February 1938, page 1.
24. Ibid., 2.
25. "The Story of Leggett and Platt ... The Main Springs of Rest," 13.

26. George S. Beimdiek, Sr., "Letter to Stockholders," 28 February 1940; Leggett and Platt Spring Bed and Manufacturing Company, Annual Report, 31 December 1939, page 1.

27. George S. Beimdiek, Sr., "Letter to Stockholders," 25 February 1941; Leggett and Platt Spring Bed and Manufacturing Company, Annual Report, 31 December 1940, page 1.

28. Harry M. Cornell, Jr., notes to publisher, 27 December 2006.

29. George S. Beimdiek, Sr., "Letter to Stockholders," 12 May 1942; Leggett and Platt Spring Bed and Manufacturing Company, Annual Report, 31 December 1941, page 1.

30. Leggett & Platt, Inc., Annual Report, 31 December 1942, cover.

31. George S. Beimdiek, Sr., "Letter to Stockholders," 5 April 1943, Leggett & Platt, Inc., Annual Report, 31 December 1942, page 1.

32. "The Story of Leggett and Platt ... The Main Springs of Rest," 13.

33. George S. Beimdiek, Sr., "Letter to Stockholders," 5 April 1943, Leggett & Platt, Inc., Annual Report, 31 December 1942, page 1.

34. Ibid.

35. George S. Beimdiek, Sr., "Letter to Stockholders," 25 March 1945, Leggett & Platt, Inc., Annual Report, 31 December 1944, page 1.

36. George S. Beimdiek, Sr., "Letter to Stockholders," 5 April 1944, Leggett &

Platt, Inc., Annual Report, 31 December 1943, page 1.

37. "L&P's Most Senior Partner," *Leggett & Platt Management Information Bulletin*, January/February 2000, page 3; George S. Beimdiek, Sr., "Letter to Stockholders," 5 April 1944, Leggett & Platt, Inc., Annual Report, 31 December 1943, page 1.

38. George S. Beimdiek, Sr., "Letter to Stockholders," 25 March 1945, Leggett & Platt, Inc., Annual Report, 31 December 1944, page 1.

39. George S. Beimdiek, Sr., "Letter to Stockholders," 27 April 1946, Leggett & Platt, Inc., Annual Report, 31 December 1945, page 1.

40. Ibid.

41. Ibid.

42. C. G. Joyce, Leggett & Platt, Inc.; "Board of Directors Meeting Minutes," 21 May 1946, page 1.

43. C. G. Joyce, Leggett & Platt, Inc.; "Board of Directors Meeting Minutes," 18 June 1946, page 1.

44. C. G. Joyce, Leggett & Platt, Inc.; "Board of Directors Meeting Minutes," 19 March 1946, page 1.

45. George S. Beimdiek, Sr., "Letter to Stockholders," 23 March 1948, Leggett & Platt, Inc., Annual Report, 31 December 1947, page 1.

46. Ibid.

47. George S. Beimdiek, Sr., "Letter to Stockholders," 11 April 1949, Leggett & Platt, Inc., Annual Report, 31 December 1948, page 1.

48. Ibid.

49. Ibid.

50. "Labor Unions in the United States," Microsoft® Encarta® Online Encyclopedia, 2007, http://encarta.msn.com/.

51. George S. Beimdiek, Sr., "Letter to Stockholders," 31 December 1951, Leggett & Platt, Inc., 1950 Annual Report, page 1.

52. Ibid.

53. "The Story of Leggett and Platt ... The Main Springs of Rest," 1950, page 15; Jack Crusa, interview by Jeffrey L. Rodengen, digital recording, 21 November 2006, Write Stuff Enterprises, Inc.

54. George S. Beimdiek, Sr., "Letter to Stockholders," 1951 Annual Report, Leggett & Platt, Inc., 31 December 1950, page 1.

55. George S. Beimdiek, Sr., "Letter to Stockholders," 10 April 1952, Leggett & Platt, Inc., Annual Report, 31 December 1951, pages 1–2.

56. Ibid.

57. Ibid.

58. "Letter to the President of the Senate and to the Speaker of the House Transmitting Report of the National Advisory Board on Mobilization Policy," President Harry S. Truman, 22 June 1951, John Woolley and Gerhard Peters, *The American Presidency Project* [online]. Santa Barbara, CA: University of California (hosted), Gerhard Peters (database), http://www.presidency.ucsb.edu/.

59. George S. Beimdiek, Sr., "Letter to Stockholders," Annual Report, 10 April 1952, Leggett & Platt, Inc., 31 December 1951, pages 1–2.

60. Ibid.

61. "Special Message to the Congress on the Steel Strike," President Harry S. Truman, 10 June 1952, John Woolley and Gerhard Peters, *The American Presidency Project* [online]. Santa Barbara, CA: University of California (hosted), Gerhard Peters (database), http://www.presidency.ucsb.edu/.

62. George S. Beimdiek, Sr., "Letter to Stockholders," 30 March 1953, Leggett & Platt, Inc., Annual Report, 31 December 1952, pages 1–2.

63. Ibid.

64. Ibid.

65. Ibid.

66. Ibid.

67. C. G. Joyce, "Minutes of Regular Directors Meeting," 16 December 1952, Leggett & Platt, Inc., page 2.

68. George S. Beimdiek, Sr., "Letter to the Board of Directors," 29 April 1953; Frank E. Ford, Jr., "Minutes of Directors Adjourned Meeting," Leggett & Platt, Inc., 29 April 1953.

Chapter Three Sidebar:
George S. Beimdiek, Sr.

1. "George S. Beimdiek, Prominent Carthage Business Man, Dies at 86," *The Carthage Press*, 11 February 1963.

2. Ibid.

3. Ibid.

4. George E. Phelps, Leggett & Platt Spring Bed and Manufacturing Company, "Board of Directors Meeting Minutes," 19 February 1938, page 1.

5. Harry M. Cornell, Sr., Leggett & Platt Spring Bed and Manufacturing Company, "Minutes of Special Meeting of Board of Directors," 8 November 1937.

6. Harry M. Cornell, Sr., Leggett & Platt Spring Bed and Manufacturing Company, "Minutes of Special Meeting of Board of Directors," 17 November 1937.

7. George E. Phelps, Leggett & Platt Spring Bed and Manufacturing Company, "Minutes of General Meeting of Board of Directors," 10 February 1938, pages 1–8.

8. Harry M. Cornell, Sr., Leggett & Platt Spring Bed and Manufacturing Company, "Minutes of the Annual Shareholders' Meeting," 31 January 1938.

9. "George S. Beimdiek, Prominent Carthage Business Man, Dies at 86."

10. G. Stephen Beimdiek, grandson of George S. Beimdiek, Sr., son of George S. Beimdiek, Jr., conversations with John Hale, summer 2007.

11. "Well-known Carthage Businessman Dies at 94," *The Carthage Press*, 9 November 2007.

12. Harry M. Cornell, Sr., Leggett & Platt, Inc., "Minutes of Directors Regular Meeting," 14 January 1959, page 2.

Chapter Four

1. Harry M. Cornell, Jr., interview by Jeffrey L. Rodengen, digital recording, 22 November 2006, Write Stuff Enterprises, Inc.

2. Herbert C. Casteel, "Letter to Chairman/Directors of Leggett & Platt," 5 November 1991.

3. Leggett & Platt, Inc., "The Story of Leggett and Platt ... The Main Springs of Rest," 1950, pages 19–22.

4. Frank E. Ford, Jr., "Minutes of Directors Regular Meeting," 15 September and 27 October 1953.

5. Harry M. Cornell, Sr., "Letter to the Stockholders," 22 March 1954, Leggett & Platt, Inc., 1953 Annual Report, pages 1–2.

6. Ibid.

7. Ibid.

8. Harry M. Cornell, Sr., "Letter to the Stockholders," 15 February 1956, Leggett & Platt, Inc., 1955 Annual Report, pages 1–2.

9. Company Accounting Records, 1956–1958, Leggett & Platt, Inc.

10. Frank E. Ford, Jr., "Minutes of Directors Regular Meeting," 23 July 1957; 29 April 1958; 28 October 1959.

11. Frank E. Ford, Jr., "Minutes of Directors Regular Meeting," 24 February 1959.

12. Frank E. Ford, Jr., "Minutes of Directors

Regular Meeting,"
25 September 1956.

13. Frank E. Ford, Jr., "Minutes of Directors Regular Meeting," 21 January 1958.

14. Frank E. Ford, Jr., "Minutes of Directors Regular Meeting," 23 September 1958.

15. Frank E. Ford, Jr., "Minutes of Directors Regular Meeting," 25 August 1959 and 13 January 1960.

16. Frank E. Ford, Jr., "Minutes of Directors Regular Meeting," 21 January 1958.

17. Frank E. Ford, Jr., "Minutes of Directors Regular Meeting," 14 January 1959.

18. W. W. Hubbard, "Report of "Annual Shareholders' Meeting," 16 January 1933; 15 January 1934; 28 January 1935.

19. Frank E. Ford, Jr., "Minutes of Special Directors Meeting," 7 February 1959.

20. Frank E. Ford, Jr., "Minutes of Directors Regular Meeting," 24 February 1959.

21. Frank E. Ford, Jr., "Minutes of Directors Regular Meeting," 29 April 1959.

22. Frank E. Ford, Jr., "Minutes of Directors Regular Meeting," 27 May 1959.

23. Frank E. Ford, Jr., "Minutes of Directors Regular Meeting," 23 June 1959.

24. Frank E. Ford, Jr., "Minutes of Directors Regular Meeting," 25 August 1959.

25. Ibid.

26. Harry M. Cornell, Jr., interviews with John Hale, summer 2007, Leggett & Platt, Inc.

27. Frank E. Ford, Jr., "Minutes of Directors Regular Meeting," 28 October 1959.

28. "Interviews with John Hale."

29. Herb Casteel, interview by Jeffrey L. Rodengen, digital recording, 21 November 2006, Write Stuff Enterprises, Inc.

30. "Interviews with John Hale."

31. Ibid.

32. Harry M. Cornell, Sr., "Letter to the Stockholders," 1958 Annual Report, 10 April 1959, Leggett & Platt, Inc., page 21.

33. Frank E. Ford, Jr., "Minutes of Directors Regular Meeting," 23 February 1960.

34. "Interviews with John Hale."

35. Frank E. Ford, Jr., personal letter to Harry M. Cornell, Jr., 6 March 2008.

36. Frank E. Ford, Jr., "Minutes of Directors Regular Meeting," 21 September 1960.

37. Ibid.

38. Frank E. Ford, Jr., "Minutes of Directors Regular Meeting," 4 November 1960.

39. Frank E. Ford, Jr., "Minutes of Directors Regular Meeting," 28 December 1960.

40. Frank E. Ford, Jr., "Minutes of Directors Regular Meeting," 30 January 1961.

41. Frank E. Ford, Jr., "Minutes of Special Directors Meeting," 18 October 1960.

42. Bill Allen, interview by Jeffrey L. Rodengen, digital recording, 22 November 2006, Write Stuff Enterprises, Inc.

43. "Results of Operations," 1962 Annual Report, Leggett & Platt, Inc.

44. Frank E. Ford, Jr., "Minutes of Directors Regular Meeting," 27 April 1960.

45. Frank E. Ford, Jr., "Minutes of Directors Regular Meeting," 23 June 1960.

46. Frank E. Ford, Jr., "Minutes of Directors Regular Meeting," 4 November 1960.

47. Frank E. Ford, Jr., "Minutes of Directors Regular Meeting," 7 July 1961.

48. Felix E. Wright, interview by Jeffrey L. Rodengen, digital recording, 21 November 2006, Write Stuff Enterprises, Inc.

49. Harry M. Cornell, Sr., "Leggett to the Stockholders—The Year in Review, The Year Ahead," 1961 Annual Report, Leggett & Platt, Inc.

50. Frank E. Ford, Jr., "Minutes of Directors Regular Meeting," 31 January 1963.

51. Frank E. Ford, Jr., "Minutes of Directors Regular Meeting," 29 March 1963.

52. Frank E. Ford, Jr., "Minutes of Directors Regular Meeting," 31 January and 26 February 1963.

53. Frank E. Ford, Jr., "Minutes of Directors Regular Meeting," 31 January 1963.

54. Frank E. Ford, Jr., "Minutes of Directors Regular Meeting," 26 February 1963.

55. "Interviews with John Hale."

56. Ibid.

57. "Expansion and Acquisition for Future Growth," 1963 Annual Report, Leggett & Platt, Inc., pages 3–4.

58. "Expansion for Growth … Modernization for Profitability," 1964 Annual Report, Leggett & Platt, Inc., page 3.

59. Harry M. Cornell, Jr., "The President's Message," 1964 Annual Report, Leggett & Platt, Inc., page 1.
60. Ibid., 2.
61. Frank E. Ford, Jr., "Minutes of Directors Regular Meeting," 26 May 1961.
62. Frank E. Ford, Jr., "Minutes of Directors Regular Meeting," 29 March 1963.
63. Ibid.
64. Frank E. Ford, Jr., "Minutes of Directors Regular Meeting," 26 February 1963.
65. Frank E. Ford, Jr., "Minutes of Directors Regular Meeting," 30 December 1964.
66. William E. Allen, "Minutes of Leggett & Platt, Incorporated Directors Meeting," 26 April 1967, pages 8–9.
67. Harry M. Cornell, Sr., Harry M. Cornell, Jr., "Letter to Our Shareholders," 1966 Annual Report, Leggett & Platt, Inc.
68. William E. Allen, "Minutes of Leggett & Platt, Incorporated Directors Meeting," 30 March 1967, pages 3–4.
69. Harry M. Cornell, Sr., Harry M. Cornell, Jr., "Letter to Our Shareholders," 1967 Annual Report, 29 March 1968, Leggett & Platt, Inc.
70. Ibid.
71. "1968 Review," 1968 Annual Report, Leggett & Platt, Inc., page 5.
72. "1969 Review," 1969 Annual Report, Leggett & Platt, Inc., page 6.
73. Ibid.
74. Harry M. Cornell, Sr., Harry M. Cornell, Jr., "Letter to Our Shareholders," 1969 Annual Report, Leggett & Platt, Inc., page 1.

75. 1969 Annual Report, Leggett & Platt, Inc.
76. "1969 Review," 5.
77. "1968 Review," 5.

**Chapter Four Sidebar:
Harry M. Cornell, Sr.**

1. Harry M. Cornell, Jr., interview by Jeffrey L. Rodengen, digital recording, 22 November 2006, Write Stuff Enterprises, Inc.
2. Ibid.
3. "The Story of Leggett and Platt ... The Main Springs of Rest," 1950, page 16.
4. "Our Hundredth Year: 1883–1983," 1983, Leggett & Platt, Inc., page 16.

**Chapter Four Sidebar:
Harry M. Cornell, Jr.**

1. Harry M. Cornell, Jr., interview by Jeffrey L. Rodengen, digital recording, 22 November 2006, Write Stuff Enterprises, Inc.
2. Ibid.
3. Frank E. Ford, Jr., "Minutes of Directors Regular Meeting," 15 July 1953.
4. Frank E. Ford, Jr., "Minutes of Directors Regular Meeting," 23 February 1960.
5. Harry M. Cornell, Jr., interview.
6. Howard Boothe, interview by Jeffrey L. Rodengen, digital recording, 21 November 2006, Write Stuff Enterprises, Inc.
7. Bill Allen, interview by Jeffrey L. Rodengen, digital

recording, 22 November 2006, Write Stuff Enterprises, Inc.

**Chapter Four Sidebar:
Wired for the Future**

1. "1969 Review," 1969 Annual Report, Leggett & Platt, Inc., page 5.
2. Harry M. Cornell, Jr., interview by Jeffrey L. Rodengen, digital recording, 22 November 2006, Write Stuff Enterprises, Inc.
3. Ibid.
4. Ibid.

Chapter Five

1. John Hale, interview by Jeffrey L. Rodengen, digital recording, 21 November 2006, Write Stuff Enterprises, Inc.
2. "A Look at the Future," 1970 Annual Report, Leggett & Platt, Inc., page 19.
3. Ibid.
4. Ibid.
5. "1970 Review," 1970 Annual Report, Leggett & Platt, Inc., page 9.
6. "Products, Markets and Marketing," 1972 Annual Report, Leggett & Platt, Inc., page 7.
7. Ibid.
8. Ibid.
9. Ibid.
10. "1970 Review," 9.
11. Ibid.
12. "A Look at the Future," 19.
13. "1971 Review," 1971 Annual Report, Leggett & Platt, Inc., page 9.
14. Harry M. Cornell, Sr., Harry M. Cornell, Jr., "To

press release, 1 August 1984, page 1.

37. "Leggett & Platt Declares Dividend Following Annual Meeting," Leggett & Platt press release, 9 May 1985, page 1.

38. "Leggett & Platt Plans to Acquire Kay Springs, Inc., Leggett & Platt press release, 4 June 1985, page 1.

39. "Leggett & Platt Begins New Discussions with Kay Springs," Leggett & Platt press release, 10 September 1985, page 1.

40. "Leggett & Platt Acquires Assets of Kay Springs," Leggett & Platt press release, 31 December 1985, page 1.

41. Gary Krakauer, interview by Jeffrey L. Rodengen, digital recording, 10 January 2007, Write Stuff Enterprises, Inc.

42. "Leggett & Platt Acquires Assets of Kay Springs," Leggett & Platt press release, 31 December 1985, page 1.

43. Wayne R. Wickstrom, interview by Jeffrey L. Rodengen, digital recording, 12 January 2007, Write Stuff Enterprises, Inc.

44. "Leggett & Platt Increases Cash Dividend and Declares 3-for-2 Stock Split," Leggett & Platt press release, 12 February 1986, page 1.

45. Harry M. Cornell, Jr., Felix E. Wright, "To Our Shareholders," 1986 Annual Report, 27 February 1987, Leggett & Platt, Inc., page 2.

46. Ibid.

47. "Leggett & Platt in the FORTUNE® 500," Leggett &

Platt press release, 24 April 1987, page 1.

48. Harry M. Cornell, Jr., Felix E. Wright, "To Our Shareholders," 1987 Annual Report, 29 February 1988, Leggett & Platt, Inc., page 2.

49. "The Leggett & Platt Difference," 1988 Annual Report, Leggett & Platt, Inc., page 4.

50. "Letter to Shareholders," 12 February 1988, Leggett & Platt, Inc., pages 1–2.

51. Ibid.

52. List of Closed Acquisitions, Mergers & Acquisitions Department, Leggett & Platt, Inc.

53. "Leggett & Platt Purchases Assets of Culp Smelting & Refining," Leggett & Platt press release, 3 May 1989, page 1.

54. "Leggett & Platt Acquires Webster," 19 April 1989, Leggett & Platt, Inc., page 1.

55. Sandy Levine, interview by Jeffrey L. Rodengen, digital recording, 7 February 2007, Write Stuff Enterprises, Inc.

**Chapter Six Sidebar:
The Arrival of Mira-Coil™**

1. Tom Wells, interview by Jeffrey L. Rodengen, digital recording, 6 February 2007, Write Stuff Enterprises, Inc.

2. Ibid.

3. Ibid.

4. "The Company and the Industry," 1978 Annual Report, Leggett & Platt, Inc., pages 8–9.

**Chapter Six Sidebar:
Exceptional Service**

1. National Association of Bedding Manufacturers, Exceptional Service Award letter to Harry M. Cornell, Jr., 19 March 1983.

**Chapter Six Sidebar:
Cornell Conference Center**

1. Commemorative Plaque, Cornell Conference Center Dedication, Leggett & Platt, Inc., 1991.

**Chapter Six Sidebar:
Together, Again**

1. Robert A. Jefferies, Jr., "Minutes of Board of Directors," 10 August 1988, Leggett & Platt, Inc., page 4.

2. Harry M. Cornell, Jr., interview with John Hale, Summer 2008, Leggett & Platt, Inc.

3. Jack D. Crusa, interview by Jeffrey L. Rodengen, digital recording, 21 November 2006, Write Stuff Enterprises, Inc.

Chapter Seven

1. Author unknown, framed quotation in the office of Harry M. Cornell, Jr., Leggett & Platt, Inc.

2. "Focused on Efficiency … A Commitment to Excellence," 1990 Annual Report, Leggett & Platt, Inc., page 9.

3. Ibid.

4. Ibid.

5. "Leggett & Platt and Dresher Announce Acquisition Plan," 20 March 1990, Leggett & Platt, Inc., page 1.
6. Ibid.
7. "Leggett & Platt Acquires No-Sag Operations," 25 July 1990, Leggett & Platt, Inc., page 1.
8. "Take Cover!" *Management Information Bulletin*, 22 February 1991, pages 1–2.
9. Ibid.
10. "Leggett & Platt Anticipates Lower Third Quarter Earnings," 2 October 1990, Leggett & Platt, Inc., page 1.
11. Harry M. Cornell, Jr., Felix E. Wright, "To Our Shareholders," 1990 Annual Report, 1 March 1991, Leggett & Platt, Inc., page 2.
12. Ibid.
13. Ibid.
14. "Focused on Efficiency ... A Commitment to Excellence," 1990 Annual Report, Leggett & Platt, Inc., page 7.
15. Harry M. Cornell, Jr., Felix E. Wright, "To Our Shareholders," 1991 Annual Report, 5 March 1992, Leggett & Platt, Inc., page 2.
16. Paul Hauser, interview by Jeffrey L. Rodengen, digital recording, 27 February 2007, Write Stuff Enterprises, Inc.
17. Harry M. Cornell, Jr., Felix E. Wright, "To Our Shareholders," 1991 Annual Report, 5 March 1992, Leggett & Platt, Inc., page 2.
18. "Leggett & Platt Sells Four Foam Operations," 1 July 1991, Leggett & Platt, Inc., page 1.

19. Harry M. Cornell, Jr., Felix E. Wright, "To Our Shareholders," 1991 Annual Report, 5 March 1992, Leggett & Platt, Inc., page 3.
20. "A Recipe for Success," *Management Information Bulletin*, 14 February 1992, Leggett & Platt, Inc., page 1.
21. "Innovation in Components ... and Beyond," 1991 Annual Report, Leggett & Platt, Inc., page 7.
22. Marcus Malcolm, interview by Jeffrey L. Rodengen, digital recording, 11 January 2007, Write Stuff Enterprises, Inc.
23. Harry M. Cornell, Jr., Felix E. Wright, "To Our Shareholders," 1992 Annual Report, 26 February 1993, Leggett & Platt, Inc., page 1.
24. Ibid.
25. Harry M. Cornell, Jr., "Letter to Shareholders," 15 June 1992.
26. "Partners in Progress," 1992 Annual Report, Leggett & Platt, Inc., page 5.
27. "Leggett & Platt Announces Proposed Acquisition," 30 June 1993, Leggett & Platt, Inc., page 1.
28. Ibid.
29. Ibid.
30. "Leggett to Acquire Armco's 50-Percent Interest in Joint Venture," 10 August 1993, Leggett & Platt, Inc., page 1.
31. Ibid.
32. Harry M. Cornell, Jr., Felix E. Wright, "To Our Shareholders," 1993 Annual Report, 28 February 1994, Leggett & Platt, Inc., page 5.
33. "Financial Highlights," 1994 Annual Report, Leggett & Platt, Inc., page 2.

34. "Products for Living," 1994 Annual Report, Leggett & Platt, Inc., page 11.
35. "A Conversation with Harry," *Management Information Bulletin*, January 1995, Leggett & Platt, Inc., page 7.
36. "Products for Living," 11.
37. Eloise Nash, interview by Jeffrey L. Rodengen, digital recording, 21 November 2006, Write Stuff Enterprises, Inc.
38. Harry M. Cornell, Jr., Felix E. Wright, "To Our Shareholders," 1994 Annual Report, 2 March 1995, Leggett & Platt, Inc., page 4.
39. "Notes to Consolidated Financial Statements," 1995 Annual Report, Leggett & Platt, Inc., page 29.
40. Harry M. Cornell, Jr., Felix E. Wright, "To Our Shareholders," 1995 Annual Report, 29 February 1996, Leggett & Platt, Inc., page 3.
41. "Creating Value Through Engineered Products," 1995 Annual Report, Leggett & Platt, Inc., page 6.
42. "Comments of Herbert C. Casteel," Leggett & Platt, Inc., newsletter, *Special Partners in Progress Edition*, May 1995, pages 2–3.
43. Comments by Harry M. Cornell, Jr.; Partners in Progress Dedication Plaque, Corporate Headquarters, May 1995.
44. "Stock Split and Increase in Cash Dividend Announced by Leggett & Platt," 9 August 1995, Leggett & Platt, Inc., page 1.

45. Harry M. Cornell, Jr., Felix E. Wright, "To Our Shareholders," 1995 Annual Report, 29 February 1996, Leggett & Platt, Inc., page 2.

46. "Management's Discussion and Analysis of Financial Condition and Results of Operations," 1995 Annual Report, Leggett & Platt, Inc., page 20.

47. 1995 Annual Report, Leggett & Platt, Inc., cover.

48. Harry M. Cornell, Jr., Felix E. Wright, "To Our Shareholders," 1996 Annual Report, 7 March 1997, Leggett & Platt, Inc., page 2.

49. "Leggett to Acquire Armco's 50-Percent Interest in Joint Venture."

50. Harry M. Cornell, Jr., Felix E. Wright, "To Our Shareholders," 1996 Annual Report, 7 March 1997, Leggett & Platt, Inc., page 2.

51. "Expanding Business Platforms, Balanced Growth"; "Aluminum Die Castings," 1996 Annual Report, Leggett & Platt, Inc., page 11.

52. Ibid.

53. Dan Hebert, interview by Jeffrey L. Rodengen, digital recording, 10 January 2007, Write Stuff Enterprises, Inc.

54. Harry M. Cornell, Jr., Felix E. Wright, "To Our Shareholders," 7 March 1997; 1996 Annual Report, Leggett & Platt, Inc., page 3.

55. Ibid.

56. "Leggett and Steadley Sign Merger Agreement," 9 September 1996, Leggett & Platt, Inc., page 1.

57. Duane Potter, interview by Jeffrey L. Rodengen, digital recording, 20 February 2007, Write Stuff Enterprises, Inc.

58. Ernie Jett, interview by Jeffrey L. Rodengen, digital recording, 21 November 2006, Write Stuff Enterprises, Inc.

59. Harry M. Cornell, Jr., interview with John Hale, summer 2007, Leggett & Platt, Inc.

60. "Leggett and Steadley Sign Merger Agreement."

61. Harry M. Cornell, Jr., Felix E. Wright, "To Our Shareholders," 1996 Annual Report, 7 March 1997, Leggett & Platt, Inc., page 2.

62. "Expanding Business Platforms, Balanced Growth;" "Aluminum Die Castings."

63. Ibid.

64. Harry M. Cornell, Jr., Felix E. Wright, "To Our Shareholders," 1997 Annual Report, 9 March 1998, Leggett & Platt, Inc., page 2.

65. "Leggett Acquisition Program Continues," 9 January 1997, Leggett & Platt, Inc., page 1.

66. "Team, Product and Company Growth," 1997 Annual Report, Leggett & Platt, Inc., page 5.

67. Ibid., 9.

68. Ibid., 13.

69. Harry M. Cornell, Jr., Felix E. Wright, "To Our Shareholders," 1997 Annual Report, 9 March 1998, Leggett & Platt, Inc., page 2.

70. Robert A. Jefferies, Jr., Michael Glauber, interview by Jeffrey L. Rodengen, 27 February 2007, Write Stuff Enterprises, Inc.

71. "Expanding Business Platforms, Balanced Growth;" "Leadership Recognition," 1996 Annual Report, Leggett & Platt, Inc., page 12.

72. Harry M. Cornell, Jr., "Chairman's Special Message," 1997 Annual Report, Leggett & Platt, Inc., page 4.

73. Ibid.

74. Ibid.

75. John A. Hale, (as reported to Write Stuff Enterprises, Inc.) summer 2008, Leggett & Platt, Inc.

76. "Notes to Consolidated Financial Statements," 1998 Annual Report, Leggett & Platt, Inc., page 37.

77. Dennis Park, interview by Jeffrey L. Rodengen, digital recording, 21 November 2006, Write Stuff Enterprises, Inc.

78. Ibid.

79. Harry M. Cornell, Jr., "Chairman's Special Message," 1999 Annual Report, Leggett & Platt, Inc., page 1.

80. "Notes to Consolidated Financial Statements," 1999 Annual Report, Leggett & Platt, Inc., page 47.

81. Harry M. Cornell, Jr., Felix E. Wright, David S. Haffner, "To Our Fellow Shareholders," 1999 Annual Report, 28 February 2000, Leggett & Platt, Inc., page 5.

82. "Leggett Added to S&P 500," 1999 Annual Report, Leggett & Platt, Inc., overlay sheet.

83. "Engineered Products, Manufacturing Solutions," "Recognized Leadership," 1998 Annual Report, Leggett & Platt, Inc., page 8.

84. Leggett & Platt, Inc., e-mail message to editor and researcher, 11 April 2007.

85. Harry M. Cornell, Jr., Felix E. Wright, David S. Haffner, "To Our Fellow Shareholders," 1999 Annual Report, Leggett & Platt, Inc., page 4.

**Chapter Seven Sidebar:
Making a Fortune**

1. 1985 Annual Report, Leggett & Platt, Inc., overlay sheet.

2. Cable News Network, "*FORTUNE®* 500 1955–2006," http://money.cnn.com/ (accessed 3 May 2007).

3. Ibid.

4. Time, Inc., "Fortune Corporate Reputation Industry Reports," *FORTUNE®* Datastore, http://www.timeinc.net/fortune/datastore/reputation/cr_report.html (accessed 3 May 2007).

5. Felix Wright, interview by Jeffrey L. Rodengen, digital recording, 21 November 2006, Write Stuff Enterprises, Inc.

6. Duane Potter, interview by Jeffrey L. Rodengen, digital recording, 21 November 2006, Write Stuff Enterprises, Inc.

7. Harry M. Cornell, Jr., interview by Jeffrey L. Rodengen, digital recording, 21 November 2006, Write Stuff Enterprises, Inc.

**Chapter Seven Sidebar:
Artistic Spirits**

1. John Hale, "As Reported to Write Stuff," summer 2008, Leggett & Platt, Inc.

2. *Management Information Bulletin*, May 1995, Leggett & Platt, Inc., page 5.

**Chapter Seven Sidebar:
Felix E. Wright**

1. Felix E. Wright, interview with John Hale, Summer 2007, Leggett & Platt, Inc.

2. Ibid.

3. Human Resources Department Employment History of Felix E. Wright, Leggett & Platt, Inc.

4. Felix E. Wright, "From the Chief Operating Officer," 1978 Annual Report, Leggett & Platt, Inc., page 5.

5. Human Resources Department Employment History of Felix E. Wright.

6. Felix Wright, *Management Information Bulletin*, "The L&P Culture," May/June 1998.

7. Felix Wright, interview by Jeffrey L. Rodengen, digital recording, 21 November 2006, Write Stuff Enterprises, Inc.

8. "The L&P Culture."

**Chapter Seven Sidebar:
The Student Learner Program**

1. "L&P Machine Products Receives 2000 Missouri Industry of the Year Award," *Mid-America Commerce and Industry*, 1 August 2000, http://findarticles.com/p/articles/mi_qa3698/is_200008/ai_n8915626/.

2. National Career Pathways Network, "Previous EWSLA Winners from 1995–2006," http://www.cord.org/ewsla/previous-winners/.

3. David Rice, Student Learner Program, summer 2007, Leggett & Platt, Inc.

4. David Rice, Student Learner Program data, as reported to David Ballew, summer 2007, Leggett & Platt, Inc.

**Chapter Seven Sidebar:
Cornell's Closing Statement**

1. Harry M. Cornell, Jr., "Chairman's Special Message," 1997 Annual Report, Leggett & Platt, Inc., page 4.

Chapter Eight

1. David S. Haffner, interview by Jeffrey L. Rodengen, digital recording, 27 February 2007, Write Stuff Enterprises, Inc.

2. Business Segment Descriptions, 2000 Annual Report, Leggett & Platt, Inc., inside cover.

3. "Financial Highlights," 2000 Annual Report, Leggett & Platt, Inc., inside cover.

4. "Leggett Works," 2000 Annual Report, Leggett & Platt, Inc., inside cover.

5. Harry M. Cornell, Jr., Felix E. Wright, David S. Haffner, "Fellow Shareholders," 2000 Annual Report, 27 February 2001, Leggett & Platt, Inc., page 2.

6. "Leggett & Platt Expects Earnings Decline Despite Strong Sales Growth," 11 September 2000, Leggett & Platt, Inc., page 1.

7. "Fellow Shareholders."

8. "Leggett & Platt Announces Performance Improvement Plan and Stock Repurchase Authorization," 20 September 2000, Leggett & Platt, Inc., page 1.

9. Matthew J. Flanigan, interview by Jeffrey L. Rodengen, digital recording, 21 November 2006, Write Stuff Enterprises, Inc.

10. "Fellow Shareholders," 3.

11. Ibid., 2–4.

12. Ibid., 3.

13. Flanigan, interview.

14. "Leggett Leadership," 2001 Annual Report, Leggett & Platt, Inc., page 6.

15. "A Conversation with Leggett," International Opportunity, 2001 Annual Report, Leggett & Platt, Inc., page 24.

16. Ibid.

17. Ibid.

18. Harry M. Cornell, Jr., Felix E. Wright, David S. Haffner, "To Our Shareholders," 2001 Annual Report, 25 February 2002, Leggett & Platt, Inc., page 3.

19. Ibid., 3–4.

20. "Leggett & Platt Announces 2007 Results," Leggett & Platt press release, 24 January 2008, page 3.

21. Felix E. Wright, David S. Haffner, Karl G. Glassman, "To Our Shareholders," 2002 Annual Report, 28 February 2003, Leggett & Platt, Inc., page 2.

22. Ibid., 3.

23. Harry M. Cornell, Jr., Felix E. Wright, David S. Haffner, "To Our Shareholders," 2001 Annual Report, 25 February 2002, Leggett & Platt, Inc., page 5.

24. The Sarbanes–Oxley Act Community Forum, "Introduction to Sarbanes-Oxley," http://www. sarbanes-oxley-forum.com/ (accessed 17 May 2007).

25. Felix E. Wright, David S. Haffner, Karl G. Glassman, "To Our Shareholders," 2002 Annual Report, 28 February 2003, Leggett & Platt, Inc., page 3.

26. "Strategy—'How Will We Get There?' 'Sterling Rod Mill,'" 2002 Annual Report, Leggett & Platt, Inc., page 11.

27. Felix Wright, interview by Jeffrey L. Rodengen, digital recording, 20 February 2007, Write Stuff Enterprises, Inc.

28. Mike Glauber, interview by Jeffrey L. Rodengen, digital recording, 27 February 2007, Write Stuff Enterprises, Inc.

29. Ibid.

30. Ibid.

31. Ibid.

32. Ted Enloe, interview by Jeffrey L. Rodengen, digital recording, 20 February 2007, Write Stuff Enterprises, Inc.

33. "Opportunity—'Where Will Growth Come From? Asia/China,'" 2002 Annual Report, Leggett & Platt, Inc., page 16.

34. Felix E. Wright, David S. Haffner, Karl G. Glassman, "To Our Shareholders," 2002 Annual Report, 28 February 2003, Leggett & Platt, Inc., page 2.

35. Felix E. Wright, David S. Haffner, Karl G. Glassman, "To Our Shareholders," 2003 Annual Report, 28 February 2004, Leggett & Platt, Inc., page 5.

36. Ibid.

37. Ibid.

38. "Leggett Announces Acquisition of RHC Spacemaster," 10 July 2003, Leggett & Platt, Inc., page 1.

39. Bill Weil, interview by Jeffrey L. Rodengen, digital recording, 22 November 2006, Write Stuff Enterprises, Inc.

40. "Leggett Announces Acquisition of RHC Spacemaster."

41. Felix E. Wright, David S. Haffner, Karl G. Glassman, "To Our Shareholders," 2003 Annual Report, 28 February 2004, Leggett & Platt, Inc., page 5.

42. Ibid.

43. Ibid., 4.

44. Ibid., 11.

45. Felix E. Wright, David S. Haffner, Karl G. Glassman, "To Our Shareholders," 2004 Annual Report, 28 February 2005, Leggett & Platt, Inc., page 13.

46. "Management's Discussion and Analysis of Financial Condition and Results of Operations," 2004 Annual Report, Leggett & Platt, Inc., page 23.

47. Felix E. Wright, David S. Haffner, Karl G. Glassman, "To Our Shareholders," 2004 Annual Report, 28 February 2005, Leggett & Platt, Inc., page 12.

48. "Leggett & Platt to Provide Die-Castings for Briggs & Stratton," Leggett & Platt press release, 27 September 2004, page 1.

49. Felix E. Wright, David S. Haffner, Karl G. Glassman, "To Our Shareholders," 2004 Annual Report, 28 February 2005, Leggett & Platt, Inc., page 14.

50. Felix E. Wright, David S. Haffner, Karl G. Glassman, "To Our Shareholders," 2005 Annual Report, 28 February 2006, Leggett & Platt, Inc., page 2.

51. "Leggett Announces Five Acquisitions," Leggett & Platt press release, 12 October 2005, pages 1–2.

52. "Notes to Consolidated Financial Statements," 2005 Annual Report, Leggett & Platt, Inc., page 26.

53. Ibid., 27.

54. Felix E. Wright, David S. Haffner, Karl G. Glassman, "To Our Shareholders," 2005 Annual Report, 28 February 2006, Leggett & Platt, Inc., page 5.

55. "Financial Highlights," 2005 Annual Report, Leggett & Platt, Inc., page 1.

56. "Management's Discussion and Analysis of Financial Condition and Results of Operations," Executive Overview: Restructuring and Asset Impairments, 2005 Annual Report, Leggett & Platt, Inc., page 26.

57. Karl Glassman, interview by Jeffrey L. Rodengen, digital recording, 27 February 2007, Write Stuff Enterprises, Inc.

58. Felix E. Wright, David S. Haffner, Karl G. Glassman, "To Our Shareholders," 2006 Annual Report, 27 February 2007, Leggett & Platt, Inc., page 11.

59. "The Road Ahead," 2006 Annual Report, Leggett & Platt, Inc., pages 2–9.

60. David S. Haffner, interview by Jeffrey L. Rodengen, digital recording, 27 February 2007, Write Stuff Enterprises, Inc.

61. "Where We Are Headed ... What We Are Doing to Get There," 2006 Annual Report, Leggett & Platt, Inc., pages 3 and 7.

62. Dave DeSonier, interview by Jeffrey L. Rodengen, digital recording, 21 November 2006, Write Stuff Enterprises, Inc.

63. Vincent Lyons, interview by Jeffrey L. Rodengen, digital recording, 27 February 2007, Write Stuff Enterprises, Inc.

64. Leggett & Platt, Inc., e-mail message to editor and researcher, 8 March 2007.

65. "Leggett & Platt and Invention Machine Announce Strategic Relationship to Accelerate Innovation and Product Development," 11 July 2007, Leggett & Platt, Inc.

66. Lyons, interview.

67. Ibid.

68. Ibid.

69. Ibid.

70. *Management Information Bulletin*, 31 May 2007, Leggett & Platt, Inc., page 1.

71. "An Important Message from Harry M. Cornell, Jr., Felix E. Wright," *Special Edition Management Information Bulletin*, 20 February 2008, Leggett & Platt, Inc.

72. "Leggett & Platt Announces Share Repurchase Authorization, Board Changes, & Quarterly Dividend," 21 February 2008, Leggett & Platt, Inc., page 1.

73. Ibid.

74. "Leggett & Platt Announces Divestiture of Prime Foam Operations," Leggett & Platt press release, 3 April 2007, page 1.

75. Ibid.

76. "Growing the Partnership," March 2007, Issue 39, Leggett & Platt, Inc., page 1.

77. Jack Crusa, interview via e-mail with Crystal Hacker, 29 November 2007, Leggett & Platt, Inc.

78. "Growing the Partnership," April 2007, Issue 40, Leggett & Platt, Inc., page 1.

79. Joe Downes, interview with Crystal Hacker, Spring 2008, Leggett & Platt, Inc.

80. Management Reports to the Board of Directors, 1 August 2007, Russell J. Iorio, Leggett & Platt, Inc., pages 6–10.

81. "Leggett Reports Second Quarter EPS of $.33," Leggett & Platt press release, 19 July 2007.

82. "Leggett & Platt Announces New Strategy Including Divestitures and 39 Percent Dividend Increase," Leggett & Platt press release, 13 November 2007.
83. Ibid.
84. Ibid.
85. Ibid.
86. Ibid.
87. Ibid.
88. Ibid.
89. Ibid.

**Chapter Eight Sidebar:
The Sterling Steel Mill**

1. Joe Downes, senior vice president of Leggett & Platt and president of the Industrial Materials segment, discussions with John Hale and David Ballew, summer 2007.
2. Ibid.
3. Ibid.

**Chapter Eight Sidebar:
David S. Haffner**

1. David S. Haffner, interview by Jeffrey L. Rodengen, digital recording, 27 February 2007, Write Stuff Enterprises, Inc.
2. Ibid.
3. Ibid.
4. "Leadership Team," 2001 Annual Report, Leggett & Platt, Inc., page 13.
5. "Board of Directors," 2006 Annual Report, Leggett & Platt, Inc., page 62.

6. Haffner, interview.
7. Ibid.

**Chapter Eight Sidebar:
Oscar "Bud" Hougland**

1. "L&P's Most Senior Partner," *Management Information Bulletin*, January/February 2000, Leggett & Platt, Inc., pages 2–3.
2. Saundra Snowden, e-mail to Bonnie Young, 10 August 2007.

**Chapter Eight Sidebar:
Looking to the East**

1. Felix Wright, interview by Jeffrey L. Rodengen, digital recording, 20 February 2007, Write Stuff Enterprises, Inc.
2. Paul Hauser, interview by Jeffrey L. Rodengen, digital recording, 27 February 2007, Write Stuff Enterprises, Inc.
3. Wright, interview.
4. Dennis Park, interview by Jeffrey L. Rodengen, digital recording, 21 November 2006, Write Stuff Enterprises, Inc.
5. Wright, interview.
6. Park, interview.

**Chapter Eight Sidebar:
Community Outreach**

1. Public Affairs & Government Relations Department records, Leggett & Platt, Inc.

2. Human Resources Department employment records, Leggett & Platt, Inc., 2008.
3. Public Affairs & Government Relations Department records, Leggett & Platt, Inc.
4. Ibid.

**Chapter Eight Sidebar:
Investor Relations**

1. "Investor Relations," *Management Information Bulletin*, January/February 2000, Leggett & Platt, Inc., pages 1–2.

**Chapter Eight Sidebar:
Supplier of the Year**

1. "F/T to Honor Jabs, L&P," *Furniture Today*, 4 October 2007.
2. "Local Industry Exec Receives High Honor," *The Carthage Press*, 8 October 2008.

**Chapter Eight Sidebar:
American Furniture
Hall of Fame
Foundation, Inc.**

1. American Furniture Hall of Fame Foundation, Inc., 9 October 2007, http://www.furniturehalloffame.com.
2. Felix E. Wright, speech at the induction ceremony of the American Furniture Hall of Fame, October 2007.

INDEX

Page numbers in italics indicate photographs